南京师范大学
国家"211工程"三期重点学科建设项目
"语言科技创新及工作平台建设"

《语言科技文库》

总主编　李葆嘉

计算语言学研究系列　　陈小荷主编
语义语法学研究系列　　李葆嘉主编
汉语方言学研究系列　　刘俐李主编
古代汉语学研究系列　　黄　征主编
语言教学与研究系列　　肖奚强主编
语言新专题研究系列　　倪传斌主编
跨学科名作译著系列　　李葆嘉主编

语篇对话性的理论及应用

Dialogicity in the Text: Theory and Practice

李曙光 著

世界图书出版公司
北京·广州·上海·西安

图书在版编目（CIP）数据

语篇对话性的理论及应用/李曙光著．—北京：世界图书出版公司北京公司，2012.5
ISBN 978-7-5100-4573-8

I. ①语… II. ①李… III. ①语言学—研究 IV. ①H0

中国版本图书馆 CIP 数据核字（2012）第 067214 号

语篇对话性的理论及应用

著　　者：李曙光
责任编辑：丁　冬

出　　版：世界图书出版公司北京公司
出　版　人：张跃明
发　　行：世界图书出版公司北京公司
（地址：北京朝内大街137号　邮编：100010　电话：64077922）
销　　售：各地新华书店和外文书店
印　　刷：三河市国英印务有限公司
开　　本：711mm×1245mm　1/24
印　　张：8.75
字　　数：190 千
版　　次：2012 年 5 月第 1 版　2012 年 5 月第 1 次印刷

ISBN 978-7-5100-4573-8/H · 1297　　　　　定　价：25.00 元

版权所有　　翻印必究

《语言科技文库》总序

李葆嘉

当代语言学已经进入了一个科学与技术的互补时代,信息处理水平成为衡量国家现代化水平的重要标志之一。知识世界的载体是语符系统,信息处理的根本对象是语言信息处理。与计算机的出现使得语言符号有可能成为数据处理对象相似,神经科学实验仪器设备的应用,使得在大脑神经层面探讨语言机制成为可能。这些无疑都引导语言研究走向科技化,"语言科技新思维"(李葆嘉 2001)应运而生。所谓"语言科学"包括理论语言学、描写语言学、历史语言学、应用语言学等分支学科,所谓"语言技术"指语言研究的现代技术手段,包括语言信息处理、语音实验分析,以及语言的神经、心理和行为实验分析的技术手段等。就语言信息处理而言,又可以分为语料库研制技术、知识库研制技术、知识挖掘和抽取技术、句法信息处理技术、词汇信息处理技术、语音信息处理技术、语义信息处理技术、语用信息处理技术等。

2001 年 5 月,南京师范大学文学院创办了史无前例的"语言科学及技术系",率先迈出了从传统文科教育范型向现代科技教育范型转变的步伐。"十五"期间,南京师大"211 工程"重点学科建设项目"语言信息处理与分领域语言研究的现代化"(陈小荷教授主持),以基础平台建设、资源建设和理论探索等为主,迈出了语言科技研究的一大步。

"十一五"期间,南京师大文学院、外国语学院和国际文化教育学院联袂申报"211 工程"三期重点学科建设项目。该项目以"语言科技"为引导,以"多学科交叉、跨院系整合、开放型营运"为理念,建设具有前瞻性、原创性、成长性的语言科技高级工作平台。以典型课题的工作原理为核心,进行资源开发和系统研制,拓展语音科技、二语习得的神经机制研究、言语能力受损儿童的语言能力研究等新方向。同时造就新一代学术领军人物和培养一批高层次复合型人才，以期形成一支高水平的交叉学科团队。该项目设计，体现了工作平台建设、理论创新、应用研究、人才培养、团队建设的学科发展一体化思路。其旨趣在于，加速语言研究从传统文科范型向现代科技范型的转变，以引领 21 世纪语言科技的新潮流。

作为新兴交叉学科项目，通过教育部组织的专家匿名评审，"语言科技创新及工作平台建设"（2008～2011）获批，总投入 1 000 万元。总体而言，这一"语言科技创新"团队，分支学科齐全，专业知识互补。涵盖了理论语言学、计算语言学、语义科技、语音科技、实验方言学、历史语言学、神经语言学、二语习得研究、话语行为语言学等领域。这一期间，项目组成员获批的国家级基金项目达 20 多项。该项目理念之前瞻、实力之雄厚、工程之浩大、经费之保障，为学界瞩目。

2008 年秋，本项目以南京师范大学语言科技研究所为实施单位正式启动。主要有三大任务：建设一个领先性的语言信息科技实验室、建立一个独创性的语言科技工作平台、撰著一套有特色的语言科技文库。

从实验室方案设计到设备招标采购，再到实验室用房改造，经过 8 个月的努力，2009 年 12 月，语言信息科技实验室建成，为语言研究从传统范型向科技范型的转变提供了基本保障。该实验室划分为实验工作区、科研工作区和管理服务区。实验工作区建有语音实验与计算室、神经认知实验与计算室、课堂话语实录室三个专门实验室。科研工作区建有语义科技工作室、语音科技工作室、方言实验工作室、知识工程工作室Ⅰ（先秦词汇）、知识工程工作室Ⅱ（中古词汇）、知识工程工作室Ⅲ（敦煌俗语言文字）、语言习得神经机制工作室、语言习得中介机制工作室，以及参研工作室。管理区服务包括办公室、管理室、编辑室和交流室。出席"语言科技高层论坛暨语言信息科技实验室落成仪式"（2009 年 12 月 14 日）的专家认为，该实验室体现了语言学跨学科研究的当代性和先进性，具有整体性、科技型、开放型三个特点，处于全国领先地位，是"语言科技新思维"的又一体现。同时认为，该实验室的科研工作涵盖了四个二级学科、四个博士学位点，有稳定明确的研究方向，有合理的设计规划和很好的科研基础；整体设计合理，功能齐备。以教育部重点实验室建设标准衡量，很多方面超过了指标。

语言科技工作平台是基于工作原理（课题定位—理论方法—技术路线—关键技术—评估方式）而建设的高级平台。一方面，从语言信息、语言知识和语言机制三个层面，围绕典型课题进行设备配置、资源建设和软件开发；一方面，将典型课题研究与工作平台建设融为一体，依据典型课题建设的子平台应具有解决同类课题的功能。

建设语言科技工作平台的目标是要实现语言研究手段的技术化和模型化，总体设计包括三个二级平台和八个子系统。

一、语言信息工作平台 1. 语义科技工作系统（李葆嘉教授主持）：基于词汇语义－句法语义的一体化研究思路，开发"人－机交互语义标注工具"，研制"深度语义标注信息库"；研制"幼儿（2~6）日常话语跟踪语料库"，完成幼儿语义系统和话语行为分析研究。2. 语音科技工作系统（顾文涛教授主持）：研制"多语言、多语境、多语用的语音语料库"，基于声学信号分析、感知实验和数学建模，完善语音韵律理论与相关技术应用。3. 方言实验工作系统（刘俐李教授主持）：完成"网络版汉语方言有声语料库"，拟定系统的可操作性语音、词汇、语法实验模型和研究方法，进一步完善新兴交叉学科"实验方言学"。

二、语言知识工作平台 1. 先秦词汇统计与知识检索系统（陈小荷教授主持）：研制"先秦文献语料库"、"专名知识库"、"汉语词汇档案库"等，开发先秦文献自动分词算法、古籍版本异文自动发现算法、同指专名检索软件工具等，完成"先秦汉语词汇统计与知识检索"。2. 中古词汇统计与知识检索系统（董志翘教授主持）：研制"中古文献语料库"、"专名知识库"、"中古汉语词汇档案库"等，开发中古文献自动分词和标注工具等，完成"中古汉语词汇统计与知识检索"。3. 敦煌俗语言文字统计与检索系统（黄征教授主持）：研制"敦煌文献资料库"、"敦煌文献俗词语档案库"，开发相应工具，完成"敦煌文献资料与知识检索"。

三、语言机制工作平台 1. 二语习得的神经机制研究系统（倪传斌教授主持)：研制"英语受蚀词汇库"等，基于行为学、脑成像和脑电三维度模型，进行中国人英语习得与磨蚀的神经机制研究，完成"基于神经机制的英语个性化学习分析系统"。2. 二语习得的中介机制研究系统（肖奚强教授主持）：研制"留学生汉语口语中介语语料库"，基于中介语理论、对比分析理论、偏误分析理论以及二语习得影响因素等，完成"留学生汉语习得的中介机制研究"。

这一工作平台，既是科技研究平台，也是人才培养平台，即一个现代化的科学研究和人才培养工作体系。

作为本项目的文本成果，《语言科技文库》包括计算语言学研究、语义语法学研究、汉语方言学研究、古代汉语学研究、语言教学与研究、语言新专题研究六个系列。其总体特征为：领域的开拓性、理论的原创性、选题的新颖性、方法的交叉性、考据的精审性、成果的应用性。在研究过程中，除了数据采集分析、资源建设和软件开发，更重要的还是要有新思路、新理论和新材料。陈小荷提出的先秦文献信息处理新方法，从先秦典籍注疏文献中挖掘出用于自动分词和词义消歧的知识，再注入已开发的古汉语分词和词性标注工具中去，所取得的先秦古籍版本异文自动发现、先秦词汇知识自动挖掘等成果均具开拓性。李葆嘉提出的语义语法学理论和话语行为理论，基于研制专用语料库或语义信息库和技术手段，开拓了语义网络建构、深度语义分析和话语行为研究等新的领域。刘俐李建构的实验方言学理论和方法，为方言学向现代科技方法的转型研究提供了新路，并取得了一系列新成果。黄征多年来从事敦煌文献及其俗词语文字研究，古代汉语学研究系列中的敦煌文献校录整理，以及敦煌写本字词考释、以古佚和疑伪经为中心的敦煌佛典词语和俗字研究、两汉声母系统研究等新见迭出。肖奚强基于汉语中介语语料库的二语习得研究，在对外汉语教学研究界已经产生了影响。钱玉莲的汉语介词与相应英语形式比较研究等专著各有亮色。倪传斌依据语言测试和认知实验等数据，从行为学、生理学和语言学三个层面分析影响中国英语学习者外语磨蚀的相关因素。刘宇红基于隐喻的理论探讨，对各类隐喻形式的结构、特性和解读规律进行了多视角的深入探讨。

《语言科技文库》所收论著，由作者在 2008 年 12 月申报选题，

2011年始逐步完稿。系列主编审读了书稿，主要就其学术价值、章节安排、内容关联、行文表述、图表绘制等方面，提出审阅意见。此后，作者们对书稿又进行了修改和润色。《语言科技文库》的作者，大多数是具有博士学位的年轻教师。对于我们这些20世纪80年代走进语言学研究领域的而言，出版论著可能已不足为道。然而，对于年轻学者而言，其论著的出版既是几年来研究的结晶，也是对其继续探索的促进。换而言之，"211工程"重点学科建设的目的之一，就是为年轻教师搭建一个可持续发展的科研和教学平台。学科带头人的主要任务之一就是提携后进。

尽管从根本上来说，科学或学术研究是一种个人的探索行为，然而复杂问题的研究，无疑需要群体协作。"学科建设"或团队合作模式，是20世纪90年代后期出现的一个新概念。这种模式涉及总体规划、多方协调，是需要付出精力和心血的。2008年，通过投票方式推举我担任该项目总负责时，就意识到自己成了一个"劳动班委"。2009年，前往安徽大学拜访黄德宽教授时，曾谈到"学科负责人的任务就是规划设计，争取项目经费和提供科研设备设施"，得到黄教授的赞许。2010年，申报江苏省高校哲学社会科学重点研究基地时，评审专家柳士镇教授提问的"作为一个交叉学科项目，各学科之间的协调是怎么考虑的，有什么做法"，可谓一语中的。作为后学，深知交叉研究之艰、学科整合之难。相关学科之间的整合协调需要借助行政机制，但凭借行政方式并非就能完成。当时的回答是，目前做到的是建成了一个可以合作研究的场所，至于学科之间的进一步沟通合作应有较长过程。有一点很明确，只有通过交叉项目，相应学科才能渗透，合作者才能逐步磨合。我们只是在一步步探索。

十一五期间的"211工程"建设项目即将完成，但是学科建设的任务并没有结束。2010年，"语言信息科技研究中心"被评审为江苏省高等学校哲学社会科学重点研究基地，为"语言科技"这一交叉领域注入了新的建设活力。重点研究基地建设，除了"跨院系整合、多学科交叉、开放型运行"理念，需要凸显"合作性攻关"。围绕交叉性项目，实施计算语言学、语音科技、神经语言学、语义科技等力量的联合攻关计划。只有通过全面开放以及和与国内外同行的合作交流，才有望建成具有影响的语言科技研究、人才培养和学术交流基地。

十年前，我（2001）曾写道："语言科技"的内涵是以理论研究为指导，以描写研究为基础，以应用研究为枢纽，促使语言研究向计算机应用、认知科学和现代教育技术领域等延伸，沟通文理工相关学科以实现语言研究过程及其成果的技术化。"语言科技"的外延为语言工程科技、语言教育科技和语言研究科技。其中，"语言研究科技"是将语言研究活动与资源建设、软件开发相结合，其目标是实现语言学自身的科技化。还应包含语言实验、数据处理这些实验语音学、神经语言学研究的科技手段。

虽然语言学家不可能也不必要都转向语言计算或实验研究，尽管描写、考据和内省始终是最基本的方法，但是具有一定的语言科技意识却非常必要。语言学家只有了解有哪些可供利用的资源、软件或仪器，才能提高其研究深度、精度和效率。语言学家也只有了解到信息处理的语言研究需求，才有可能为之提供可资应用或参考的基础成果。"语言科技"是21世纪语言学研究的潮流。

此为出版缘起。是为总序。

2011 年 8 月谨识于南都

辛　序

欣闻曙光的博士论文经过整理以"语篇对话性的理论及应用"为题即将纳入南京师范大学"211工程"建设项目"语言科技文库"系列丛书由世界图书出版公司出版，作为导师我感到由衷的高兴并十分乐意作序。

曙光是我指导的第一位博士研究生，他思维敏捷、勤奋好学、朴素低调，作为一名锐意进取的年轻人，这些品质难能可贵。在硕士阶段，他专注于乔姆斯基的形式语言学研究，在语言学基础理论与研究方法上打下了扎实的基础。完成硕士学位论文以后，为了更加全面了解乔姆斯基的整个学术事业，曙光将兴趣点从乔姆斯基所关注的人类语言知识中的"柏拉图问题"转向了乔姆斯基和当今语言学家及公共知识分子所普遍关注的另一个问题——有关人类知识的"奥威尔问题"。

作为有关人类知识的两个大哉问，所谓"柏拉图问题"，用罗素的话来说就是"尽管人类在其短暂的一生中与世界接触如此之少，为何他们的知识却又如此之丰富？"与之相对，所谓"奥威尔问题"则是"尽管现实中的证据如此之丰富，为什么人们却所知甚少？"可以说，乔姆斯基的整个事业就是围绕以上两个问题展开的：缘于对第一个问题的不断追问，乔姆斯基在上世纪中期与一批志同道合的学者一起在人类语言以及心智研究领域发起了一场影响深远的"认知革命"，从而建立了其著名的生成语言学理论，并且随着研究的深入而不断修正这一理论，为人类语言及心智的研究不断注入新的动力；对于第二个问题，虽然乔姆斯基认为它不是一个真正的科学问题，但是为了揭露以美国为代表的资本主义世界虚伪的愚民与强权本质，他对美国的内政外交以及受资本主义意识形态控制的大众传媒进行了深刻的反思和批判，让人们更加清楚地认识了其真相和本质。虽然乔姆斯基反复强调，在他的学术生涯中，这两个方面的努力相互之间没有什么必然联系，而且只有第一个方面才是真正的科学研究，但是他对奥威尔问题的探究客观上使他当之无愧地成为致力于对美国各类政治话语进行批评性分析的伟大实践者。

我于上世纪90年代初负笈英伦，受导师Henry G. Widdowson的影响，对当时正在兴起的批评性话语分析产生了浓厚的兴趣，回国后一直致力于这方面的研究。在进行理论介绍的同时，试图从以巴赫金为代表的文艺理论家那里汲取营养来拓宽批评性话语分析的理论视野，并且围绕新闻等公共语篇的批评性分析开展了一系列的研究。批评性话语分析的宗旨在于，通过对语篇尤其是新闻、广告等公共语篇进行微观语言学分析的基础上，考察话语所传达的某些思想与使这些思想得以存在的社会条件之间的关系，并揭示往往不为人们所觉察的语言、权力和意识形态之间的某些联系，从而提高人们的批评性思维及读写能力，使其更好地理解语言以及社会生活，最终促进公平世界秩序以及和谐社会的构建。

一生以罗素为楷模的乔姆斯基1971年受邀在剑桥大学三一学院设立的罗素讲座中发表系列演讲，以纪念这位刚刚逝去的伟大哲学家，演讲后来以"知识与自由问题"为题结集出版。从该演讲可以看出，乔姆斯基认为知识分子的使命有两个：一个是"努力理解这个世界"，另一个是"改造这个世界"，目的是让人们获得更多的自由与尊严。由此可见，乔姆斯基的基本诉求与批评性话语分析的根本宗旨具有高度的一致性。因此，当曙光2004年暑假同我谈起他想要转向乔姆斯基所关注的奥威尔问题时，我感到十分高兴，并且鼓励他大力拓宽阅读面，在批评理论与篇章语言学两个方面进行知识储备。当时我申请的国家社科基金项目"新闻语篇的互文性分析——英汉报纸新闻转述言语的比较研究"获得立项，我就邀请曙光在进行有关批评性话语分析基础文献阅读的同时积极参与到项目的研究中来，因为对新闻语篇尤其是英语世界的新闻语篇进行批评性分析也是认识奥威尔问题的有效途径。虽然乔姆斯基对西方的大众传媒进行了大量的批评性分析，但他只是凭常识在进行解读，没有提出过系统的理论。所以，我建议曙光把目光投向前苏联文艺批评家巴赫金，从他的对话理论中梳理出可以用于对非文学语篇进行批评性分析的理论框架。曙光欣然接受了我的建议，经过刻苦的文献阅读和积极创新的思考之后,决定以"语篇对话性理论及其在新闻语篇分析中的应用"为自己的博士论文选题,从而才有了现在这本厚实的学术专著。

虽然国内外关于巴赫金对话理论的研究已经相当成熟,但曙光在对巴赫金的大量著述进行研读的同时,以巴赫金所提倡的"对话式阅读"对其著作进行积极的读解,在对他的以语篇对话性为核心的超语言学理论进行系统梳理的基础上,得出巴赫金对话理论的精髓在于其所倡导的"反向性阅读"精神这一结论,并以此为指导提出:如果以"事实性"或者"虚构性"为标准来考察我们社会生活中的各类语篇,以"虚构性"为特征的小说等文学语篇与以"事实性"为基本诉求的新闻语篇构成一个连续统的两端,其他类型的语篇则处于连续统中要么靠近小说语篇要么靠近新闻语篇的位置。对各类语篇的对话性进行解读,简单来说就是要对其进行反向性读解,即从小说语篇解读出"事实性"与"客观性",而从新闻语篇中解读出"虚构性"。可以说,曙光对于巴赫金理论的理解颇具创意,其基本诉求与批评性话语分析高度一致,这为他对新闻语篇的对话性进行批评性分析构建了独特的理论视角。

另外,为了弥补巴赫金理论在微观语言分析上的不足,曙光在本书中将巴赫金的超语言学理论置入韩礼德的系统功能语言学理论中进行重新语境化,即以系统功能语言学理论为基础对巴赫金超语言学的对话性分析框架进行适当的发展。在此过程中,他重点对"声音"、"表述"以及"对话关系"这三个关键概念进行了认真的阐述,并且对在语篇中能够标引出"异质性声音"的语言资源进行了较为系统的描述,从而成功构建起一个可操作的对语篇对话性进行有效分析的框架。在此基础上,通过对英国出版的《星期日电讯报》的两个头版硬新闻语篇的分析,验证了重新语境化后的对话性分析框架的可操作性,同时也通过对话性分析揭示了硬新闻语篇产制过程中所承诺的客观性和中立性原则的"虚构性"本质。应该说,本书无论对于篇章语言学还是新闻传播学的研究都具有较高的参考价值。

目前,曙光又埋头研读乔姆斯基的语言学著作,打算利用篇章语言学的理论来对乔姆斯基的语言学著作进行批评性分析。虽然对于学术著作进行批评性分析在篇章语言学领域已不是十分新颖的课题,但是以乔姆斯基的语言学语篇为对象的批评性分析似乎还不多见,这在很大程度上可能跟乔姆斯基的著作比较晦涩难懂有着很大的关系,因为任何有效的分析首先要对分析对象有着深刻的理解。所以,曙光目前的任务主要有两个:一是对乔姆斯基各个时期的著作进行细致的研读,获得尽可能透彻的理解;二是要继续关注篇章语言学尤其是批评性话语分析的新进展,努力更新理论工具与分析框架。虽然这两个方面的任务都十分艰巨,但是我坚信曙光一定能够很好地实现自己的目标,因为这本书就是他学术水平和科研能力的一个见证。

最后,我预祝曙光顺利完成自己的研究计划,取得新的成果!

辛斌
2011 年 8 月 6 日
于南京龙江金信花园

Abbreviations & Notational Conventions

Abbreviations

MPL	*Marxism and the Philosophy of Language*
PDP	*Problems of Dostoevsky's Poetics*
PSG	*The Problem of Speech Genres*
CGL	*Course in General Linguistics*
SFL	Systemic Functional Linguistics
CDA	Critical Discourse Analysis
DS	direct speech
IS	indirect speech
QDS	quasi direct speech
QIS	quasi indirect speech
FIS	free indirect speech
NRSA	narrative report of speech act

Notational Conventions

Rep.	reporting voice
O	other's voice
Rep.$_r$	reporting voice responding
O$_i$	other's voice initiating
Pr.$_i$	the Prince's voice initiating
Anti-NGO$_r$	anti-wind farm non-governmental organization's voice responding
Con-NGO$_r$	conservation non-governmental organization's voice responding
Gov.$_{r/i}$	governmental voice both responding and initiating
Opp.$_r$	the Opposition leader's voice responding
Unspec.	unspecified voice
→	supporting ostensively
←	confronting blatantly
--▸	supporting in disguise
◂--	confronting in disguise

Contents

Introduction 1
Chapter 1 Bakhtin's Translinguistics 14
  1.1 Bakhtin's understanding of language 14
    1.1.1 Language, sign, consciousness and ideology 15
    1.1.2 The object of language-study 16
  1.2 Bakhtin's translinguistics 21
    1.2.1 Discourse, text and utterance 21
    1.2.2 Utterance, context and speech genres 24
  1.3 Translinguistics and textual analysis 32
    1.3.1 Discourse, text and utterance in contemporary linguistics 32
    1.3.2 Discourse, text and utterance in our discussion 36
    1.3.3 Bakhtin's translinguistics and textual analysis 37
  1.4 Summary 39
Chapter 2 The Compatibility between Translinguistics and Hallidayan *SFL* 42
  2.1 Non-Aristotelian philosophical tradition 42
  2.2 Translinguistics and *SFL*: context, function, register and genre 45
    2.2.1 Context of situation: Bakhtin, Malinowski and Halliday 45
    2.2.2 Linguistic functions: Bühler, Bakhtin and Halliday 46
    2.2.3 Register and genre: Bakhtin, Halliday and Martin 48
  2.3 Instantiation and realization: *SFL* bridging translinguistics and linguistics 52
  2.4 A double-oriented functional model of textual analysis 56

2.4.1 A theory-driven top-down dialogic look at text ········· 57
2.4.2 A data-driven bottom-up linguistic look at text ········· 58
2.5 Summary ········· 60
Chapter 3 Modeling Dialogicity on Hallidayan *SFL* ········· 62
3.1 Bakhtin's idea of textual dialogicity ········· 62
3.1.1 Dialogue, dialogicity and dialogism ········· 62
3.1.2 The mode of dialogicity ········· 65
3.1.3 Problems with Bakhtin's mode of textual dialogicity ········· 66
3.2 Recontextualizing Bakhtinian dialogicity in the context of Hallidayan *SFL* and the postmodern theories ········· 67
3.2.1 From subject and utterance to voice: participant of textual dialogue ········· 68
3.2.2 The dialogic relationship between voices ········· 79
3.2.3 Dialogic markers in the text ········· 83
3.2.4 Functions of dialogic relationships in the text ········· 84
3.3 Summary ········· 85
Chapter 4 Dialogic Markers in Print News of English ········· 87
4.1 Voice, difference, and source in news text ········· 87
4.2 Dialogic markers of speech reporting in news text ········· 90
4.2.1 Speech reporting: a fundamental feature of human language ········· 91
4.2.2 News text: report about others' words ········· 91
4.2.3 Bakhtin's understanding of speech reporting ········· 93
4.2.4 Dialogic markers in speech reporting ········· 97
4.3 Modality as dialogic markers in news text ········· 105
4.3.1 Modality and dialogicity ········· 106
4.3.2 Modality resources as dialogic markers ········· 107
4.4 Conjunction resources as dialogic markers in news text ········· 110
4.5 Negatives as dialogic markers in news text ········· 113
4.6 Summary ········· 115
Chapter 5 Dialogic Interactions in Print News of English ········· 119
5.1 The dialogic relations in print news ········· 119

5.2　Genres and social functions of print news ················· 123
5.3　A dialogic analysis of hard news text (1) ················ 124
    5.3.1　The distribution of different voices in hard news text (1) ··· 127
    5.3.2　The interactions among the foreign voices in hard news text (1) ··· 129
    5.3.3　Framing: the reporter's voice taking foreign voices under its control ·· 133
5.4　A dialogic analysis of hard news text (2) ················ 141
    5.4.1　The distribution of different voices in hard news text (2) ··· 143
    5.4.2　Evaluation as sides-taking ·························· 145
    5.4.3　Sides-taking through ventriloquation ················ 146
5.5　Summary ··· 160
Conclusion ·· 166
References ·· 174

List of Figures & Tables

Figures

Figure 0.1	Cline of textual factuality and fictionality	7
Figure 3.1	Textualization of voice in a Hallidayan mode	75
Figure 3.2	Dialogic relationship between textual voices	82
Figure 3.3	Dialogic relationship between textual voices revisited	83
Figure 4.1	Realization of Bakhtinian linear and pictorial speech reporting	95
Figure 4.2	Xin Bin's continuum of speech reporting	97
Figure 4.3	A continuum of speech reporting modeled on Bakhtin's and Xin Bin's	98
Figure 5.1	Cline of dialogic relationship between voices	119
Figure 5.2	The dialogic interactions among foreign voices in hard news text (1)	129
Figure 5.3	Framing effect of the reporting voice in hard news text (1)	140
Figure 5.4	The textual structure of the rewritten version of hard news text (2)	154
Figure 5.5	A continuum of inter-voice control in speech reporting	155
Figure 5.6	The layout of reporting modes in hard news text (2)	157
Figure 5.7	The dialogic interactions in hard news text (2)	159

Tables

Table 2.1	Understandings of linguistic function of Bühler, Bakhtin and Halliday	47
Table 3.1	Hallidayan dialogic model	80
Table 3.2	Hallidayan dialogic model and Bakhtinian model compared	81

Table 5.1	The distribution of dialogic markers in hard news text (1)	127
Table 5.2	Voices inhabiting hard news text (1)	128
Table 5.3	The distribution of dialogic markers in hard news text (2)	143
Table 5.4	Voices inhabiting hard news text (2)	144

Introduction

In the early years of the last century, linguistics grew from a dependent branch of study in comparative historical philology into an independent discipline because Saussure, the founding father of modern linguistics, successfully and systematically adopted the structural approach to studies on language. *Structuralism* has thereupon become so influential that whatever different interpretations are placed on the exact meaning of the word, as Robins (2001: 225) argues, "few linguists would now disclaim structural thinking in their work." The influence of Saussurean structuralism, however, is not confined to the linguistic circle which includes such great names as Hjelmslev, Chomsky, Halliday and so forth, but has instead been so widespread that it actually provides a framework for the humanities, or at least for "organizing and orienting any 'semiological' study, any study concerned with the production and perception of 'meaning'" (Pettit, 1977: vi). Mostly in this sense, Greenberg (1973) argues that for nearly over a century, social scientists have consciously turned to linguistics for direction and thus confirmed "linguistics as a pilot science". Thus the structural framework derived from Saussurean linguistics, the primary semiological discipline, dominated the analysis of the literary arts, the analysis of the non-literary arts and the analysis in social psychology and social anthropology, and so forth during much of the latter half of the twentieth century (especially in France) (Unger, 2004).

When Saussure's new understandings of language were heralded as a linguistic revolution in western countries, they also met with an enthusiastic reception in Russia where a new nation state was built by drawing inspiration from Marx in the first quarter of the last century. Through Jakobson and his colleagues, Saussure's influence was firmly established and spread, and thus Russian literary formalism came into being, which in turn anticipated the later prosperity of continental structuralism (Hutchings, 2004). But in the same country and almost in the same period of time, together with his friends and students, Mikhail Bakhtin, an enigmatic thinker in Former Soviet Union, who is believed to "have left an indelible mark on our intellectual and scholarly landscape" (Gardiner, 2003: ix), mounted an assault on the philosophical foundations of Saussurean structural linguistics, which he believes has inherited heavily from Leibniz's rationalism and abstract objectivism and turned the living language into a dead object for scientific and objective study by severing it from its context of use—taking *langue* as its exclusive object for systematic study and ignoring *parole* (i.e. the actual speech) and its social, historical and cultural connections. Through criticizing Saussure, Bakhtin tries to push the studies on language back onto the right track by drawing enough insights from German philosophical traditions to which, among others, Kant, Marx, Humboldt, Husserl, Bühler and Cassier made great contributions. In sharp contrast to Saussure, who is believed to insist on the choice of the bifurcation of the synchronic observation on language rather than the diachronic model, and on the choice of the bifurcation of static langue rather than the dynamic parole as the legitimate object for his linguistic study, Bakhtin gives more emphasis to the dynamic dimensions of language: in his eyes, language can only exist in its use; that is, it is always socially situated and constructed. Studies on language have to focus on actual speech—the living language rather than the dead one. As is widely known, Bakhtin's criticisms of Saussurean linguistics are primarily made in his seminal book *Marxism and the Philosophy of Language* (*MPL*), the only monograph exclusively on language problems published under the name of Volosinov, a key member of the now-widely-accepted Bakhtin Circle.[1] Although Bakhtin has clearly elaborated in this book his positions on the philosophical foundations of language problems and accordingly made a relatively specific study on speech reporting, a common mechanism shared by human languages, he does not give a name to the way of studying living language in its context of use that he has strongly advocated.

His different understandings of language problems from Saussure actually have formulated the ontological and methodological foundations for his *translinguistics*, a competing way of studying language problems against Saussurean structural linguistics, which is firstly advanced in *Problems of Dostoevsky's Poetics* (*PDP*) where discourse of Dostoevsky's novels is discussed (Bakhtin, 1984: 181).[2] Although the notion of translinguistics is still pointed at Saussurean "pure linguistics", Bakhtin's purpose then is obviously to explore the polyphonic nature of Dostoevsky's novels that he believes are full of dialogic relationships between different voices. These dialogic relationships, according to him, "cannot be measured by purely linguistic criteria" (Bakhtin, 1984: 182), but belong to the realm of translinguistics. That is to say, when the concept of translinguistics is advanced, it is closely related to the discussion on the discourse of Dostoevsky's novels rather than encompassing the issues of language use in a wider range. In addition, unlike Saussurean linguistics, whose object and way of doing things have been clearly defined once it was proposed, translinguistics remains on the level of making general commitments to do what Saussurean pure linguistics fails and is unable to do. And moreover, Bakhtin's translinguistic analysis of novel text relies heavily upon the insights and competence of the analyst rather than concrete linguistic evidence. As Lynne Pearce (1994: 66) points out, "it is interesting to see how, in tacit acknowledgement of this, Bakhtin resorts to words like 'feel' to describe the reader's task (e. g. , 'This process has to do with the 'feel' we have for distancing...' [Bakhtin, 1981: 419])." It is generally believed that a textual analysis which relies too much on the analyst's personal "feel" rather than detailed and sufficient linguistic description is strongly redolent of running impressionistic poetic comments; that is, according to Halliday (2000: F42), it cannot be accepted as a rigorous analysis at all.

Though it is generally believed that *The Problem of Speech Genres* (*PSG*) is another significant work (apart from *MPL*) on the "pure" language problems, unfortunately, in this place Bakhtin focuses exclusively on *utterance* and *genre*, as if he has simply forgotten the notion of translinguistics he once proposed in *PDP*. Most probably, that is why the concept of translinguistics receives relatively less attention in the circle of scholars working on Bakhtinian linguistic legacy.[3] This lack of concern is well reflected in the four-volume collection of the seminal research papers, edited by Gardiner in 2003, on Bakhtin's ideas concerning philosophy, anthropology, literary criticism, linguistics, psychology, history and even political science in the last thirty years. In this collection, entitled *Mikhail Bakhtin*, only one paper, *Answering as Authoring: Mikhail Bakhtin's Translinguistics*, contributed by Michael Holquist, is on the topic of Bakhtin's translinguistics. Insightful as it is, the paper only focuses on the metaphysical foundation of translinguistics, failing to demonstrate the implications of translinguistics as an analytical tool for doing concrete analysis for its object in a similar way Saussurean linguistics can do.[4] In the Chinese world, researchers also mainly focus on the philosophically-semiologically-and-poetically-oriented interpretations of Bakhtin's theory about discourse or translinguistics, for example, Hu Zhuanglin (1994b; 2001), Wang Jiaxing (1998), Yang Xichang (1999), Ling Jianhou (2000; 2001; 2002), Ning Yizhong (2000), Bai Chunren (2000), Feng Lin (2001), Li Bin (2001), and Liu Hanzhi (2004), to name just a few.[5] That is to say, translinguistics is seldom interpreted in a linguistically-oriented way.[6]

The objective of this book, therefore, is to make a relatively more linguistically-oriented interpretation of Bakhtinian translinguistic ideas dispersed in his works written over several decades. Thus under our focus will be the subject of translinguistics, its connections with the contemporary canonical linguistic theories which share with it a similar philosophical foundation for observing language, and its applicability as a theoretical framework to analyzing hard news text.

To incorporate the linguistic findings into Bakhtin's translinguistics and thus turn the latter into a more workable framework for analyzing texts on the basis of due lexico-grammatical observations is what we mean by *recontextualizing* Bakhtin's translinguistics. The recontextualization of it in the setting of contemporary linguistics and media studies is partly motivated by Bakhtin's hypothetical assertion that any actual speech (i.e. any utterance or text) is full of dialogic relationships between various voices that can only be measured by translinguistics. Given that non-literary texts such as hard news reportings are encompassed in his classification of utterances or texts, they are expected to be dialogic in nature and their dialogicity can be analyzed by the framework provided by translinguistics. It is understood that although Bakhtin has theoretically taken the so-called public discourse including hard news text into his translinguistic consideration, he himself limits his dialogic reading to novel texts (especially those of Dostoevsky's). Sometimes he seems even to be distracted to make some seemingly self-contradictory statements. For example, he tends to argue that poetic forms like the epic and certain kinds of lyrics and some non-literary texts such as hard news reports are essentially monologic, for they enforce a singular, authoritative and finalized voice upon the world. Only novels and indeed only certain kinds of novels are truly dialogic, and thus "submit to unfinalized and infinite dialogue" (Bakhtin/Volosinov, 1986: 122-3; Bakhtin, 1986: 150- 2; Allen, 2000: 26; Pearce, 1994: 64). Thus if the public texts such as hard news reportings can be read in a dialogic manner, Bakhtin's hypothetical assertion that any text is heteroglossic and dialogic in nature can receive empirical support. In so doing, translinguistics can be developed into a framework that possesses stronger theoretical force and accordingly has a wider-range coverage. That is to say, aiming at a linguistically-oriented interpretation of translinguistics, we will start our discussion by accepting Bakhtin's hypothetical assertion that any text is dialogic in nature and anticipates that the monologic hard news text can also be read dialogically. If this gets done, Bakhtin's self-contradiction will be resolved by developing translinguistics into a more general framework for textual analysis. [7] Our recontextualization of Bakhtin's translinguistics in the setting of modern linguistics is actually also allowed by Bakhtin himself, who does have acknowledged the existence of complementarities between translinguistics and "pure linguistics" by saying that "they must complement one another" but, of course, at the same time he still maintains "they must not be confused" (Bakhtin, 1984: 181). Unfortunately, Bakhtin fails to spare due efforts to demonstrate to us how linguistics complements his translinguistics or vice versa. Although in his later years, he seems to return to this topic by making several insightful observations on the differences and connections between linguistics and translinguistics, they are conducted mainly in the form of note-making rather than being fully developed (Bakhtin, 1986: 114, 118, 120, 122). The reason for his laconism on this problem may be partially because he did have plans to work on this subject but his old age failed him. But what is more important is that he consistently insists on a philosophical observation of the things in his vision. That is, even his analysis of Dostoevsky's novel discourse is for the ultimate purpose to understand the philosophical problems like the relationship between "I" and "other", and the relationship between "words" and "world". That is why he maintains that "our analysis must be called philosophical mainly because of what it is not: it is not a linguistic, philological, literary, or any other special kind of analysis (study)" (Bakhtin, 1986: 103). [8] But Bakhtin's laconism on the interface between his translinguistics and linguistics and his "reluctance" or even "contemptuousness" to remain at somewhat specific levels of doing things by confining himself within the borders of a certain discipline do not necessarily mean that it is unnecessary and impossible for us to focus on the junctures and intersections between linguistics and translinguistics in order to make translinguistics, whose metaphysical and social dimensions have been fruitfully developed and interpreted, settle on a concrete materialized linguistic foundation. In this sense we are enabled and entitled by Bakhtin to interpret his translinguistics in the context of certain modern linguistic theories. It should be noted at this juncture that among different schools of modern linguistics, Halliday's *Systemic Functional Linguistics* (*SFL*) is found to be compatible with Bakhtinian translinguistics because they share a lot in the understanding of human language use by both emphasizing that language should be observed from a sociological perspective. The stratificational model of human language of *SFL* and its systematic in-depth and fruitful observations of the lexico-grammatical resources of language make a solid foundation for Bakhtin's translinguistics to be developed into a workable framework for analyzing texts other than novels. That is to say, the combination of translinguistics and Hallidayan *SFL* can enhance the linguistically-oriented potential of translinguistics for textual analysis.

The choice of hard news text as the setting to reinterpret Bakhtin's translinguistics and as empirical evidence to test the validity of our recontextualized model of translinguistics is made on the basis of another rationale. According to journalist training textbooks and canonical media theories, hard news texts are expected to report facts. The core maxim of the highly acclaimed professionalism in the journalistic circle is the principle of objectivity and the ethical bottom line is to be free of bias against or in favour of what is reported (Tuchman, 1978: 160-1; Lau, 2004: 702-3; Pötter, 2004). That is to say the authorial effect and fictionality of hard news text are supposed to be reduced to the lowest level, which is in sharp contrast with the novel texts that are believed to be fictional in nature—the story and its characters (especially what they say, do and think about) usually do not have their corresponding real matches in the world out there, and thus fictionality is generally considered the hallmark of a typical novel. [9] Thus the commonsensical relationship between hard news reportings and novels as far as factuality, fictionality and authorial control are concerned can roughly be illustrated by the following figure.

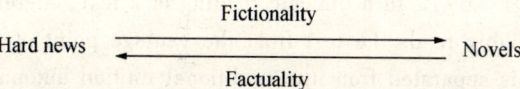

Figure 0.1 Cline of textual factuality and fictionality[10]

Given that translinguistics theorizes on utterance or text that is believed to be full of voices from others in its context of use and thus dialogic and heteroglossic in nature, novel texts are then impossible to be taken under the complete control of the authors as they are generally expected, viz, not everything in the novel is simply created out of the mind of the author and at the mercy of his authorial will. Therefore, in Bakhtin's translinguistic analysis of Dostoevsky's novel discourse, the traditional omnipotent authorship gets deconstructed. In Dostoevsky's novels, according to Bakhtin, the characters are made to hold equal status with the author rather than being tightly controlled by the author—the relationship between the author and the character is understood to be that between "I" and "thou" (Bakhtin, 1984: Ch. 2). The author's voice and the voices from the characters interact with one another and thus a polyphonic effect is produced. The deconstruction of the authorship is actually in a measure in agreement with the postmodern mentality, which makes a productive context for a plethora of fruitful interpretations, reinterpretations, developments and even appropriations of Bakhtin's categories and concepts (Allen, 2000: 56-60, 69-76). But it seems to be against our common sense that the characters or heroes hold the equal status with the author and are actually in a measure independent of the latter. That is why Bakhtin's unusual interpretation of the relationship between the author and the heroes in Dostoevsky's novels triggers heated discussions among literary critics (Zeng Jun, 2004: 44-9). During these discussions, however, it is easy to be overlooked that in Bakhtin's analysis of Dostoevsky's texts, two types of authors have been distinguished: the author-as-creator and the author-as-person. "As 'a constitutive moment of the work', the status of the former is relegated to the past upon completion of the text. The notion of author-creator for a given work thus effectively dissolves, leaving in its stead the author-person as 'a constitutive moment of the ethical, social event of life', who may then offer insights into the work from decidedly different perspectives than formerly—as critic, psychologist, or even moralist" (Danow, 1991: 69). In a dialogic reading of a text, therefore, the analyst most probably reads the text from the vantage point of the author-as-person, who is separated from the traditional unified autonomous *author*. When reading the text from the point of view of the author-as-person, the reader tends to read the text by shifting his visions from the fictional plane to the actual world, in which the heroes acquire independent lives and engage in dialogues with the author-as-person on equal terms. This is quite evident in Bakhtin's reading of Dostoevsky's novels in *PDP*. Thus, Danow argues that " [i]n elaborating the relationship of the author to his hero, Bakhtin constantly shifts his discussion from the plane of the fictional to the actual world. Oddly, he frequently refers to the character in a work as a human being, bearing a biography akin to the author and, therefore, as being the bearer of his own destiny" (Danow, 1991: 71). [11] Another reason why Bakhtin reads Dostoevsky's novel as "the actual" may be because he believes that Dostoevsky's artistic perception of the world is characterized by the fact that he sees and represents the world in the category of coexistence. That is, he "treats every social and political question on the plane of the present-day", which Bakhtin thinks "is explained not only by his position as a journalist, which required that everything be treated in the context of the present", but "is explained precisely by the above characteristic of Dostoevsky's artistic vision" — "all is simultaneous, everything co-exists" (Bakhtin, 1984: 29-30). That is to say, in Bakhtin's eyes, the polyphonic-dialogic novel texts of Dostoevsky have something essential in common with journalistic texts: coexistence of diverse and contradictory materials in the cross-section of a single day. Therefore, it is safe to say that Bakhtin in a measure reads Dostoevsky's novel as news.

Bakhtinian dialogic reading of Dostoevsky's novel texts from a translinguistic perspective actually constitutes one of the major theoretical and practical resources for Critical Discourse Analysis (CDA), advocated by linguists such as Roger Fowler (Fowler, 1991; 1996) and Norman Fairclough (Fairclough, 1992a; 1995). In order to make clear social determinations and effects of discourse which are characteristically opaque to participants in social interactions, CDA analysts read texts (especially the so-called public texts including hard news texts) in the way of deconstructing what we usually take for granted, for instance, the objectivity of news and the academic discourse. In so doing, they intend to reveal the ideological domination and power relations lying behind our "common sense", and thus to reduce the extent to which we are subject to ideological control. If "novels as fiction" can be accepted as common sense and Bakhtinian translinguistics can be used to read novel texts in a critical way by denaturalizing the canonical understanding of novels (their fictionality and authorship), then can translinguistics allow us to read hard news texts critically? Or can hard news text be read as fiction in which reporters exert a tight control over what is reported as a "creative novelist" does to his heroes rather than just working as a recorder? If the answer is "yes", then the critical significance of translinguistics is established without arguing, for it can provide us with an analytic framework to read critically any text in the cline from the factual hard news to the highly fictional novel. And it should be noted in passing that considering dialogic readings of literary text have already been fruitfully made by a host of literary critics following Bakhtin, it is empirically advisable for our linguistically-oriented recontextualization of translinguistics to be conducted in the setting of print hard news text of English, an important genre that makes up one of the two poles of the cline as far as factuality and fictionality are concerned, if we want to attain a translinguistic analytical framework with a wider coverage.

Determined by our major objective, the body of our book consists of five chapters: (1) Bakhtin's Translinguistics; (2) The Compatibility between Translinguistics and Hallidayan *SFL*; (3) Modeling Dialogicity on Hallidayan *SFL*; (4) Dialogic Markers and Relationships in Print News of English; and (5) Dialogic Interactions in Print News of English. In the first chapter, Bakhtin's translinguistics is given a relatively systematic account by piecing together his understandings and observations on language dispersed in the works over several decades. In Chapter 2, the compatibility between Bakhtinian translinguistics and Hallidayan *SFL* is demonstrated from the following two aspects: (1) their shared non-Aristotelian philosophical tradition; and (2) their understandings on context, function, register and genre. Since Bakhtinian translinguistics and Hallidayan *SFL* have so much in common and *SFL* is found to be able to bridge the gap between translinguistics and pure linguistics, *SFL* constitutes an adequate setting for us to recontextualize Bakhtinian translinguistics into a more workable framework for textual analysis, which will be conducted in a double-oriented manner. On the basis of the first two chapters that serve as the theoretical foundations of our discussion, Chapter 3 is set for the development of a workable dialogic model for analyzing hard news text, with the participants of textual dialogue (i. e. *voice*) clearly defined and *the dialogic relationship* highlighted in the translinguistic framework that is modeled on Hallidayan *SFL*. Chapter 4 provides linguistic resources for a bottom-up dialogic reading of text, in which an inventory of so-called dialogic markers are made and at the same time the local dialogic interactions between voices are also discussed in the form of exemplification. Chapter 5 constitutes a crucial part of the book in that the analytic framework developed in the previous chapters is used to analyze two authentic hard news texts, through which the feasibility and applicability of the dialogic model are tested and global observations and interpretations of dialogic relationships among textual voices are consequently attained. By analyzing these two concrete hard news texts, it is found that news reporters usually wrap up their bias mainly in the following two ways: (1) framing the competing voices to invoke their evaluations; and (2) ventriloquating what they want to say through sources. In so doing, the principle of objectivity and factuality of news report is in a measure deconstructed and hard news texts are thus found to have something in common with novels in the sense that they are both under the due manipulation of the author/reporter.

The whole book is concluded with a brief discussion of the implications of Bakhtinian translinguistics for news-text-reading as well as a summary of its main points. Likewise, the limitations of our discussion are admitted and further necessary studies on the issue proposed.

Notes:

[1] In the English world, the authorship of the book is of controversy. For example, Morson and Emerson (1989: 2) argue that the book cannot be Bakhtin's simply because he bluntly declares his "lifelong dislike of Marxism" (Danow, 1991: 7; Matejka et al., 1986: ix-xi), and Hirschkop (2001) even contends that it is Volosinov who influenced Bakhtin to take a linguistic turn rather than the vice versa. In recent years, it seems that the controversy has been suspended and people seem to have lost their interest in it; the ideas embodied in the book are attributed to the so-called Bakhtin Circle; that is, it is considered the collective work of the circle (Brandist et al., 2004). But here we still follow

Clark and Holquist (1984: 146-70) who argue convincingly that the book should be accredited with Bakhtin. Therefore, in our following discussion, *MPL* was just referenced in the way that Bakhtin's and Volosinov's names co-occur with a slash between them when they are noted in the parenthetical brackets. Another "excuse" for our so doing is that the authorship of the book is not quite relevant in our discussion, for it is undeniable that the ideas in the book anticipate the understandings of language in Bakhtin's later works.

[2] Bakhtin's actual term was "metalinguistics". Because of the numerous meanings associated with this term in contemporary studies of language and because, as Clark and Holquist (1984: 10) have noted, the term *meta-* has become so banal in Western scholarship, we shall follow their lead and use the term "translinguistics" (cf. Wertsch, 1991: 51).

[3] Only in comparison with Bakhtinian translinguistics are the word "linguistics" and its derivative "linguistic" narrowly used to refer to Saussurean structural linguistics; in other places, they are used in a more general sense referring to the issues concerning human language.

[4] It should be noted that Saussurean linguistics is not confined to the linguistic ideas in Saussure's *Course in General Linguistics* (*CGL*), but refers to the various schools of linguistic theories engendered by structural methods and concepts provided by this seminal book. It is believed that the linguists such as Bloomfield, Chomsky, Hjelmslev and Halliday inherit Saussure's structural model of language study though they are quite different from each other on some essential points and have made some revolutionary developments on Saussure's model of linguistic study. Thus Saussurean linguistics in our discussion is sometimes used to refer to the canonical linguistics (or in Bakhtin's word, pure linguistics) which is characterized by systematic studies on language issues envisaged by the textbooks in general linguistics such as Lyons (1981), Robins (1989), and Fromkin & Rodman (1993).

[5] Among the references listed at the end of this book, the works published or written in the Chinese language (including the Chinese translations of foreign works) are separated from those in English; these works are also listed according to the alphabetical order of the authors' names in Chinese.

[6] Xin Bin (2002) interpreted Bakhtin's theory on language from the perspective of pragmatics, which makes a good example for recontextualization of Bakhtinian translinguistics in the contemporary linguistic setting. Xin's interpretation focuses on the pragmatic implications of Bakhtin's observation on language, while the notion of translinguistics has not been mentioned. Wang Wenzhong (2002) only focuses on Bakhtin's genre theory (an important part of translinguistics), its relations with Speech Act Theory, and the classification of genres as well as differences between cultures.

[7] Researchers such as David Lodge (1990: 90) have already pointed out the self-contradiction in Bakhtin's poetry-novel opposition as far as dialogicity is concerned— "If language is innately dialogic" (Lodge, 1990: 95), as Bakhtin would seem to be arguing in many instances, "how can there be monologic discourse?" (ibid.) He even argues that "monologic discourse is a kind of fiction or illusion" (ibid.) and what Bakhtin is really trying to say is that certain types of writing (e. g., the lyric, and the epic) tend to suppress and conceal the inherent dialogicity of spoken discourse.

[8] During an interview conducted by Viktor Duvakin, when asked, "So (in the 1920s) you were more of a philosopher than a philologist?", Bakhtin answered promptly, "More of a philosopher. And such have I remained until the present day. I am a philosopher. A thinker." Bakhtin's own testimony shows us that "his certified profession (philology, the academic field of linguistics and literary scholarship) served him somewhat as a refuge and cover" (Emerson, 1997: 6-7). Researchers such as Lynne Pearce (1994: 46) even argue that "although ostensibly writing about Dostoevsky and Dostoevsky's novels, it is plain to see that what he [Bakhtin] is really doing is constructing his own 'world view'."

[9] It should be noted that the literary texts called novels are really heterogeneous in type, and the sub-types of realistic novels (especially the so-called historical novels) are claimed to represent the actual social events and be objective (Booth, 1961). But " [o]ne characteristic feature of literary texts arguably is their fictionality. People usually agree that literary texts, even if they attempt to represent reality in some form or another, are ultimately products of a writer's imagination and that at least the characters and their conversations are fictitious. Thus, some of the characters in Sir Walter Scott's historical novels for example, are pure inventions although they are situated in authentic historical contexts, and they have fictitious conversations with historical figures who actually existed" (quoted from an online course about English literature that is available at the website: http://www.anglistik.uni-freiburg.de/intranet/englishbasics/Home01.htm). As for the relationship between novel and reality, Milan Kundera (1986: 42) has made such an observation as this: "A novel examines not reality, but existence. And existence is not what has occurred, existence is the realm of human possibilities, everything that man can become, everything he's capable of. Novelists draw the map of existence by discovering this or that human possibility."

[10] The arrows indicate an increase of the concerned criterion on the scale, which implies that the difference between hard news text and novel text is not absolute and categorical but just a matter of degree: the fictionality in hard news text is expected to be minimized and its factuality maximized; the fictionality in novel text is expected to be maximized and its factuality minimized.

[11] Lynne Pearce (1994: 66) has made a similar observation of Bakhtin's dialogic reading of Dostoevsky's novels by arguing that "implicit in Bakhtin's conceptualization of the speaking subject in the novel, then is his or her closeness to the speaking subject in the 'real world'—both historical subject and literary character are animated and defined by their inscription in the languages of others: 'Discourse in the novel is structured on an uninterrupted mutual interaction with the discourse of life' (Bakhtin, 1981: 383)." And according to Emily A. Schultz (1990: 78), when talking about Dostoevsky's discourse in *PDP*, Bakhtin argues that the author's discourse about a character in Dostoevsky's novels is organized as discourse about someone actually present, someone who hears him (the author) and is capable of answering him. That is to say, for the most part of time, Bakhtin reads Dostoevsky's novels at a factual plane.

Chapter 1 Bakhtin's Translinguistics

As we have mentioned in the introduction, Bakhtin is mostly considered one of the greatest theorists in literary criticism, philosophy, and anthropology (Clark & Holquist, 1984; Gardiner, 1992; Morris, 1994; Nielsen, 2002), but his contributions to the understanding of human language are also of undeniable importance. Though he himself prefers to be regarded as a philosopher, he is absolutely qualified as a linguist in every sense of the word (Paducheva, 1998; Zhang Huisen, 1999; White, 2003; Georgakopoulou, 2005). Dispersed in his various works concerning aesthetics, philosophy, literary criticism, cultural studies and so on, Bakhtin's concepts of language, on the whole, center on the dialogic nature of discourse, which can be grouped under the name of translinguistics he first advanced in *PDP* (Bakhtin, 1984: 181-204).

Since this book is intended to recontextualize Bakhtin's translinguistics into a workable analytical model to explore the dialogicity of text (especially a model that can incorporate hard news reporting, the type of text which is believed to lie at the positive extreme of the cline of texts as far as factuality is concerned), it is quite necessary to firstly make a relatively adequate account of what Bakhtin's translinguistics is mainly about. For example, what is his understanding of language? What is the subject of translinguistics? And in what respects is it related to modern linguistics and textual analysis?

1.1 Bakhtin's understanding of language

Though there still exist some controversies, it is accepted by most scholars that Bakhtin is the real author of the linguistic monograph *MPL*, which was published in the name of both his friend and student Volosinov. It is in this book that Bakhtin formulates his unique understandings of human language and the role it plays in social interactions. First published in 1929 when Saussurean linguistics was right on the peak and dominated almost all the talk on language issues in Europe, including the former Soviet Union where Bakhtin and his circle did their thinking on various topics about human issues, this book aims to look at things which are discarded and misunderstood by the mentalities confined to the paradigm set by Saussure's *CGL*.

1.1.1 Language, sign, consciousness and ideology

In Bakhtin's view, language is the purest and most sensitive medium of social interactions and thus is the most fundamental and characteristic of human beings as a species. Although he places language into the bigger picture of the general sign system for consideration, the study of language, he believes, can illuminate the mysteries of intermental functioning as well as intramental functioning of human beings, because human actions for the most part are mediated actions and various kinds of sign systems (natural language included) constitute those mediational means (Wertsch, 1991). For that reason, Bakhtin suggests that the analysis of human speech act can throw some new light on the complex phenomenon called "social psychology" in Marxism and considered by the majority of Marxists as the link between the material basis and the mental creativity of man. He argues that the Marxist "social psychology", removed from the actual process of verbal interaction, risks turning into the metaphysical or mythic concept of "collective soul", "collective inner psyche", or "spirit of the people" (Bakhtin/Volosinov, 1986: 19). In short, speech act and the rules that govern its systematic usage in society were recognized by Bakhtin as the framework of human behavior and assigned a central role in the framework of Marxism itself (Matejka et al., 1986: 3). That is to say, Bakhtin believes that language-in-use plays a central role in the human world, and that it not only mediates inner-human mental functioning and inter-human interaction but also bridges the gap between the spiritual world and the material one. In addition to this tool-oriented understanding of human language, language together with other modes of signs, is ontologically regarded as the constituting components of social reality and has its material forms, e.g. sound and graphological existence (Bakhtin/Volosinov, 1986: 11). It is because of this very nature of signs (language as its typical form) that human consciousness and its supreme form, ideology, acquire their solid social and material bases. In Bakhtin's words:

Consciousness takes shape and being in the material of signs created by an organized group in the process of its social intercourse. The individual consciousness is nurtured on signs; it derives its growth from them; it reflects their logic and laws. The logic of consciousness is the logic of ideological communication, of the semiotic interaction of a social group. If we deprive consciousness of its semiotic, ideological content, it would have absolutely nothing left. (Bakhtin/ Volosinov, 1986: 13)

If we take the belief as true that human consciousness or even social ideology consists of various kinds of meanings and values, it is safe to say that Bakhtin holds the position that meaning mainly exists in the process of human verbal intercourse (in a more popular term verbal interaction or communication). Language as the most important sign system of consciousness and ideology, therefore, can be better (or even only) understood from a sociological perspective. On the basis of critical acknowledgement of the sensible ingredients of what he calls individualistic subjectivism originating with Wilhelm von Humboldt, Bakhtin's sociological looking at language pays enough attention to the three elements in language, i. e. the properties of creativity, social function and value of individuals. But at the same time he emphasizes that individuals cannot be separated from the social group and the most significant thing that deserves our thinking is the dynamics among social members or in his word "me" and "other". This is the very point at which he is divided from Saussure and from which his understanding of utterance and discourse makes its departure for the theory of translinguistics.

1.1.2 The object of language-study

In order to establish a different paradigm from Saussure's linguistics, Bakhtin approaches it critically in his *MPL* and often uses lengthy quotations from Saussure's *CGL* as antitheses to his own views. He particularly challenges Saussure's dichotomy between *la langue* (language system) and *la parole* (speech act/utterance), and he seriously questions the conceptual separation of synchrony from diachrony in the investigation of verbal communication.

In his review of Saussure's linguistics, especially his emphasis on the arbitrary nature of linguistic signs and value-difference-based understanding of meaning, Bakhtin traces Saussure's views on language back to the philosophical-linguistic sources originating from Leibniz's conception of universal grammar, and, above all, from the Cartesianism and rationalism of the 17th and 18th centuries. Here are his words:

> The idea of *the conventionality, the arbitrariness of language*, is a typical one for rationalism as a whole, and no less typical is the *comparison of language to the system of mathematical signs*. What interests the mathematically minded rationalists is not the relationship of the sign to the actual reality it reflects nor to the individual who is its originator, but the *relationship of sign to sign within a closed system* already accepted and authorized. In other words, they are interested only in the *inner logic of the system of signs itself*, taken, as in algebra, completely independently of the ideological meanings that give the signs their content. (Bakhtin/Volosinov, 1986: 57-8; italics in the original)

This giving too much priority to the system at the expense of the language user (the speaker/writer) and almost equating language with the mathematical sign system is a typical way of thinking of abstract objectivism. In addition to that, Saussure also draws heavily on the sociology of Durkheim, who abstracts his social reality from the myriad social phenomena, which he believes constitutes the only legitimate object of sociology and can be studied in a similar way that natural sciences can be dealt with (Baert, 2002 [1998]: 7-8). Modeling his linguistic object on Durkheim's social reality, Saussure abstracts linguistic system from social verbal interactions and assigns the former the status of the only legitimate object of linguistics and sweeps the latter into a dark corner. In this way, Saussure believes that language can be studied scientifically and a real discipline named linguistics thereby be established. Although in *CGL* Saussure acknowledges the potential existence of the study of speech, he denies it the term linguistics and confines linguistics only to the objective linguistic structure/system itself (i. e. his *la langue*) in the name of avoiding confusion (Saussure, 2001: 8-17, 96-8).

But to Bakhtin, the first thing that needs questioning is the objectivity of Saussure's linguistic system, viz the degree to which the system of

Saussure's self-identical linguistic norms (i. e. the system of language) may be considered a real entity. In Bakhtin's view, none of the representatives of abstract objectivism would ascribe concrete material reality to the system of language. It is true that their system is expressed in material things (in signs of course), but as a system of normatively identical forms, it has reality only in the capacity of the social norm. Although they constantly stress (and it is one of their basic principles) that the system of language is an objective fact external to and independent of any individual consciousness, Bakhtin argues that represented as a system of self-identical, immutable norms, the system can be perceived in this way only by the individual consciousness and from the point of view of that consciousness. What he does mean here is that the objectivity of the linguistic system is conventional in nature, radically different from that of the real concrete existence, and it is agreed, assigned, recognized, observed, and interpreted by social subjects. This objectivity is based on human subjectivity. More importantly, Bakhtin suggests that "if we were to look at language in a truly objective way—from the side, so to speak, or more accurately, from above it, we would discover no inert system of self-identical norms. Instead, we would find ourselves witnessing the ceaseless generation of language norms" (Bakhtin/Volosinov, 1986: 66). That is, from a truly objective viewpoint (from above, taking a historical perspective), "the one that attempts to see language in a way completely apart from how it appears to any given individual at any given moment in time, language presents the picture of a ceaseless flow of becoming" (ibid.). There is no real moment in time when Saussure's synchronic system of language could be constructed. Hence to the historian of language, with his diachronic point of view, a synchronic system is not a real entity, but it only serves as a conventional scale that registers the deviations occurring at every real instant in time. In this way, Bakhtin destroys the basis of the objectivity of linguistic system which is enshrined as the only legitimate object of study in Saussure's *CGL*. At the same time, he also points out that any system of social norms possesses the same property, including Durkheim's social structure.

It is necessary to note at this juncture that Bakhtin does not deny the existence of the objective linguistic system as a social and cultural common wealth for a community, but what he lays emphasis on is the point that this mode of existence of language as a system of stable identical forms depends on the consciousness of each member of any given language community. It is a pure abstraction but not a reality, that is, a constructed objective entity rather than real-life existence. In real life, the fact is that the speaker's focus of attention is brought about in line with the particular, concrete utterance he is making. What matters to him is applying a normatively identical form in some particular, concrete context. In other words, what the language user really cares is the new and concrete meaning his utterance acquires in the particular context rather than the identity of the form. Bakhtin has emphasized more than once that the life of language consists in its concrete use in a concrete context (namely, "living speech" or in his more frequently used term "utterance") rather than in the abstract system of identical forms. In his own words:

> The linguistic consciousness of the speaker and of the listener-understander, in the practical business of living speech, is not at all concerned with the abstract system of normatively identical forms of language, but with language-speech in the sense of the aggregate of possible contexts of usage for a particular linguistic form... In point of fact, the linguistic form, which, as we have just shown, exists for the speaker only in the context of specific utterances, exists, consequently, only in a specific ideological context. In actuality, we never say or hear *words*, we say and hear what is true or false, good or bad, important or unimportant, pleasant or unpleasant, and so on. *Words are always filled with content and meaning drawn from behavior or ideology.* That is the way we understand words, and we can respond only to words that engage us behaviorally or ideologically. (Bakhtin/Volosinov, 1986: 70; italics in the original)

It is quite apparent that the way in which Bakhtin views language is an out-and-out social one. First, he takes both the speaker and the listener (rather than the traditionally solitary speaker) into his consideration. Although Saussure also includes the listener into his famous head-speech-circuit (Saussure, 2001: 11-2), the act of communication is represented as a pure psychological phenomenon, that is, the transmission of the concept pure and simple through the sound waves. The understanding, or to be exact, receiving of the concept on the part of the listener is only an act of copying the original one triggered by the stimulus of sound wave. But in Bakhtin's view, that is only a passive way of understanding or even, it cannot be considered an act of understanding in the true sense of the word. In real-life communication, there is actually no such kind of puppet listener. The listener does play an active constitutive role in the generation of the living speech. As an intrinsic social interaction, utterance is constructed between socially organized persons, and even in the absence of a real addressee (written verbal communication for instance), he will be presupposed in the person, so to speak, of a normal representative of the social group to which the speaker belongs. The real case is that: when the speaker/addressor plans his speech, he is supposed to anticipate the apperceptive background of the listener/addressee, and the listener/addressee's possible response thereby shapes the speaker/addressor's speech; when the listener/addressee tries to figure out the speaker's speech, he does not only recover what the speaker's inner concept of his words, but more importantly gives his evaluation (in Bakhtin's words, what is true or false, good or bad, important or unimportant, pleasant or unpleasant) to the received speech. Second, the basis on which the speaker anticipates the listener's apperceptive background and the listener gives evaluation to his partner's speech is constructed by the actual conditions of the given speech event. These conditions range from the immediate social situation to the broader social-cultural or ideological context. That is why Bakhtin insists on bringing *context* into the picture of real-life verbal interactions. In his view, any kind of utterance—even the kind of utterance that is not a referential message (communication in the narrow sense) but the verbal expression of some need (e. g. hunger), is socially oriented in its entirety. It is determined immediately and directly by the participants of the speech event (i. e. both explicit and implicit participants) in connection with a specific situation, which shapes the utterance, dictating that it sounds one way rather than the other. In short, only when a speech is located in the social context can it be turned into a social reality (Bakhtin/Volosinov, 1986: 86).

It is widely accepted to be one of the constant lines running through Bakhtin's works concerning human language that "verbal interaction is the basic reality of language" (Bakhtin/Volosinov, 1986: 94) and the unit of verbal interaction is living speech act (in his own term, "utterance").

We need to note in passing that the view that individual utterances rather than the language system are what constitute the actual, concrete reality of language is the sensible understanding of language Bakhtin accredits to the school of individualistic subjectivism. If the study on language is only confined to the constructed abstract system of forms and ignores the reality of language—living utterance, Bakhtin argues, it can at most reveal part of the story of language, which will inevitably lead to some misconceptions about language, especially the language existing in various forms in human daily interactions.

1.2 Bakhtin's translinguistics

In contrast to Saussure's linguistics designating language system as its only legitimate object, Bakhtin proposes that a due paradigm of study on language, which aims at the living real-life discourse as its legitimate object, be established. And he (Bakhtin, 1984: 181) names such kind of study on language-in-use *translinguistics*.

1.2.1 Discourse, text and utterance

It is quite accepted now in linguistic circles that if Ferdinand de Saussure is considered the father of linguistics, Bakhtin should be regarded as the father of discourse. At a time when language was conceived as an abstract system (of linguistic signs), Bakhtin highlighted the communicative function of language, and drew his attention to language in use, namely, *discourse* (Podestá, 2001). But our problems here are "What does Bakhtin really mean when he uses the term *discourse* in his translinguistics?" and "What is the relationship between his discourse and the other two frequently used terms *utterance* and *text*?" The clarification of these questions, we believe, can in a measure be instrumental in understanding his theory of translinguistics.

The above mentioned three terms (i.e. *discourse*, *utterance* and *text*) are generally believed to be the English translations of the corresponding Russian words слово, высказывание, and текст in Bakhtin's original works. Some scholars believe that Bakhtin sometimes uses these three terms to refer to the same phenomenon. Such usages of the three terms (especially utterance and discourse) do exist in Bakhtin's works. A good case in point is his *MPL*, in which *discourse* is used interchangeably with *utterance, and sometimes even with word* (Zhao Yifan, 1993; Ling Jianhou, 1999, 2000). Bakhtin himself did once admit his "love for variations and for a diversity of terms for a single phenomenon" (Bakhtin, 1986: 155), but at the same time he also adds that in his using the terms there are "the multiplicity of focuses" and this has the function of "bringing distant things closer without indicating the intermediate links" (ibid.). That is, when talking about different topics, Bakhtin may have different focuses even though the same term is used, for his topics are really very extensive. For instance, when his focus is on relatively specific topics on language issues, these three terms receive their different treatments by acquiring different senses behind the lines in his works, but when his focus is raised to the level of the total human issues the term of discourse and text gain a broader sense of referring to "all thoughts in the human sciences and philosophy in general" (Bakhtin, 1986: 103). The latter usage of discourse and text is what the post-modern theorists such as Foucault are dwelling upon. Discourse and text in this sense is used to refer to semiotic elements of social practices, including language (written and spoken and in combination with other semiotic resources, for instance, music in singing), nonverbal communication (facial expressions, body movements, gestures, etc.) and even visual images (for example, photographs, films, etc.) (Hanks, 1989). This concept of discourse can be understood as a particular perspective on these various forms of semiosis—it sees them as moments of social practices in their articulation with other non-discursive moments (Bakhtin, 1986: 103; Chouliaraki & Fairclough, 1999: 38).

In addition to this broad understanding of discourse and text, within the theory of translinguistics Bakhtin also uses these terms in their relatively narrow sense and associates with them different contents. Discourse is used by Bakhtin to refer to the total phenomena of language-in-use. Here is what he exactly says when he proposes the term translinguistics:

> We have entitled our chapter "*Discourse* in Dostoevsky", for we have in mind *discourse*, that is, language in its concrete living totality, and not language as the specific object of linguistics, something arrived at through a completely legitimate and necessary abstraction

from various aspects of the concrete life of the word. But precisely those aspects in the life of the word that linguistics makes abstract are, for our purposes, of primary importance. Therefore the analyses that follow are not linguistic in the strict sense of the term. They belong rather to metalinguistics [translinguistics], if we understand by that term the study of those aspects in the life of the word, not yet shaped into separate and specific disciplines, that exceed—and completely legitimately—the boundaries of linguistics. (Bakhtin, 1984: 181; italics in the original)

It is safe to say that an analogy between translinguistics and linguistics is implied here; that is, just as the abstract language system constitutes the legitimate object of study for Saussure's linguistics, the concrete discourse (language in its concrete living totality) qualifies itself as the legitimate object of study for translinguistics.

Within the theory of translinguistics, another related analogy between Saussure's linguistic and translinguistics is also drawn by Bakhtin when he elaborates his genre theory in *PSG*. Just as linguistics selects sentence as the unit of analysis, translinguistics chooses *utterance* as the unit of living speech communication (discourse). To be more specific, Bakhtin defines *utterance* as the unit of discourse. At this juncture, we need to note in passing that we can find a similar distinction in Austin and Ducrot. Austin holds that a sentence is a grammar entity, abstract and not realized whereas an utterance is an actual manifestation of language produced by a speaker under definite circumstances. He also explains that the sentence is contained in an utterance. Ducrot refers to the sentence as a phrase and defines the utterance as a fragment of discourse and he adds that it is the study of the utterance which will lead to a full understanding of the units of language as a system, that is, the word and the sentence. (Podestá, 2001)

Considering the central role played by sentence in linguistics in which linguistic theory is built on the basis of revealing its properties, utterance occupies the same status as the key concept in translinguistics. Since there exist such similarities between the two ways of language studies, Bakhtin has to acknowledge some practical significance of Saussure's abstract linguistics, which in other places is under his strong criticism. He even says,

"Of course, metalinguistics [translinguistics] research cannot ignore linguistics and must make use of its results" (Bakhtin, 1984: 181). Therefore, the relationship between linguistics and translinguistics is that "[t]hey must complement one another, but they must not be confused" (ibid.). In this sense, it is safe to say that Bakhtin's translinguistics is established analogically out of Saussurean linguistics, and ironically this is strongly reminiscent of poststructuralism that also launches a destructive reaction to Saussurean structuralism by depending on the tools provided by the latter. That is why Rutland argues that "*Marxism and the philosophy of Language* challenges the premises of Saussure's linguistics while adhering to the latter's fundamental principles" (Rutland, 2003).

The third important term we need to spare some space for is the concept of *text* in translinguistics. As has just been mentioned above, like discourse, text also has its broad sense and its narrow one. In the broad sense, it is used to refer to any semiotic practice and its production in human society; but when it is confined within the boundaries of translinguistics, it is used in the way of "text as utterance" (Bakhtin, 1986: 104-5, 161-2). To be more specific, Bakhtin uses them to refer to the same thing, that is, the living verbal communication in any form (oral or written) (Bakhtin, 1986: 104; White, 1998: 58).[1]

Before we close this subsection, it is necessary to note that, in Bakhtin's works, discourse and text branch into two levels of studies. The higher level is a broad and macroscopic one, which focuses on exploring the dynamics between language and ideology, knowledge, power, institution, the system of civilization, etc., thus working in close connection with the post-modern discourse theorists represented by Foucault; the lower level places more emphasis on the concrete properties of verbal communication.

1.2.2 Utterance, context and speech genres

From the above discussion, we may have formed a vague picture of Bakhtin's translinguistics, which begins its journey from the place Saussure's linguistics sets as its finishing line. In the odyssey of translinguistics, in Bakhtin's view, utterance as the basic analytical unit can serve as the signpost and milestone. A clearer picture of translinguistics, therefore, depends on a due understanding of utterance.

In *PSG*, Bakhtin elaborates three principal properties of utterance on the basis of the comparison made between sentence and utterance, because to define precisely the relationship between the two can give us a clearer picture of both. Different from sentence, utterance possesses the finalized wholeness of representation, addressivity and expressivity.

As a unit of the collective abstract language system, the boundaries between sentences are never determined by a change of speaking subjects. When a sentence is put into the frame of the changing of speaking subjects, it is not the abstract sentence any more, but has been transformed into an entire utterance. For example,

(1) A: Why do you love her?
B: *She is **beautiful***.
A: But beauty won't endure.
...

(2) A: She is a good girl. *She is beautiful*. But she doesn't care much about it. What is in her mind is how to cultivate a good disposition.
B: She must be a very respectable figure in your class.
...

According to Bakhtin, "*She is beautiful*" in (1) is a concrete utterance because it belongs to a concrete speaking subject, namely, speaker B. What is more important is that the boundaries on either side of the very wording in question are marked clearly by the changing of the speaking subject, and in this case, these two positions are both held by speaker A. But the same wording "*She is beautiful*" in (2) is only a sentence, though it is a relatively complete thought, directly correlated with the other three thoughts expressed by their corresponding sentences in (2) of the single speaker A within his utterance as a whole. In this case, the speaker pauses at the end of a sentence in order then to move on to his next thought, continuing, supplementing, and substantiating the preceding one. "The sentence itself is not correlated directly or personally with the extraverbal context of reality (situation, setting, prehistory) or with the utterances of other speakers; this takes place only indirectly through its entire surrounding context, that is, through the utterance as a whole" (Bakhtin, 1986: 73-4). Apart from this formal feature, that is, the changing of speaking subject, Bakhtin identifies a second important attribute of the wholeness of utterance. This second feature is the specific *finalization* of the utterance, which, of course, is thought to be inseparably linked to the first. Finalization here approximately means the exhaustiveness of what the speaker wants to say at the very moment of speaking; what he has said is a complete response to other's utterance, and at the same time he is waiting for the other party's response to his own. In (1), for instance, speaker B's wording "*She is beautiful*" is directed at speaker A's question "*Why do you love her?*", which as a complete utterance indicates that the reason is nothing but "*She is beautiful.*" Speaker B here has expressed all that he wants to say and what he wants and needs to do is anticipate a comment on his reason from his partner, speaker A. But in the case of (2), within the whole utterance, the wording "*She is beautiful*" can only express part of what speaker A wants to say at the moment. That is, it does not exhaust the topic of speaker A in this turn. But the first and foremost criterion for judging the *finalization* of an utterance, in Bakhtin's words, is "the possibility of responding to it or, more precisely and broadly, of assuming a responsive attitude toward it" (Bakhtin, 1986: 76).

An utterance cannot only be responded to, but respond to other utterances. That is, each utterance should be directed at a listener, or in Bakhtin's term, an addressee. The addressee is the person, from whom the addressor/speaker expects a response. According to Bakhtin, the addressee plays a very important role in the formation of the addressor's utterance in the way that when constructing an utterance, the addressor tries actively to determine response from the addressee and moreover, tries to act in accordance with the response he anticipates, so this anticipated response, in turn, exerts an active influence on the addressor's utterance. For instance, when speaker B in (1) tries to respond to speaker A's utterance, he at the same time takes speaker A's possible response into consideration, thus the utterance "*She is beautiful*" answering to speaker A's utterance preceding it (i.e. *Why do you love her?*) and simultaneously anticipating speaker A's utterance following it (i.e. *But beauty won't endure*). This kind of anticipating property of utterance is termed *addressivity* by Bakhtin. In Bakhtin's view, the role played by the addressivity of utterance in planning, constructing (and especially choosing genre of) the utterance is more evident in the case of verbal interaction in written form. "For example, genres of popular scientific literature are addressed to a particular group of readers with a particular apperceptive background of responsive understanding; special educational literature is addressed to another kind of reader, and special research work is addressed to an entirely different sort. In these cases, accounting for the addressee (and his apperceptive background) and for the addressee's influence on the construction of the utterance is very simple: it all comes down to the scope of his specialized knowledge" (Bakhtin, 1986: 96).

The third basic property of utterance is its expressive aspect, that is, "the speaker's subjective emotional evaluation of the referentially semantic content of his utterance" (Bakhtin, 1986: 84). In Bakhtin's eyes, there can be no such thing as an absolutely neutral utterance. The speaker's evaluative attitude toward the referential content of the utterance (e. g. the proposition) also plays an important role in the choice of lexical, grammatical, and compositional means of the utterance. The evaluative overtones of the utterance are actually the position the addressor takes when he responds to other's utterances, suggesting his agreement or disagreement, acknowledgement or resistance, affirmation or criticism, and so on. In addition to the attitude toward other's utterance, of course, the addressor also holds a certain attitude toward the thing he is talking about. In short, the addressor's utterance includes evaluative attitudes toward both the referential content and other's utterance at a single stroke. This kind of *expressivity* is directly realized by tonic recourses (or in Bakhtin's word *accent*) in oral interactions; but in written cases, it will mainly depend on lexico-grammatical recourses and this will be discussed in detail in the following chapters.

The above discussed properties of utterance are closely related to each other; that is, each depends on the existence of the other. The wholeness of utterance characterizes the expressive and addressive aspects of the utterance; the attitude adopted and the addressivity anticipated by the utterance presuppose the unique existence of the very utterance and its subject behind. These properties of utterance which distinguish utterance from sentence, however, are assigned by the concrete context and belong to certain genres.

It is generally acknowledged that any approach to language through a social perspective should take into consideration the situation immediate or even broader in which the verbal communications actually take place. These situations are usually given the umbrella name *context* in the studies on language issues. Putting language forms in concrete context for consideration is the main point on which Bakhtin diverges from Saussure (Xin Bin, 2002). In *MPL*, Bakhtin argues that when an addressor speaks, what matters to him is applying a normatively identical form in some particular, concrete context. "For him, the center of gravity lies not in the identity of the form but in that new and concrete meaning it acquires in the particular context" (Bakhtin/Volosinov, 1986: 67-8), because the meaning of a language form "is determined entirely by its context" (Bakhtin/Volosinov, 1986: 79). In fact, there are as many meanings of a language form as there are contexts of its usage. But on the contrary, linguists working with the school of abstract objectivism only focus their attention on the identity of language forms by removing them from their contexts; this forces these linguists to see only the dead and alien word. (Bakhtin/Volosinov, 1986: 67-82) Later, in *PSG*, Bakhtin further reiterates the important role played by context in connecting the linguistic sentence with translinguistic utterance. Here are his words:

> Any sentence can act as a complete utterance, but then, as we know, it is augmented by a number of very essential non-grammatical aspects that change it radically. And this circumstance also causes a special syntactic aberration. When the individual sentence is analyzed separately from its context, it is interpreted to the point of becoming a whole utterance. As a result, it acquires that degree of finalization that makes a response possible. (Bakhtin, 1986: 82)

From here we can see that in Bakhtin's view, it is utterance rather than sentence that has its concrete context. If a sentence enters a concrete context which is not shared by other sentences and is attributed to a concrete speaking subject, it will not be a sentence anymore, but has become an utterance par excellence. For in the context, sentence can be linked to extra-language reality, it gains evaluative overtones and also is connected to the words of others, hence its entrance to the domain of translinguistics. In a given context, sentence can acquire the properties of utterance, whereas if we look at this process of becoming the other way round, we can say that utterance can be realized by sentences in a concrete context.

When a sentence becomes an utterance in a particular and concrete context, it will not belong to nobody any more, but belong to a unique speaking subject. Its uniqueness exists in its acquisition of another two meanings (i. e. expressive and responsive overtones) in addition to its own referentially semantic content. Thus, in a context, corresponding to its above mentioned three properties, utterance possesses three kinds of meanings: (1) the referentially semantic content of the theme; (2) the addressor's plan (or speech will) and his evaluative attitude toward the semantic content of the theme; (3) the addressor's evaluative attitude toward the addressee and his utterance (or even other's utterances related to the theme) (Bakhtin, 1986: 76-100). Among these three meanings, in Bakhtin's view, the first meaning is possessed by sentence, thus being abstract and belonging to nobody or to everybody (it is the meaning speakers of a community share with one other) (Bakhtin/Volosinov, 1986: 100). The second and third aspects of meaning, however, make an utterance a historical phenomenon and render it unique in that it carries with it distinctive evaluative features from other utterances. The unique evaluative features and its relationship with other utterances constitute what Bakhtin calls the dialogicity of a given utterance, the central place of which in Bakhtin's theory and potentials of which for text analysis will constitute our topic in the following chapters. [2]

Although Bakhtin reveals the individual uniqueness of utterance and regards it as the basis which the dialogicity of utterance is built on, he also maintains that there are relatively stable types of utterances in each sphere of human society in which language is used. These relatively stable types of utterances are termed *speech genres* in *PSG*.

In Bakhtin's eyes, speech genres are determined by the myriad types of human activities. Considering the fact that the various possibilities of human activities are inexhaustible, and even each sphere of activity contains an entire repertoire of speech genres, the wealth and diversity of speech genres are correspondingly boundless. Thus when talking about speech genres we have to lay special emphasis upon the extreme heterogeneity of them. In fact, just as Bakhtin specifies, the categories of speech genres include short rejoinders of daily verbal interaction, everyday narration, writing (in all various forms), the brief standard military command, the elaborate and detailed order, the fairly variegated repertoire of business documents, the news reportings, and the diverse world of commentary, the diverse forms of scientific statements and all literary genres. It is true that speech genres and the utterances they contain are so heterogeneous that there is seemingly no common level at which they can be studied. That is probably the reason why Saussure sweeps them into the stuff that cannot be studied linguistically and analytically. But while emphasizing the extreme heterogeneity of speech genres and the attendant difficulty of determining the general nature of utterance, Bakhtin also insists on the relative regularity lying behind multifarious and dynamic speech genres. He actually identifies two major categories of speech genres, that is, the primary and the secondary speech genres. The former (e. g. daily verbal interactions, correspondence, etc.) refers to the genres that have taken form in unmediated speech communion; the latter are built on the basis of the former by absorbing and digesting them. Thus the latter, that is, secondary or complex speech genres refer to those arising in more complex and comparatively highly developed and organized cultural communications (primarily written) that are artistic, or scientific, or sociopolitical, and so on: for example, novels, dramas, all kinds of scientific research, major genres of commentary, news reportings, and so forth. Making secondary speech genres of primary ones is not a simple process of adding one constituent utterance of primary genres to another. When the primary genres enter into complex ones, they will be altered and assume a special character, for they have lost their immediate relation to actual reality and to the real utterances of others. To illustrate this, Bakhtin (1986: 62) gives us a clear example, by saying that "rejoinders of everyday dialogue or letters found in a novel retain their form and their everyday significance only on the plane of the novel's content. They enter into actual reality only via the novel as a whole, that is, as a literary-artistic event and not as everyday life. The novel as a whole is an utterance just as rejoinders in everyday dialogue or private letters are (they do have a common nature), but unlike these, the novel is a secondary (complex) utterance."

From this we can see that an utterance of secondary speech genre is usually hybrid in that it is a mixture of various primary genres by absorbing and altering them into a concrete whole. Thus a study of speech genres can throw enough new light upon the nature of utterances. This is what the generic intertextuality and interdiscursivity in Critical Discourse Analysis

(CDA) mainly addresses (Xin Bin, 2000: 91-4, 191-252; Fairclough, 1992a: 124-30). According to Bakhtin, since any research whose material is concrete language (discourse/text analysis is a good case in point) inevitably deals with concrete utterances (written or spoken) belonging to various spheres of human activity: chronicles, contracts, texts of law, news reports, various literary, scientific, and commentarial genres, official and personal letters, rejoinders in everyday dialogue, etc., it is immensely important for almost all areas of linguistics and philology to take speech genres into consideration. In short, we have to study utterances with reference to their corresponding genres. This is the only right track for translinguistic and even for linguistic studies, thus being of huge methodological significance.

Considering the enormous complexity of Bakhtin's theory on language, a brief summary of his main ideas on language and translinguistics should now be in order, though it seems to be a nearly impossible task in nature. First, through criticizing two trends in linguistic studies, namely, individual subjectivism and abstract objectivism, both of which ignore the essentially social nature of language, Bakhtin establishes his out-and-out sociological view on language. In his eyes, the only reality of language is the living speech in concrete social context (i.e. utterance) rather than the stable system of normative linguistic forms, in which the once divided two levels of the individual psyche and the social ideology are brought together. The utterance is actually the verbal interaction between social subjects, thus both its production and its comprehension are interactive, generative, and evaluative in nature (i.e. dialogic). Accordingly, his translinguistics is centered on the exploration of the properties of utterance, which is characterized by its *referential wholeness*, *expressivity* and *addressivity*. It is these properties that the dialogicity of utterance lies in. As the concrete unit of existence of language use in human society, utterances of a speech community are organized by the particular spheres of general human activity into various relatively stable types, which is called *speech genres*. Thus a new way of looking at language in use has been established around the key concept of utterance. Given written text in various forms being among the diverse forms of utterances, translinguistics will inevitably lend us due theoretical support for analyzing written texts, print hard news text of English included of course.

As far as contemporary text analysis is concerned, however, Bakhtin's translinguistics will inevitably engage in dialogues with other theories with the same interest in the present context. This engagement is not only presupposed but also promoted by his translinguistics. [3] But before entering into this dialogue, the addressivity of the participating utterance (i. e. the theory of translinguistics) requires it to take stock of itself according to the personality, so to speak, of its addressee and the context of communication.

1. 3 Translinguistics and textual analysis

When taking up this topic, we at first have to clarify in what way the term text is used in our discussion, aiming at preparing a context for a theoretical dialogue between the parities concerned.

1. 3. 1 Discourse, text and utterance in contemporary linguistics

It is quite accepted that in the linguistic circles all over the world, the trend towards shifting our eyes from the abstract linguistic system to the concrete language used by particular speakers has been established and is still gaining strength (Leech, 1983: 1-2; Gu Yueguo, 1999). But there seems to be no agreement among linguists about how to name the living speeches produced by human verbal interactions in oral and written forms. Thus the three terms, *utterance*, *discourse* and *text* are used in a little bit confusing way by scholars working with different linguistic schools.

Fortunately, it seems that the term *utterance* claims a relatively independent territory in comparison with *discourse* and *text*. It mainly inhabits the realm of pragmatics. Moreover, it is because of the distinction made between sentence and utterance that pragmatics secures an independent position from syntax and semantics. According to Levinson (2001: 18), "a sentence is only an abstract theoretical entity defined within a theory of grammar, while an utterance is the issuance of a sentence, a sentence-analogue, or sentence-fragment, in an actual context. " That is to say, the major difference between a sentence and an utterance is whether it is used by a particular person in a concrete context. But empirically, Levinson admits, the relation between an utterance and a corresponding sentence may be quite obscure; for instance, the utterance may be elliptical, or contain sentence-fragments or "false-starts" in conversations and it can also be a string of sentences paired with a context. Thus the term utterance can also be used to refer to "any stretch of talk, by one person, before and after which there is silence on behalf of that person" (Harris, 1952: 14). Holding a similar position, Saeed (2000: 13) provides us with a clear example of the speaker-dependent nature of utterance by saying: "If I say *Ontogeny recapitulates phylogeny*, this is one utterance. If another person in the same room also says *Ontogeny recapitulates phylogeny*, then we would be dealing with two utterances." This description of utterance and the difference it holds from sentence are surprisingly redolent of what Bakhtin has formulated in his translinguistics. What is shared by the modern linguists and their enigmatic predecessor, who nevertheless is seldom acknowledged as a linguist (Alpatov, 2004), is that sentence is considered to be abstract and context-independent, but utterance is the real-life language-in-use, with its meaning depending on the concrete context. Utterance can be as small as a turn-making rejoinder in a casual conversation, and as big as a complete letter, news report, novel, and so on. But there is no evidence showing that the contemporary Anglophone linguists receive any influence from Bakhtin, who however can be qualified as a forerunner of modern pragmatics (Xin Bin, 2002). However it is necessary to note that in canonical pragmatics only utterance consisting of single sentence is under focus, and to some extent the context in which the utterance-meaning is studied is mainly the artificial-mimic and *ad hoc* context postulated by the researchers (Schiffrin, 1994: 6-12). In other words, it is still characterized by too much abstraction and leaving a lot of real-life utterances untackled. The object of analysis and the context, in which the interpretation of meanings are made, therefore, among other things, distinguish Bakhtin's translinguistics from the modern pragmatics at least at the practical level. But the case in contemporary pragmatics on the Continent is a little different. For example, linguists represented by Jef Verschueren (2000) and Jacob L. Mey (2000; 2001) not only acknowledge the contribution made by Bakhtin to pragmatics but also try to develop a different understanding of pragmatics from the canonical Anglo-American pragmatics which prefers to have itself run parallel to phonology, syntax and semantics and concentrate mostly on the issues of deixis, speech acts, conversational implicature, conversational structure, presupposition, and so forth (He Ziran, 2000; Xu Shenghuan, 2001). Thus it is safe to say that Bakhtin's translinguistics has exerted some influence on the linguists who want to extend the scope of the canonical Anglo-American pragmatics by taking into consideration those relatively macro issues such as literary pragmatics, and pragmatics across cultures. If we take the vantage point of Mey, Bakhtin's translinguistics may well fall into his macro-pragmatics. But the relationship between Bakhtin's translinguistics and the modern pragmatics is so complicated that it may deserve a book-length discussion, and our project is conducted in a way which is more closely related to modern text or discourse analysis, so we will leave it at that.

Since our project works on a translinguistic analytical model, hoping that it can be used to make a dialogic reading of print hard news text, our thinking is mainly conducted in the context of text or discourse analysis. But in contemporary linguistic analyses, which take the concrete verbal interactions in both oral and written forms as their working objects, text and discourse are used in different ways by different scholars, for the frameworks they adopt and the objectives they set are usually different from one another. But roughly speaking, there are mainly two ways of understanding these two terms. Some linguists think there is no radical difference between these two terms, but they actually also show their preferences for one rather than the other. Generally, discourse is more popular with American and British linguists, and their endeavors in this field are accordingly named *discourse analysis*. This is probably influenced by Zellig Harris who first used the term in his "Discourse Analysis" published in *Language* in 1952. His focus is looking at how language is organized as "connected discourse", but his conception of discourse analysis is simply a matter of extending the scope of grammar. And actually the transformations that Harris proposes in his analysis are essentially adopted by Chomsky in the design of generative grammar (Hu Zhuanglin, 1994a: 8; Widdowson, 2004: 1-4). Linguists in continental countries usually prefer to use the term *text* when referring to the same thing analyzed, hence the *text linguistics* (Hu Zhuanglin, 1994a: 3; Huang Guowen, 2001: 4; Li Yue'e & Fan Hongya, 2002: 3). It is generally accepted that Halliday's *SFL* is mainly "designed to account for how the language is used" (Halliday,

2000: F39), that is, how "every text" — "everything that is said or written" — "unfolds in some context of use" (ibid; Zhu Yongsheng et al., 2004: 164-71). In other words, text is an instance "of linguistic interaction in which people actually engage: whatever is said, or written, in an operational context" (Halliday, 2001: 108-9). Thus it is safe to say that Halliday's text is what Bakhtin's utterance actually implies. Thus, in his framework, the terms discourse and text are not deliberately distinguished from each other, but the term text is preferred. This treatment of discourse and text is widely accepted by the leading linguists working in this field in China, for example, Hu Zhuanglin (1994a), Huang Guowen (1988; 2001), Zhu Yongsheng & Yan Shiqing (2001), Zhu Yongsheng et al. (2001), and Zhang Delu (1998).

The other schools of linguists hold that there are radical differences between these two terms. Some linguists designate the term discourse for the oral interaction, and the term text for written communication. Others assign the term discourse to the process of verbal communication, and the term text to the product or representation of this dynamic process of interaction. For example, Brown & Yule (1983) use text to refer to the verbal record of a communicative act, discourse to refer to the process itself. This "text-as-product" -and- "discourse-as-process" view actually originates with Widdowson (1979) and is later developed in his new book, *Text, Context, Pretext*, published in 2004. In this monograph based on his PhD thesis, Widdowson reiterates his position of radically differentiating discourse from text. According to him, text can come in all shapes and sizes: they can correspond in extent with any linguistic unit—letter, sound, word, sentence, and combination of sentences. He also adds that he identifies a text by its social intent not by its linguistic extent. The major difference between text and discourse is that text is inert, but discourse is activated by contextual connection, namely, using language to engage with extralinguistic reality. "Discourse in this view is the pragmatic process of meaning negotiation. Text is its product" (Widdowson, 2004: 8). Here, discourse is regarded as something higher than text to some extent: it refers not only to the production process but also to the process of interpretation or understanding, and the text is their representation or the object of interpretation. Thus according to Widdowson, there exists a paradox in the process of analyzing written texts. In the production stage, the author only interacts with the intended readers, who may well be greatly different from the actual readers (including the analysts of course); therefore the discourse reconstructed by the readers in the interpretation or understanding process is very likely to be different from that of the producing process. We may have two or even more discourses represented by the same text. To be exact, we will have as many discourses as many particular readers and many contexts for interpretation. If we accept that the readers are the legitimate participants of the discourse, then discourse is totally context-dependent, but text is just the inert and stable linguistic realization of discourse, or just the "manifestation of linguistic data" (Widdowson, 2004: 14) for the job of analysis or interpretation.

On the other hand, compared with the term text, discourse is also widely used in social theories and analysis. For example, in the works of Michel Foucault (especially Foucault (1972)), it is used to refer to different ways of structuring areas of knowledge and social practice. For instance, the discourse of "medical science" is currently the dominant one in the practice of health care, though it contrasts with various holistic "alternative" discourse (e. g. those of homeopathy and acupuncture) as well as popular "folk" discourses. Thus discourses in this sense are manifested in particular ways of using language and other symbolic forms such as visual images (Fairclough, 1992a: 3). Foucault's using of discourse is quite accepted and very influential in post-modern philosophical discussions, literary criticisms, and other interdisciplinary studies involving the problem of language.

1.3.2 Discourse, text and utterance in our discussion

Since our project is aimed at a recontextualized framework of Bakhtinian translinguistics for analyzing print hard news text in the setting of modern linguistics (Hallidayan *SFL*, and Fowler's and Fairclough's CDA in particular), our understanding and using of the three terms naturally has to fit the task. We accept Bakhtin's usage of utterance, which is intended to refer to any concrete verbal interaction in spoken or written form. And accordingly, discourse is used holistically to refer to the entirety involving all aspects of human verbal interaction. Compared with Widdowson (2004) and Fairclough (1992b), the distinction made by Bakhtin between discourse and utterance is quite similar with that made by them between discourse and text. That is, discourse is used similarly in Bakhtin's translinguistics and utterance is replaced by text in contemporary mainstream discourse analyses. But considering our object of analysis, we will keep these three terms in our later discussion: we use text to refer to the whole passage of news reporting in different types, utterance to refer to the snippet of words inserted or woven into the whole text which carries with itself an alien flavor and can be identified as belonging to other speakers than the author;[4] we use discourse to refer to the dynamic process of verbal interaction, that is, in the same sense shared by Bakhtin, Widdowson and Fairclough. Thus Bakhtin's utterance is split into two cases of usage here: *utterance as text* and *utterance as utterance* which is woven into the text. *Since our object is print news, any stretch of news report we direct our analysis at will be termed text, and any stretch of wording we identify from this text and connect it with a source and a context for interpretation will be termed utterance.* But both of them are still used in the sense of Bakhtin's utterance; that is, they both have the three properties of thematic or referential completeness, expressivity and addressivity. In short, they are dialogic in nature. It is necessary to note that this treatment of text and utterance is simply due to technical consideration, which will be demonstrated in the following chapters; and therefore, there will also be occasions when they are used interchangeably.

1.3.3 Bakhtin's translinguistics and textual analysis

We have gone to great lengths to locate our understanding of text in the context of modern mainstream linguistics. The only purpose of doing so is to show that the key related terms in Bakhtin's translinguistics can find a lot of strong resonance in the current textual or discourse analysis, which will ensure us a possibility to draw some nutrients for translinguistics from contemporary linguistic context.

As has just been mentioned above, in our discussion, different from the macro and comprehensive term *discourse*, *text* is used to refer to the concrete and stable linguistic existence produced by a particular speaker or writer, and thus textual analysis will be performed in the way that any understanding and interpretation of a text should be based on the concrete linguistic evidence such as vocabulary, grammar, text structure and so forth. It seems that we are still working in the frequently-chided paradigm of analyzing texts in the "code model" (Lähteenmäki, 1998; Bek, 1999). But our story is that we do decode the meaning behind the lines of a text in a Hallidayan sense, but this should be under the guidance of a pre-formulated thesis or hypothesis based on a comprehensive knowledge of the context in which the text is located. This methodological account will be one of our focuses in the next chapter.

It would be beyond dispute that Bakhtin never aims at a linguistically-oriented analysis when he envisages his translinguistic theory. But his contemplation on language-in-use is now accepted to be so illuminating that a relatively complete picture of human communications can be revealed by it. That is to say, even the so-called linguistically-oriented textual analysis cannot escape its influence; for in the mainstream linguistics now text is no longer considered just to be a supra-sentential unit independent of context. It is at least regarded as a semantic concept, and below this level of thinking, there is no position set for text in the territory of syntax. Saussurean paradigm never gives a place for the text as utterance in question, for it belongs not to his *langue* but to his *parole*. But the influence cast by Bakhtin's theory upon linguistically-oriented textual analysis cannot be exaggerated too much. The reasons for its limitation may be hard to pin down, but the following three factors are quite obvious. First and foremost, Bakhtin's emphasis on the dynamic nature of meaning generated by the process of human interaction forbids any explicit account of meaning, because any attempt to pin down the meaning according to linguistic evidence will actually fix only one possible way of understanding at the cost of other competing meanings achieved from different perspectives. That is why some scholars accuse Bakhtin himself of committing this kind of monologic speaking when he uses language in written form to reveal the dynamic nature of meaning and text (Zhang Jie, 2004). That is to say, there is a danger of self-deconstruction (or in folk language, self-contradiction) in Bakhtin's theory. Of course, this dilemma characterizes the whole postmodern mentality, because post-modern thinkers have to use language when they talk about crisis of linguistic representation (Eco, 1992). Secondly, although Bakhtin's *PDP* is heralded as an example of literary criticism and even of textual analysis, which is believed to have overcome the defects and errors of Russian formalists and vulgar sociopolitical critics, it fails to settle into sustained study of any one of Dostoevsky's works and remains at a persistently high level of generality (Booth, 1984: xxvi). On the one hand this high level of generality distances itself from our practice of analyzing concrete texts; on the other hand, as far as textual analysis in general is concerned, it looks relatively specific, for it confines itself only to novel text, which is typical of literary criticism rather than general textual analysis. Thus the influence exerted by this kind of "textual analysis" is comparatively limited. And as has been mentioned in the introduction, when conducting his dialogic analysis of novel text, Bakhtin relies too much upon his own insights (i.e. his personal "feel") rather than concrete linguistic analysis (Bakhtin, 1981: 419; Pearce, 1994: 66-7), but sufficient linguistic observations are usually believed to be the foundations of a linguistically-oriented textual analysis. Thirdly, although the term of translinguistics is first introduced in *PDP* when discourse of Dostoevsky's novels is discussed, it is relatively specific and underdeveloped. But when Bakhtin extends it to a general level in his *PSG* later, he fails to apply it to practical analysis of any text (literary or non-literary) (Wertsch, 1991: 79).

In short, if it is employed in analyzing texts apart from novels, especially the so-called public texts (including news texts), Bakhtin's translinguistics will have to absorb the latest developments of modern linguistics. In this connection, Halliday and his followers' *SFL* naturally comes into our vision. This is not only because it claims to aim at textual analysis, but more importantly because Bakhtin's translinguistics and *SFL* have a lot in common.

1.4 Summary

In this chapter, the observations on language made by Bakhtin in different periods of time are firstly assembled to form an organic whole, which consists of the following two essential parts: (1) the philosophical and methodological basis for translinguistics are formulated in comparison with Saussurean abstract objective linguistics; (2) instead of the abstract stable language system, the object of translinguistic studies is living speech or discourse, and the analytical unit for discourse is utterance which is inherently dialogic; the dynamic utterances can be categorized into different relatively stable genres, which mirror the various habitualized activity types in the society. If we take the first component as the philosophical basis of translinguistics, which is, as Rutland (2003) says, constructed against the model of Saussurean linguistics, then the second will be the original contributions highlighted in translinguistics. As far as textual analysis is concerned, the most significant concept in translinguistics is *dialogicity* of text, which, as has been mentioned in the introduction to our discussion, ensures Bakhtin's dialogic readings of Dostoevsky's novels in the actual plane rather than the fictional one and will also anticipate a similar dialogic reading of hard news text on the condition that more necessary recontextualizations of translinguistics have to be made in the setting of Hallidayan *SFL* and the modern media practices and theorizations.

In order to pave a smooth way for the subsequent interpretations and developments of a translinguistically-dialogic framework for textual analysis, the three important terms, namely, *discourse*, *text*, and *utterance*, have been clarified within the potential of Bakhtin's understandings of them. In this connection, the relationship between Bakhtin's translinguistics and modern linguistically-oriented textual analysis has also been considered in order to usher Hallidayan *SFL* into Bakhtinian translinguistics, for *SFL* is believed to be able to bridge the gap between Bakhtin's translinguistics and pure linguistics. This gap-filling will turn into reality Bakhtin's hypothetical acknowledgement that translinguistics and pure linguistics complement each other. In so doing, a wider-spectrum translinguistically-dialogic model that can be used to analyze hard news text will be attained.

Notes:

[1] Bakhtin's idea on the relationship between utterance and text is in a measure ambivalent. Even in the same article, he first regards "utterance as text" (Bakhtin, 1986: 104-5), and later he also views text just as a stable linguistic concept, utterance a translinguistic dynamic concept (Bakhtin, 1986: 122-3). But in other places, text is mostly treated as utterance, which is characterized by dialogic nature, for instance, on page 162 of the same book, the dialogic nature of text is discussed and obviously text is regarded as utterance there (Danow, 1991: 111).

[2] It is widely accepted that Bakhtin's philosophy is actually a philosophy of dialogue, thus *dialogism* as not only an ontological but also a methodological thread running through all his theorizations on nearly anything entering his vision

(Holquist, 2002). Thus the dialogicity of utterance or text actually constitutes the most essential and revolutionary part of his translinguistics, which deserves a special chapter in our discussion. So we will save this topic for Chapter Three after we have prepared a productive context by ushering Hallidayan *SFL* into our consideration in order to interpret textual dialogicity more fruitfully as far as reading hard news text dialogically is concerned.

[3] It is commonly accepted that Bakhtin's translinguistics is built upon the cornerstone of dialogism, which is characterized by its encouragement of dialogue, communication and accommodation between ideas, texts and utterances.

[4] But in our later discussions in Chapter Three, where the relationship between voice and utterance are considered, utterance gains more methodological significance: it will be regarded as an important unit for textual interpretation in the process of dialogic analysis of a certain text.

Chapter 2　The Compatibility between Translinguistics and Hallidayan *SFL*

　　Both looking at language from a social perspective and focusing on language use beyond the abstract linguistic structure, Bakhtin and Halliday have a lot in common. As has been discussed in the previous chapter, Bakhtin's translinguistics differs from the Saussurean abstract objectivism and the individual subjectivism represented by Vossler and Croce mainly in that Bakhtin simply takes a sociological look at language—the concrete speech in a concrete context, the dynamic and dialogic nature of meaning, the intersubjectivity between speakers, and speech genres. These aspects of language use can find strong resonance in Hallidayan *SFL*.

2.1　Non-Aristotelian philosophical tradition

　　The common ground shared by Bakhtin and Halliday can be traced back to their preferring a non-Aristotelian view on language. As is widely known, commonly accredited to Aristotle are such understandings of language as the logic-based syntactic structure, the classification of words into different categories according to its syntactic positions (i.e. part of speech), the distinction between grammar and rhetoric or poetics, the arbitrariness of language, and the concept of language as a system of rules. According to Halliday (2003: 92-115), linguists influenced by Aristotle usually agreed: linguistics is part of philosophy, and grammar is part of logic; language is normative, and meaning is related to truth; language can be represented as a system of rules, and sentences and uses can be formally analyzed for purposes of idealization (for deciding what falls within or outside its scope). The Aristotelian paradigm of looking at language is dominant for the most part of the time in linguistic history. Its way of thinking is passed on through the medieval linguists Modistae who laid the foundations for formal syntax and their French successors, the rationalist school of Port-Royal, to Saussure and Chomsky. Linguists or philosophers of language in this tradition stress the universals of human languages and thus the abstract stable system of forms becomes the chief object of their studies, the extreme version of which is embodied by the transformational linguistics founded by Chomsky. Another thing shared by the linguists in the Aristotelian tradition is that they usually take a look at language from a psychological or even a biological perspective rather than a sociological perspective; that is, language is usually observed as an inner-organism rather than an inter-organism phenomenon (Hu Zhuanglin et al., 2005: 6-9). Some defenders of this rationalist tradition even believe that unless some priori universals can unite human beings, nothing can do so, since we begin as self-enclosed individuals with no natural ties to one another (Schultz, 1990: 3-4).

In contrast to Aristotelian understanding of language, Halliday (2003: 92-115) identifies another way of looking at human language issues originating with Protagoras and Plato. This tradition regards language as a resource (rather than a formal, rule-bound system) for making, realizing, and enacting context-dependent social meanings (Thibault, 1991: 119). That is, the linguists in this tradition are concerned much more with meaning in living verbal communications than with truth value. They hold that if language has any relation to truth, it lies in its ability to demonstrate that truth is relative to the believer and the situation in which it occurs. Different from the Aristotelian linguistics, which makes linguistics part of philosophy and grammar part of logic, the linguists in the second tradition believe that linguistics is part of anthropology, and grammar part of culture. Therefore, instead of focusing exclusively on idealization and universalities, they acknowledge differences and diversities of human languages. Even within a single language, they pay more attention to the heterogeneity than homogeneity. After all, Halliday (2003: 99) warns us that there is a danger of simplification in making such a gross dualistic account of western linguistic tradition. It is hard to say that every school, every scholar and every work must belong squarely to one tradition or the other. Most of them combine ideas, in a way, from both. But the preference for either of them can be found recurring throughout the history of ideas about language. The relativist (rather than the absolutist or rationalist) way of looking at language, though comparatively marginalized, is promoted by Malinowski, Whorf and Firth, to name just a few, and is now gaining its strength. Heavily influenced by them, Halliday and his followers for the most part identify themselves with the second anthropological or sociological tradition, namely, the non-Aristotelian philosophical tradition. He chooses to regard language as an inter-organism phenomenon and to look at language from a sociological rather than a psychological perspective.

As has been discussed in the previous chapter, Bakhtin also adopts a sociological view on language; in his translinguistics, he places more emphasis on the heterogeneity of language than on its homogeneity. In his *MPL*, Bakhtin takes to task the philosophy-and-logic-based linguistic studies and reveals that Saussure's viewing language as a system of normatively identical forms can be traced back to Aristotelian philology. He simply says, "Aristotle is a typical philologist" (Bakhtin/Volosinov, 1986: 71). Moreover, for Bakhtin, the philosophical, literary and linguistic movements from Aristotle's poetics to Saussure's structuralism are implicated in the process of conceptualization of language and even literary text as a closed system. That is, language is considered a stable, monolithic entity, and correspondingly, literary text a self-sufficient authorial monologue (Gardiner, 1992: 34). In contrast to Aristotelian monological and centripetal sense of the wholeness of literature and of the harmonious interaction of all genres contained within the whole, which excludes novel from it, Bakhtin regards novel (especially those heteroglossia-saturated dialogic novels) as a revolutionary genre of utterance or discourse; the genre of novel as utterance characterized by its heteroglossia and dialogicity is believed to inherit a lot from Socrates, Plato, Menippe, Rabelais and so forth (Bakhtin, 1981: 5, 8, 62; 1984; Gardiner, 1992: 139; Lock, 2001). In Charles Lock's words (2001: 76), "The distinctive feature of novelistic discourse (i. e. dialogicity) is, in a Bakhtinian light, its transgression of Aristotelian boundaries, its disowning of Aristotelian features. To Bakhtin we can attribute the recognition that the history of the reception of the novel has been, since the Enlightenment, a willful, blind submission to the authority of Aristotle." Thus, it is safe to say that, like Halliday, Bakhtin also works in a non-Aristotelian paradigm when observing language (literary texts in particular). On the basis of analyzing Dostoevsky's and Rabelais's novels, he advances his translinguistics, which is crowned with his theory of speech genres developed in his late years. According to Schultz (1990), Bakhtin also opposes rationalism and the Whorfian concept of linguistic relativity is quite evident in his works about language. This can be regarded as another point where Bakhtin and Halliday converge.

2.2 Translinguistics and *SFL*: context, function, register and genre

As has just been discussed above, when looking at language in use, Bakhtin and Halliday both adopt a non-Aristotelian position; they both set text (or utterance as text) as a unit of analysis of human verbal interaction. Hence a comparison between the core issues in their ideas about language will be fruitful.

2.2.1 Context of situation: Bakhtin, Malinowski and Halliday

It is commonly accepted that the recognition of the central role played by context in human verbal communication characterizes Bakhtin's translinguistics. To him, "the meaning of a word is determined entirely by its context" (Bakhtin/Volosinov, 1986: 79); the major fault of abstract objectivism lies in the ignorance of context—what they did is "remove the word from the contexts" and " [fix] its meaning outside any context" (Bakhtin/Volosinov, 1986: 80). And context can help us tell a sentence from an utterance (Bakhtin, 1986: 81-5). Like Bakhtin, Halliday (who follows Malinowski) also assigns context a central position in his *SFL*. Considering Halliday's acceptance of the concept of context formulated by Malinowski, the connection between his and Bakhtin's understanding of context can be detected from the quoted part from Malinowski: "... utterance and situation are bound up inextricably with each other and the context of situation is indispensable for the understanding of the words. Exactly as in the reality of spoken or written language, a word without linguistic context is a mere figment and stands for nothing by itself, so in the reality of a spoken living tongue, the utterance has no meaning except in the context of situation" (Malinowski, 1923: 307; adopted from Hasan, 1985: 17). Here it is quite evident that Bakhtin and Halliday (accepting Malinowski) both agree that meaning is determined by context and utterance is inseparable from its context (Holquist, 2003).

Although Bakhtin and Malinowski recognize the central role played by the context of situation in human communications, it is Halliday who gives it a full development and makes the relationship between the context of situation and the meaning of utterance more concrete and easier to understand. He proposes that: "The semiotic structure of a particular situation type can be represented as a complex of three dimensions: the ongoing social activity, the role relationships involved, and the symbolic or rhetorical channel" (Halliday, 2001: 110). And he refers to these three dimensions respectively as *field of discourse*, *tenor of discourse* and *mode of discourse*, which then determine ideational, interpersonal and textual meaning of an utterance respectively. In this way, context becomes a more practical concept with concrete content and due delicacy with respect to textual analysis, hence the need for Bakhtin's translinguistics to incorporate this new development.

2.2.2 Linguistic functions: Bühler, Bakhtin and Halliday

The functional understanding of language of Bakhtin and that of Halliday meet at the point of Bühler, who is known in linguistic circles for his advocating functions of human language. According to the expressive, representative and triggering functions of language identified by Wundt, Husserl and Marty, Bühler proposes three functions that each concrete "speech event" comprises: the function of expression (expressive), the function of appeal (or conative), and the function of representation (or referential). Here, the similarity between Bakhtin's (1986) description of the three properties of utterance and Bühler's three functions of speech event is quite evident: expression corresponds to expressivity, appeal to addressivity, and representation to the referentially semantic content. According to Brandist (2004: 97-124), among others, Bakhtin is greatly influenced by Bühler not only in language issues but also in his thinking about the question of intersubjectivity in general. Bühler's attack of Husserl for taking a one-sided approach to meaning typical of the logicians (stressing only the representational function) provides Bakhtin with a framework within which his early philosophy of authorship could be translated into discursive terms. Thus dialogue could now become the discursive embodiment of intersubjective relations.

Although Bühler is believed to use language to investigate something else and his interest is probably psycholinguistics, he does in a measure exert much influence on Halliday. In Halliday's own words:

> My own *ideational* corresponds very closely to Bühler's *representational*, except that I want to introduce the further distinction within it between *experiential* and *logical*, which corresponds to a fundamental distinction within language itself. My own interpersonal corresponds more or less to the sum of Bühler's *conative* and *expressive*, because in the linguistic system these two are not distinguished. Then I need to add a third function, namely the *textual* function, which you will not find in Malinowski or Bühler or anywhere else, because it is intrinsic to language: it is the function that language has of creating text, of relating itself to the context—to the situation and the preceding text. (Halliday, 2001: 48; italics in the original)

From here, we can see that trained as a linguist, Halliday differs from Bühler and Bakhtin in that he pays much more attention to the intrinsic properties of language rather than exclusively looking at language from a sociologically extrinsic perspective. That is, he aims at explaining "the internal nature of language in such a way as to relate it to its external environment" (ibid.). The relationship among Bühler's linguistic functions, Bakhtin's meanings (or functions) of utterance and Halliday's metafunctions can be demonstrated in the following table:

Table 2.1 Understandings of linguistic function of Bühler, Bakhtin and Halliday

Bühler (psychological)	Bakhtin (translinguistic)	Halliday (linguistic)	
referential	referential	ideational	experiential
			logical
expressive	expressive	interpersonal	
conative	addressive		
		textual	

It is necessary to note here that Halliday's functions are later also identified as three types of meaning of language-in-use, namely ideational meaning, interpersonal meaning and textual meaning in his functional grammar (Halliday, 2000: F39-F40). Thus we can say that Bakhtin and Halliday most probably refer to the same thing when looking at a speech event from an outside social perspective: how the language in use interacts with the outside world and what is the dynamics between addressor and addressee. But at the same time, Halliday spares some efforts for the interactions taking place within the language itself, hence the textual dimension.

2.2.3 Register and genre: Bakhtin, Halliday and Martin

There would be no dispute about the understanding that both Bakhtin and Halliday try to observe the mass of irregular and diversified concrete utterances (or texts) which Saussure excludes as an impossible task from his scientific studies on language. Differing from Saussure, they both hold that behind the seemingly chaotic myriad of utterances lie some stable patterns of human verbal interaction. That is, above Saussure's system of forms, the stable types of utterance (or text) can also be found.

With respect to the problem of the diversity of texts, Halliday places his focus on the variability of the context of situation, for he agrees that "the language we speak or write varies according to the type of situation" (Halliday, 2001: 32). On the basis of adequate theorization and generalization, he finds that types of communicative situation differ from one another mainly in the following three dimensions: first, what is actually taking place; secondly, who is taking part; and thirdly, what part the language is playing, and he summarizes them correspondingly under the three headings of *field of discourse*, *tenor of discourse* and *mode of discourse*. These three variables identified by him actually make the concept of the context of situation proposed by Malinowski much clearer and more applicable to analyzing and understanding text. The configuration of the three variables that determines the meaning of a text and its linguistic choices (i.e. in folk terminology, the choices of sentence patterns, words, etc.) is called *register*. Halliday also defines this crucial term (i.e. *register*) "as the configuration of semantic resources that the member of a culture typically associates with a situation type" (Halliday, 2001: 111). According to him, the relationship between register and text is that the latter is an instance of the former— "it [register] defines the variety of which the particular text is an instance" (Halliday, 2001: 145). This relationship of instantiation implies that both being the concepts at the same level

(i. e. the level of semantics), the myriad of texts can be subsumed under various registers, which are considered relatively stable and conventionally recognized by the members of a speech community. But the relationship between text and register is actually complicated by the recognition that several distinct types of situation may be detected in a particular text, especially the text belonging to what Halliday calls open-registers (Halliday & Hasan, 1985: 40). But this complication does not invalidate the theoretic significance of register. Researches show that people can indeed produce and identify distinctive registers as appropriate to different types of situation (Fowler, 1996: 190).

Compared with the context of situation, its twin concept of the context of culture inherited from Malinowski is less theorized and developed by Halliday; for he thinks when meaning potential is interpreted in the context of culture it will be the entire semantic system of the language and " [t]his is a fiction, something we cannot hope to describe" (Halliday, 2001: 109; Leeuwen, 2005: 6). This inadequacy in Halliday's theorization on the context of culture, however, is recognized by his student Martin and has become one of the key issues within his concern from mid-1980s. By abstracting away from the plane of register Halliday's *rhetorical genre*,[1] Gregory's (1967) *functional tenor* and Ure & Ellis's (1977) *role*, Martin (1985) proposes an independent plane of generalization, the concept of *genre* (Hu Zhuanglin, 1994b). According to him, genres are how things get done when language is used to accomplish them. They range from literary to far from literary forms and are used to embrace each of the linguistically realized activity types which comprise so much of our culture. Genre is situated at the level above register and constrains the possible combinations of field, mode and tenor variables of the context of situation; and it has schematic structures (Martin, 1985). Different from registers, genres are then believed to be "the staged purposeful social processes through which a culture is realized in a language" (Martin & Rothery, 1986: 243; adopted from Swales, 2001: 41). Although Martin tries to introduce the concept of genre (which is comparatively ignored or integrated into register by Halliday) into the conceptualization of the context of culture, this idea of his remains vague to some extent before he associates himself with Bakhtin's theory of speech genres (Hu Zhuanglin, 1994b). Martin (1992: 494) finds that " [w]hile acknowledging metafunctional diversity in terms strikingly similar to those developed by Halliday, Bakhtin places emphasis as well on the integration of these meanings as speech genres which evolve and differentiate themselves in different spheres of human activity. " Thus Martin accordingly formulates his theory of genre by drawing heavily upon Bakhtin's theory of speech genres, which can be best embodied by the opening paragraph of his *PSG*:

> All the diverse areas of human activity involve the use of language. Quite understandably, the nature and forms of this use are just as diverse as are the areas of human activity... Language is realized in the form of individual concrete utterances (oral and written) by participants in the various areas of human activity. These utterances reflect the specific conditions and goals of each such area not only through their content (thematic) and linguistic style, that is, the selection of the lexical, phraseological, and grammatical resources of the language, but above all through their compositional structure. All three of these aspects—thematic content, style, and compositional structure—are inseparably linked to the *whole* of the utterance and are equally determined by the specific nature of the particular sphere of communication. Each separate utterance is individual, of course, but each sphere in which language is used develops its own *relatively stable types* of these utterances. These we may call *speech genres*. (Bakhtin, 1986: 60; italics in the original)

Inspired by this Bakhtinian understanding of speech genres, Martin proposes a separate stratum above Halliday's register, because he believes that Halliday puts too much emphasis on the connection between the register and the semantic components of the text, and pays insufficient attention to the dynamic inter-connections among the texts and registers. Addressing such inadequacy of Halliday by accepting Bakhtin's theory of speech genres, Martin names this separate plane *genre*. As far as the relationship between genre and register is concerned, Martin (1992: 493-7) argues that compared with Halliday, Bakhtin takes a more holistic cultural perspective on text-type and interprets context as a system of social processes, which is characterized by dialogic interactions and theorized as heteroglossia and dialogicity. Thus it is quite necessary to join Bakhtin's genre theory to Halliday's theory of register; for they in reality complement each other.

Drawing on these two complementary sources, Martin proposes an integrated model of the operation of language in human social interactions by separating genre from register. In his stratified model (Martin, 1992: 495), *genre* is used to realize *the context of culture* and *register* to realize *genre*; and register is then realized by *the linguistic system*. Using Hjelmslev's terms, Martin points out that the register functions as the expression form of genre, and language functions as the expression form of register.

Agreeing with Bakhtin (1986: 60-2), Martin maintains:

> The number of recognizably distinct genres in any culture may be quite large, but not unmanageably so. In contemporary western culture we can informally name many spoken genres whose patterns of meaning are more or less predictable, such as *greetings*, *service encounters*, *casual conversations*, *arguments*, *telephone enquiries*, *instructions*, *lectures*, *debates*, *plays*, *jokes*, *games* and so on; and within each of these general types, we could name many more specific genres. (Martin & White, 2005: 33; italics in the original)

As for the relationship between genre and text, Martin accepts Halliday's concept of instantiation, but differing from Halliday, who designates text at the other end of the cline (one end of which is the generalized meaning potential, namely the system), Martin argues that instead of concrete texts, the end of the cline which is in opposition to the other end filled by *the system* should be occupied by the concrete readings of texts, because different readers will be socially positioned differently and interact differently with a certain text (and with its author behind the scene), hence different subjectified understandings of the text (Martin & White 2005: 24-5). It is quite obvious that Martin accepts Bakhtin's idea of a dialogic active understanding of a text that is proposed in his *MPL* (Bakhtin/ Volosinov, 1986: 102-3). Furthermore, Martin and his colleagues also give Halliday's interpersonal system a significant development by drawing heavily on Bakhtin's dialogism, thus an important branch of *SFL* named *Appraisal Theory* being established (Martin & White, 2005). In short, the fact that Bakhtin's translinguistic theory serves as a new resource for *SFL* linguists to develop their ideas strongly suggests that Bakhtin's translinguistics is highly compatible with Hallidayan *SFL*.

2.3 Instantiation and realization: *SFL* bridging translinguistics and linguistics

In the above two subsections, we have found Bakhtin's translinguistics and Hallidayan *SFL* have a lot in common concerning the major issues about human language-in-use. But Bakhtin, who possesses a wider-range of interests in human issues such as philosophy, ethics, literary criticism, anthropology, linguistics and so forth, is believed to focus on the philosophical thinking in the form of literary criticism. He is not talking about language for language's sake, and his shifting from the traditional philosophical, ethical and literary concerns to linguistic issues is quite in agreement with the linguistic turn in western philosophical practice (Hirschkop, 2001). Thus, it is quite understandable that his socially-and-philosophically-oriented translinguistics is not designed to deal with the language issues in a concrete and systematic way. Trained as a linguist, Halliday's interests, however, are mainly directed to language within and without. His theory of language is certainly linguistically-oriented.

Although Halliday is believed to have inherited a lot of Saussure's legacy, his *SFL* is also different from Saussure's conception of linguistics in that it takes into consideration both system and text (i. e. Saussure's *parole*). That is, Halliday tries to build a new type of linguistics (or a functional grammar) which is "at once both a grammar of the system and a grammar of the text" (Halliday, 2000: F48). Here is what he says when he talks about the relationship between system and text:

> We follow Saussure in his understanding of the relationship between the system of language and its instantiation in acts of speaking; although not in his implied conclusion, that once the text has been used as evidence for the system it can be dispensed with—it has served its purpose. This mistake (whether due to Saussure or to his interpreters) haunted linguistics for much of the twentieth century, making it obsessed with the system at the expense of the text. (ibid.)
>
> For a linguist, to describe language without accounting for text is sterile; to describe text without relating it to language is vacuous. (Halliday, 2003: 196)

That is to say, system cannot be observed separately from text, and vice versa; for they are the things of the same level (or stratum) and forms a cline from the potential to the actual instance: system is the meaning potential; text is the actual choice made by the speaker or writer from the potential. In short, the relationship between text and system is that of intrastratal instantiation (Muntigl & Horvath, 2005: 217-8). Considering the fact that the text is dynamic in that it connects with the concrete context of communication and even a written text can be read in different ways, the systems of language cannot be autostable and closed, but only metastable—"they persist only through constantly changing by interpenetration with their environment" (Halliday, 2002a: 358). That is, "[t]he system is permeable because each instance (i. e. text) redounds with the context of situation, and so perturbs the system in interaction with the environment" (Halliday, 2002a: 359). In order to give us a clearer picture of the relationship between system and text, Halliday draws an analogy between the system-text relation and the climate-weather relation. Here is his account:

> A climate is a reasonably stable system; there are kinds of climate, such as tropical and polar, and these persist, and they differ in systematic ways. Yet we are all very concerned about changes in the climate, and consequences of global warming. What does it mean to say the climate is changing? Climate is instantiated in the form of weather: today's temperature, humidity, direction and speed of wind, etc., in central Scotland are instances of climatic phenomena. As such they may be more, or less, typical: today's maximum is so many degrees higher, or lower, than average—meaning the average at this place, at this time of year and at this time of day. The average is a statement of the probabilities: there is a 70 per cent chance, let us say, that the temperature will fall within such a range. *The probability is a feature of the system (the climate); but it is no more, and no less, than the pattern set up by the instances (the weather), and each instance, no matter how minutely, perturbs these probabilities and so changes the system.* (ibid. ; italicized by the author of this book)

In an article entitled "On the 'Architecture' of Human Language" published in 2003 as the introduction to one of his ten-volume collected works edited by Jonathan Webster, Halliday (2003: 1-29) elucidates and reiterates his idea on system and structure again. Language is the most powerful among all human semiotic systems—systems of meaning; and language belongs to the highest order of complexity, "being semiotic and social and biological and physical: meaning is socially constructed, biologically activated and exchanged through physical channels" (Halliday, 2003: 2). Language is the greatest source of power because it resides in its organization as a huge network of interrelated paradigmatic choices; the system of language is thus this huge network of choices, theorized as meaning potential. The complexity of language also lies in the fact that it is a layered system; the relationship between the different layers or strata is theorized as *realization*. For instance, meanings are realized as wordings, and wordings realized as sound (or soundings). The interstratal realization ensures the connection between the top order meaning system and the bottom order physical system. Among the strata of systems, the emergence of the stratum of lexicogrammar is crucial not only from a *phylogenetic* perspective but also from an *ontogenetic* one (Halliday, 2002a: 355-60). [2] It supplies the space in which meanings could be organized in their own terms. At this stratum, the syntagmatic composition, which forms the major concern of Saussurean structure, is fundamental; and the structure of clause rank is central because it carries the main burden of integrating the various kinds of meanings—that is, the selections in the various meaning systems—into a single frame. Thus, it can be accepted that the clause rank and its compositional structure provide a point at which Halliday's system dovetails with Saussurean structural linguistics. But it is necessary to note at this juncture that in Halliday's view, syntagmatic composition is the simplest and most accessible form of organization for any system whether material or semiotic, not just for the syntactic system. Another point we have to be cautious about is that although Saussure perhaps does not confine his system to structure or forms, his dyadic separation of paradigmatic relation from syntagmatic relation and giving the latter his priority do promote the later practice of confusing system with structure. With respect to the relationship between system and structure, Hallidayan linguists share the understanding that paradigmatic systems form the meaning potential from which speakers make their choices to realize their communicative purposes, but the structures are the output of these choices being combined together according to the syntagmatic compositional principles (Halliday, 2002a: 196-217; Zhu Yongsheng & Yan shiqing, 2001: 10; Hu Zhuanglin et al., 2005: 66-70).

Intrastratal instantiation and interstratal realization are the two important mechanisms of language identified by Halliday. The former makes it possible for us to observe against the background of linguistic system the seemingly chaotic instances of concrete language-in-use discarded by Saussure but valued by Bakhtin; the latter enables us to have a clearer picture of how the fictional system gains its blood and flesh and is incarnated into a concrete text or utterance. Thus if we bring Saussure, Bakhtin and Halliday into the same scene, it seems that Halliday can serve as a good mediator. Hence *SFL* bridges translinguistics and Saussurean linguistics (cf. Ongstad, 2004: 77). And Bakhtin does allow the room for this kind of bridging when he advances his translinguistics by saying:

> Of course, metalinguistic [translinguistic] research cannot ignore linguistics and must make use of its results. Linguistics and metalinguistics [translinguistics] study one and the same concrete, highly complex, and multi-faceted phenomenon... (Bakhtin, 1984: 181)
>
> Language as a system has an immense supply of purely linguistic means for expressing formal address: lexical, morphological (the corresponding cases, pronouns, personal forms of verbs), and syntactical (various standard phrases and modifications of sentences). (Bakhtin, 1986: 99)

Unfortunately, Bakhtin stops the topic where he makes this generous "reconciliation" and leaves the task of incorporating linguistic findings into his translinguistics to Halliday. But this "commissioning" happens beyond the notice of the two parties concerned, though they had been contemporary with each other for a long time before the year of 1975.

In this section, we have found that Bakhtin's translinguistics is quite compatible with Hallidayan *SFL*, because they are not only in the same non-Aristotelian tradition but also share a lot in their ideas about context, function of language, genre, linguistic means as resources from which choices can be made and so on. This compatibility enables us to bring Bakhtin's insights about utterance (or text) into full play in textual analysis by employing the tool kit supplied by Hallidayan *SFL*, which translinguistics is "notoriously" short of. This tool kit is actually the functional grammar based on the "systemic" theory formulated by Halliday and his followers. The necessity of this tool kit in doing textual analysis even in a Bakhtinian translinguistic model is motivated by the fact, pointed out by Halliday, that " [a] discourse [text] analysis that is not based on grammar is not an analysis at all, but simply a running commentary on a text" (Halliday, 2000: F42). That is why we have to develop Bakhtin's key ideas on the dialogicity of text in the context of *SFL*. But before we tackle this Herculean task in the next chapter, a brief account of the methodology of textual analysis we will adopt in this book should be in order.

2.4 A double-oriented functional model of textual analysis

The approaches to textual or discourse analysis are as diverse as the understandings of what a discourse or text is, or to be exact, the methods adopted by analysts are determined by their concepts of text or discourse. According to the linguistic theory used as analytical basis, Schiffrin (1994) identifies six approaches to discourse analysis in the mainstream linguistics: analysis based on speech act theory, on interactional sociolinguistics, on the ethnography of communication, on pragmatics, on conversation analysis, and on variation analysis which stems from studies of linguistic variation and change. But this is far from being the complete picture of textual analysis. For up to now, textual analysis is still a discipline of becoming, which is influenced by a variety of theories from different disciplines (such as linguistics, semiotics, psychology, anthropology, sociology, literary criticism, and information science) rather than a unified single theory, and follows no established approaches or steps. But it seems to be a common practice that each analyst usually makes explicit beforehand the theories he employs, the perspective he takes and the steps he follows (Huang Guowen, 1988: 7; Huang Guowen & Ghadessy, 2006: 12-3; Schiffrin, 1994: 1; Gee, 1999: 4-5; Jørgensen & Phillips, 2002: 1-3). Therefore, in addition to the adopted theories discussed above, it is quite necessary for us to clarify other methodological aspects of our project—to analyze the dialogic nature of print hard news text for the purpose of testifying the validity of the translinguistic framework in which our textual analysis of print hard news is conducted.

2.4.1 A theory-driven top-down dialogic look at text

The foregoing discussions of this book have shown that we will take Bakhtin's translinguistics as the starting point of looking at print hard news text. Connecting any real text with its concrete context and putting it into different genres, translinguistics mainly explores the dialogic nature of text. Thus when we follow this kind of observation of text, we really bear some preformulated "prejudice" about text or in van Dijk's (2001: 96) words, our analysis of the text is basically an "analysis with an attitude".

According to Lynee Young & Harrison (2004: 1-2), this kind of looking at text with preformulated theses is typical of CDA (Critical Discourse Analysis). The framework of CDA, according to Chouliaraki & Fairclough (1999: 60) can be summarized synoptically into the following steps:

1. A problem (activity, reflexivity).
2. Obstacles to its being tackled:
   (a) analysis of the conjuncture;
   (b) analysis of the practice re its discourse moment [sic]:
      (i) relevant practice(s)?
      (ii) relation of discourse to other moments?
         —discourse as part of the activity
         —discourse and reflexivity;
   (c) analysis of the discourse:
      (i) structural analysis: the order of discourse
      (ii) interactional analysis
         —interdiscursive analysis
         —linguistics and semiotic analysis.
3. Function of the problem in the practice.
4. Possible ways past the obstacles [sic].
5. Reflection on the analysis.

It is quite obvious that to the scholars with this school discourse is actually used to refer to semiotic elements of social practices (Chouliaraki & Fairclough, 1999: 38); the analysis of it should be put into the large framework of the overall human activities and conducted in the way of problem-solving-and-feedback-reflection; and the analysis itself should be interactional—interacts with other disciplines and practices. In other words, this kind of analysis is more socially-oriented than linguistically-oriented, and linguistic analysis, if there is any case of it, is put at the bottom of their observation. By analyzing different public discursive events in this top-down fashion, they try to explore the hidden and habitualized relations between language and power and the ways in which language is used to produce, maintain, and reproduce positions of power through discursive means (Xin Bin, 2000: 14-57, 2005: 6-7; Fairclough, 2001: 1-13).

Since the Bakhtinian dialogic relations between utterances within a text are hidden between the lines, only a critical reading, which is characterized by reading and responding to it in an active or dialogic way (or in Fowler's (1996) word "defamiliarization" of the text), can expose this textual dialogicity. Thus we will follow this top-down critical reading of print hard news text advanced and practiced by CDA analysts, hoping to discover some social motivations for textual dialogicity.

2.4.2 A data-driven bottom-up linguistic look at text

Although any in-depth textual analysis should start from a holistic theoretic point, this so-called top-down reading has to be based on concrete linguistic observations (especially lexico-grammatical descriptions). Only stressing the importance of language but rarely considering linguistic details, is the common error shared by those macro-discoursal analyses represented by Foucault (Cook, 1999: 52). And in a measure, Bakhtin's theory on discourse and utterance is commonly believed to be in the same vein (Fairclough, 1992a: 46-7). A textual analysis without concrete linguistic descriptions is considered a series of *ad hoc* impressionistic statements which can hardly be accepted as cogent interpretations and explanations; for they are drifting rather than consolidated. In the eyes of linguists, especially Halliday (2000), a textual analysis without detailed grammatical analysis cannot be regarded as an analysis at all.

But linguistic analysis is also theory-based, and not all the linguistic theories are fit for a linguistic description for textual interpretations and explanations. According to Young & Harrison (2004: 4), among various linguistic theories, "*SFL* provides a solid methodology that can, as Gregory (2001) states, help preserve CDA from ideological bias—a view which echoes Martin's (2000) that one of the strengths of *SFL* for CDA is to ground concerns with power and ideology in detailed analysis of texts in real contexts of language use, thereby making it possible for the analyst to be explicit, transparent, and precise."

The reason why *SFL* is able to provide textual analysis in CDA paradigm with a solid methodology as far as linguistic analysis is concerned has actually been discussed in the above sections (Li Zhanzi & Gao Yihong, 2002; Xin Bin, 2005: 54-6). At this juncture, it is necessary to get its main principles reiterated. The concept of stratification and realization of language use in the human society enables *SFL* to join the macroscopic observation of language in the social and cultural context with the microscopic analysis of language. And the functional grammar formulated under this guiding principle serves as a powerful analytical tool for making detailed observations of the text in question. Therefore with the help of its functional grammar we can identify the lexico-grammatical resources selected to realize the dialogic relations among different utterances within the text, thus the power relations between the subjects of the utterances and the ideological struggles behind the lines being revealed or reconstructed. Although this Hallidayan interstratal realization is accused of being another type of Saussurean codification and considered incompatible with Bakhtin's translinguistics (Bek, 1999), this incompatibility or in Bek's word "misconception" is actually overstated. The grounds for Bek's accusation may mainly come from the early works of Halliday concerning the analysis of literary texts. At that time Halliday did once emphasize an objective linguistic description of text without any influence of a preformulated thesis (Halliday, 1964; Fowler, 1986: 2-3, 1996: 3-4), but Halliday himself has changed this idea for a long time, and this change is promoted by his developing the functional modules of his *SFL* (Hu Zhuanglin, 2000: 115-9). The functional understanding of language use actually presupposes a holistic view of language in combination with its context, thus overriding the practice that regards the bottom-up objective description as the only legitimate method of textual analysis. And the target of the analysis is far more than the de-codification of the meaning codified in the linguistic expressions by the writer. As early as 1976, Halliday & Hasan pointed out:

> The linguistic analysis of a text is not an interpretation of that

text; it is an explanation. This point emerges clearly, though it is often misunderstood, in the context of stylistics, the linguistic analysis of literary texts. The linguistic analysis of literature is not an interpretation of what the text means; it is an explanation of why and how it means what it does. (Halliday & Hasan, 2001: 327-8)

That is to say, to Halliday, textual analysis should be conducted at two levels. Its lower-level target is to interpret what it means, which can be achieved by linguistic analysis of the text based on a workable grammar; the higher level of it is to evaluate the text and explain why and how the text can mean what it does, and this can be achieved by taking the context of situation and culture into consideration on the basis of linguistic analysis. Thus, he identifies the following six steps usually adopted in textual analysis: observation, interpretation, description, analysis, explanation, and evaluation (Huang Guowen & Ghadessy, 2006: 26-8). And more importantly, in textual analysis, the analysis cannot actually be separated from interpretation and explanation: they are interwoven into each other and conducted simultaneously though from opposite directions (Hu Zhuanglin, 2000: 116).

Thus a fruitful and cogent analysis of a text can only be achieved in a way in which detailed analysis based on a workable and powerful grammar (here of course Halliday's functional grammar) should be conducted under the guidance of a theory which is able to connect the lexico-grammatical descriptions with the context of communication. In our discussion, Bakhtin's translinguistics is held to serve this guiding purpose. In other words, when doing a bottom-up linguistic analysis of a text we have to bear in mind the holistic connection with the context of communication, and when conducting a top-down translinguistic observation of the text, we have to base them on sufficient concrete linguistic analysis. This is what we mean by a double-oriented functional model for analyzing the dialogicity of texts including hard news text that we will focus on later.

2.5 Summary

In this chapter, the compatibility between Bakhtin's translinguistics and Hallidayan *SFL* is established by showing that they have a lot in common as far as the following four aspects are concerned: the non-Aristotelian philosophical tradition; the recognition of and emphasis on the role played by context in linguistic matters; the functional observation on language; and the genre-bound nature of actual speech. As a linguistic theory that takes both system and instance into its consideration, *SFL* actually functions as a bridge to fill the gap between Bakhtin's translinguistics and Saussurean linguistics that is characterized by systematic observations of the lexico-grammatical resources of language. And as a linguistic theory aiming at analyzing real text, *SFL* can also make it possible for translinguistics to incorporate into it the more linguistically-oriented achievements made by mainstream schools of textual analyses, especially the methodological nutrients from CDA, which is believed to have already inherited a lot from translinguistics.

But more importantly, the compatibility between translinguistics and *SFL* makes it possible for us to develop a more practical framework for analyzing textual dialogicity (the most essential and revolutionary component of translinguistics that is the backbone of Bakhtinian analysis of text), for *SFL* can ensure us a real analysis of text that is based upon convincing linguistic evidence.

Notes:

[1] It is generally believed that Halliday just regards *genre* as an aspect of *mode*, one of the three variables of register (Halliday, 2001: 144-5).

[2] What Halliday means here can be roughly understood in this way: the emergence and growth of lexico-grammatical mechanisms in human language is so significant that it distinguishes the human species from other creatures (i. e. phylogenetically) and indicates a successful transformation of a linguistically mature human being from a pre-linguistic infant (i. e. ontogenetically).

Chapter 3   Modeling Dialogicity on Hallidayan *SFL*

In the previous two chapters, we made a preparatory account of Bakhtin's translinguistics and its compatibility with Hallidayan *SFL* in order to build a productive context for a special account and necessary development of Bakhtin's model of textual dialogicity (the most essential and revolutionary part of translinguistics), which will be given a detailed consideration in this chapter.

3.1   Bakhtin's idea of textual dialogicity

3.1.1   Dialogue, dialogicity and dialogism

When we talk about Bakhtin's theory on language-in-use, the three terms *dialogue*, *dialogism* and *dialogicity* are frequently used, but they have received little special differentiation and even been used interchangeably sometimes, though they are quite different from one another.

In the context of modern linguistics, no one would deny that the oral communication precedes the written one, and that dialogue is the basic form of oral communication. The canonical type of dialogue is talk in face-to-face interaction between spatiotemporally co-present individuals based on shared linguistic and world knowledge. Given the fundamental role it plays in accounting for human communication, dialogue is commonly appropriated and extended to cover a much wider range of communicative phenomena. For instance, in the modern world, telephone conversations, electronic real-time interactions are also regarded as dialogues (Linell, 1998: 13). In Bakhtin's translinguistics, all human verbal communications can be regarded as dialogues, that is, everything is dialogized in his eyes. He insists that:

Dialogue, in the narrow sense of the word, is, of course, only one of the forms—a very important form, to be sure—of verbal interaction. But dialogue can also be understood in a broader sense, meaning not only direct, face-to-face, vocalized verbal communication between persons, but also verbal communication of any type whatsoever. A book, i. e. , a *verbal performance in print*, is also an element of verbal communication. It is something discussable in actual, real-life dialogue, but aside from that, it is calculated for active perception, involving attentive reading and inner responsiveness, and for organized, *printed* reaction in the various forms devised by the particular sphere of verbal communication in question (book reviews, critical surveys, defining influence on subsequent works, and so on). (Bakhtin/Volosinov, 1986: 95; italics in the original)

It is quite clear that Bakhtin has extracted what he believes to be the essence of dialogue and broken through the limits of co-presentness of participants and the medium involved, which are once held to be design features of canonical dialogues. Thus dialogues can now take place between speakers and listeners living hundreds or thousands of years apart. They can also happen in the way that one participant addresses the other orally, but is responded in written form, or vice versa. This essentiality of dialogue, which is found in any form of human verbal communication and thus makes it dialogized, is *dialogicity*.

From the previous chapters, we can see that the central task of translinguistics is to explore "language in its concrete living totality" (i. e. discourse) (Bakhtin, 1984: 181), and the unit for analyzing discourse is utterance. The three properties of utterance (especially its addressivity and expressivity) identified by Bakhtin are actually derived from the context of communication, in which one speaker's concrete utterance comes into contact with, or "interanimate", the utterance of another. This propensity carried by utterance of interanimation or interaction between utterances is actually what dialogicity refers to (Linell, 1998: 8-9; Wertsch, 1991: 54). Thus, dialogicity is actually the umbrella name used to summarize the latter two properties of utterance (that is, addressivity and expressivity), which of course is the essential reality extracted from the canonical dialogues. It is the dialogicity of utterance that makes one utterance come into contact with or interanimate another. It is also this dialogic property of utterance that makes translinguistics differ from Saussurean linguistics. In Bakhtin's works, dialogicity of utterance is explored by observing the dialogic relationships among utterances and "must become one of the chief objects of study for metalinguistics [translinguistics]" (Bakhtin, 1984: 185). Thus the study of discourse is actually the study of dialogic relationships (Schultz, 1990: 21).

In the English world and even in the English translations of Bakhtin's works, the term of *dialogism* is often used interchangeably with *dialogicity*, or one is used at the absence of the other (Kristeva, 1986: 34-61; Marková & Foppa, 1991: 259, 2003: 29-51; Ongstad, 2004: 65-6). However, according to Per Linell (1998: 8), dialogism as an epistemology or an analytical framework should be kept distinct from, on the one hand, dialogicity and, on the other hand, dialogue. Roughly speaking, dialogism is a way of looking at things. Bakhtin's philosophical establishments are believed to center on this epistemological principle, which gives priority to interaction, openness, and processes over stability, closure, and products. In his early philosophically-oriented works, influenced by Kant and phenomenological traditions, Bakhtin tries to solve the rupture caused by philosophical dualism between subject and object, or mind and world. He argues that the world exists "as an event (and not as existence in ready-made form)" (Bakhtin, 1986: 162). In this event, according to Bakhtin, there are two subjects— "I" and "other", rather than a subject and an object. Once the "other" being acknowledged as subject, the relationships between "I" and "other" can be dialogized, that is, become communicative and interactive. Thus dialogue is considered to be the mode of the existence of the world; only through the perspective of dialogism, which is characterized by its emphasis on intersubjectivity, can the world be understood (Holquist, 2002: 14-39).

During the process of interaction between "I" and "other", language is absolutely essential, so it is inevitable for Bakhtin to turn his eyes to language. In *MPL*, therefore, Bakhtin argues that language can only be studied from the perspective of the relationship between "I" and "other". In the collective where speaker and listener (one of the various forms of "I" and "other") participate, language circulates neither as an abstract system of linguistic forms, as in the Saussurean "langue", nor as isolated monologic utterances, viz "parole", but rather as a social event of language—interaction—which comes about in the contact between utterance and counter-utterance (Lachman, 2004: 46-7). Thus it is safe to say that translinguistics is derived from looking at language from the perspective of dialogism as an epistemology, which constitutes the philosophical foundation of translinguistics and makes possible the extraction of dialogicity from human communications.

3.1.2 The mode of dialogicity

Given that the dialogicity of utterance is embodied in and engenders different modes of dialogic relationships, the study on the dialogicity of utterance is actually the study on dialogic relationships in verbal communications.

In Bakhtin's translinguistics, utterance is characterized by its three properties of referential wholeness, addressivity and expressivity and demarcated by the changing of concrete speaking subjects. Therefore, in a context of communication, only an utterance as a whole can come into contact with another utterance at the same level. That is, dialogic relationships can only exist between utterances, rather than sentences, which are the unit of analysis in pure linguistics. In other words, within one single utterance, there will be no dialogic relation. For example, if the two judgments of "*Life is good*" and "*Life is not good*" are united as thesis and antithesis in a single utterance from a single speaking subject, the relation between them is only logical; only when they are separated into two different utterances (that is, spoken by two different speaking subjects) can dialogical relationship arise (Bakhtin, 1984: 182-3). Thus this kind of relationship between utterances from concrete speaking subjects is termed "inter-utterance dialogicity" in the present book for the convenience of discussion, though Bakhtin himself has never used such a name.

Besides the dialogic mode mentioned above, Bakhtin has identified another type of dialogic relations within a single utterance rather than between utterances. For example, in his *PDP*, Bakhtin acknowledges that:

> Dialogic relationships are possible not only among whole (relatively whole) utterances; a dialogic approach is possible toward any signifying part of an utterance, even toward an individual word, if that word is perceived not as impersonal word of language but as a

sign of someone else's semantic position, as the representative of another person's utterance; that is, if we hear in it someone else's voice. Thus dialogic relationships can permeate inside the utterance, even inside the individual word, as long as two voices collide within it dialogically (microdialogue, of which we spoke earlier). (Bakhtin, 1984: 184)

Thus the wholeness of utterance together with its unique subject is now divided into various semantic positions or voices. Consequently dialogic relationships can also be identified within one's own utterance as whole. This newly-discovered property of utterance is termed "double-voicedness" and constitutes the chief object of investigation for Bakhtin into the discourse of Dostoevsky's novels and the chief object of study for translinguistics (Bakhtin, 1984: 185). With his moving forward to consider the novel discourse as a genre in general, Bakhtin insists that virtually all utterances are double-voiced or even multiple-voiced because they result from borrowing another's words marked by another's voice (Bakhtin, 1981: 275-331).

In the present discussion, we will abandon the term "double-voicedness" used by Bakhtin and other scholars to refer to the dialogic mode within a single utterance, because of the misgiving that the word "double" will be understood superficially as "two". But the fact is that utterances are possibly triple-voiced, or quadri-voiced; that is, it is highly possible that they contain more than two voices. Thus this kind of dialogic relation is termed "intra-utterance dialogicity" in our discussion for the avoidance of possible confusion and for some technical convenience.

3.1.3 Problems with Bakhtin's mode of textual dialogicity

When we discussed above the two types of dialogic relations identified by Bakhtin, we encountered some ambivalence or even contradictions in Bakhtin's account. When addressing the differences between sentence and utterance, Bakhtin insists that only an utterance as a whole, which is associated with a concrete speaking subject, possesses dialogicity, namely, dialogic relations can only exist between utterances rather than within a single utterance. But leaving this context, Bakhtin maintains that dialogic relations can also be found within any single utterance (Bakhtin, 1984:

184). When talking about the so-called intra-utterance dialogic interactions, it seems that Bakhtin has shifted his focus from the notion of concrete speaking subject (which was previously held as a criterion for identifying utterance) to the notion of *voice*, a concept that is essential for dialogic analysis of text and thus later dominates nearly all the Bakhtinian topics. Therefore, a successful dialogic analysis of a text (or an utterance) relies on the identification of different voices within it. But the problem seems to be that Bakhtin himself not only fails to define his frequently-used term *voice*, but also does not bother to delineate the relationship between *subject*, *utterance*, and *voice*, the three fundamental concepts in his translinguistic observation of the dialogicity of a text. Even if we cannot say that Bakhtin ignores this necessary transition from utterance to voice when taking an omnipresent dialogic view at texts belonging to different genres, his ambivalence or at least too much laconism on the issue is quite evident. Therefore, it is necessary for us to fill this gap left by Bakhtin in the following sections of this chapter through some due discussions on what *voice* used by Bakhtin and others really means and more importantly how it gets realized in a text.

At this juncture, it is necessary to note again that as far as textual analysis is concerned, Bakhtin's dialogic observations of utterances or texts are believed to remain at the level high above detailed linguistic analysis, which renders some of his insightful statements on language-in-use under a bit of suspicion of being *ad hoc*, arbitrary, and selective.

3.2 Recontextualizing Bakhtinian dialogicity in the context of Hallidayan *SFL* and the postmodern theories

As has been said in the previous chapter, a more workable framework for dialogic analysis of text derives from the combination of Bakhtin's translinguistics with modern linguistics, and among various linguistic theories Hallidayan *SFL* is the first choice to make a good dovetail connection to it. It is well known that *SFL* is constructed on the bases that among others grammar should be semantic-driven, and language is stratified and multifunctional. Thus it enables us to develop in a measure a linguistically-oriented model of dialogicity.

3.2.1 From subject and utterance to voice: participant of textual dialogue

In this section, from a different perspective and in greater detail, we will consider the problems entailed in Bakhtin's theory of dialogicity, especially the constitutive elements of the dialogic relations. In order to make our discussion more concrete, we accept that the dialogic relations presuppose dialogues in the broader sense identified by Bakhtin. Given that dialogic relations can exist not only between utterances but also within any single utterance, it can also be accepted that we accordingly have inter-utterance dialogues and intra-utterance dialogues. The first question we have to ask naturally is who participates in these non-canonical dialogues. The answer to this question, however, has already been supplied in the previous section that the participants of the dialogues are actually different voices rather than speaking subjects and utterances. But why does this so happen?

As we have already mentioned above, there is a strong trend towards decentering of the canonical social subject in Bakhtin's dialogism. To him, the social subject is not autonomous anymore, and its existence depends on others; that is to say, the existence of "I" presupposes the existence of "other". In his world, there is no place for a self-centered social subject. The "I" can only be perceived from the perspective of "other"; the subject is an internally complex and socially-and-discursively constituted entity which bears little similarity to the fully autonomous, rational and curiously incorporeal being postulated by Descartes or Kant: "A single consciousness is *contradicto in adjecto*. Consciousness is in essence multiple. *Pluralia tantum*" (Bakhtin, 1984: 228; adopted from Gardiner, 1992: 74). In short, against Cartesian individualism, Bakhtin's dialogism only recognizes the existence of intersubjectivity and dialogue rather than subjectivity and monologue (Holquist, 2002: 155; Nielsen, 2002: 47-50). But when talking about dialogic relations in translinguistics, Bakhtin's attitude towards subject or subjectivity is rather ambivalent. The decentering of subject entailed in his dialogism, however, finds its clear expression in postmodern theories,[1] which is thought to originate with Nietzsche (Zima, 2002: 53-9), renouncing "the bourgeois concept of a singular, stable subjectivity clearly differentiated from the outside world" (Agger, 1998: 36) and advocating that "the self or subject has become a contested terrain, with permeable boundaries between it and the external world" (ibid.). And among those subjectivity-or-individuality-decentering theories, Foucault's theory of discourse is representative and most relevant. In this connection, therefore, we accept Foucault's idea of the relationship between social subject and discourse in our discussion.

According to Foucault, the social subject that produces a statement is not an entity which can exist outside of and independently of discourse. It should not be regarded as the source of the statement, words, or discourse (i.e., it is not as identical with the author). He argues that:

> [T]he subject of the statement should not be regarded as identical with the author of the formulation—either in substance, or in function. He is not in fact the cause, origin, or starting-point of the phenomenon of the written or spoken articulation of a sentence; nor is it that meaningful intention which, silently anticipating words, orders them like the visible body of its intuition; it is not the constant, motionless, unchanging focus of a series of operations that are manifested, in turn, on the surface of discourse through the statements. It is a particular, vacant place that may in fact be filled by different individuals; but, instead of being defined once and for all, and maintaining itself as such throughout a text, a book, or an *œuvre*, this place varies—or rather it is variable enough to be able either to persevere, unchanging, through several sentences, or to alter with each one. (Foucault, 1972: 95)

Thus, in Foucault's view, the traditional understanding of the relationship between the subject and the utterance or discourse should be reversed in the way that it is the discourse that constitutes and defines the subject. Or in folk language, it is not the subject who speaks, but it is the discourse who speaks about the subject. Given that discourse is totally institutionalized, the social subjects are not the real-life individuals now, but are different social positions defined by the conventions in different institutions in human society (Halliday, 2003: 56-7; Liu Yameng, 2005: 151). In other words, as Fairclough once pointed out, what Foucault wants to emphasize is that discourse plays a major role in the constitution of social subjects and the questions of subjectivity, social identity, and "self-hood" correspondingly ought to be of major concern in theories of discourse and language, and in discursive and linguistic analysis. Thus, "Foucault's work is a major contribution to the decentering of the social subject in recent social theories, the view of the subject as constituted, reproduced and transformed in and through social practice, and the view of the subject as fragmented" (Fairclough, 1992a: 44). For us, the real significance of Foucault's understanding of subject as subject position constituted by discourse is that in the dialogic reading of an utterance, what we have to identify is not the subjects in the traditional sense of the word anymore but different subject positions, which can be decoded from the linguistic resources contained in the utterance, because these subject positions can actually be recognized as different semantic or ideological positions (i. e. voices) in the utterance or text we will analyze. [2]

Another reason for us to abandon the term of subject in doing news-text analysis is that news texts are highly institutionalized. They are usually produced by a group of people in a highly organized manner. That is, behind a news text there tend to be a team of speaking subjects, so it offers a classic case of language produced by multiple parties: sources, journalists, editors, newsreaders and so forth. Drawing upon the ethno-linguist Dell Hymes' (1974) and sociologist Erving Goffman's (1974) findings, Allan Bell (1991: 36-44) identifies four roles institutionalized in news production, they are *principal*, *author*, *editor* and *animator*. But as textual analysts, it is impossible for us to identify clearly the impact on the text exerted by these different roles, for it is a common practice that they are not allowed to be credited with authorship of views or utterances in the text, especially in those so-called hard news texts. Or in folk language, the analyst mostly can only hear different voices but cannot see the speakers. For instance, in the following short snippet of news report, we can only hear some different voices, with some of them difficult to be assigned a definite source (let alone a concrete speaking subject).

(1) Unions for refuse collectors are threatening to strike over what they say is a rising tide of violence that has seen one in five of Britain's 40,000 binmen injured in physical attacks at work and more than two thirds verbally abused. They blame the violence on growing

frustration with complex regulations requiring people to minimize waste and separate recyclable materials. If households fail to sort their waste or put out too much, binmen are ordered not to take it. (*The Sunday Telegraph*, 14/05/2006: 1)

In this text, it is not difficult to identify at least four different voices: (1) the reporting voice—reporting the whole event; (2) voice from unions for refuse collectors—saying there is a rising tide of violence that has seen one in five of Britain's 40,000 binmen injured in physical attacks at work and more than two thirds verbally abused; (3) voice still from the unions—blaming the violence on some people's growing frustration with complex regulations requiring them to minimize waste and separate recyclable materials; (4) unspecified voice ordering binmen not to take the waste which has not been sorted or over-discharged. But it is almost impossible to make sure whether the piece is kept intact or not after the reporter submitted his work to the editors at different levels concerned in the news-producing organization (i. e. the newspaper *The Sunday Telegraph*), and who made the remarks to the reporters, the chairman, the vice chairman or spokesman of the union if there is any of them. It is also hard to know from the text who it is that makes the stipulation requiring the binmen to refuse to collect the waste under certain conditions. Even though we can identify a concrete speaker behind some utterances sometimes, it is hard to say whether all that he is speaking is what he really wants to say. It is very likely that as a member of the organization he has to say what the organization wants him to say though he may hold a quite different opinion on the issue. In this sense, the most utterances in news text are impersonal rather than personal; they are disciplined utterances rather than spontaneous ones like those in casual conversations.

As an important genre of so-called public discourse or text, news text is believed to be characterized by its objectivity and authenticity. Though it is far from being a simple issue to tell sometimes who is the real speaker or author of the voice, it is quite significant to identify the institutionalized *sources* of various voices included in news text, because the manipulation of sources has been found to be of substantial importance in the studies concerning news production and reception that are shaped by the power relations in social interactions (Zang Guoren, 1999). Researchers like

Thompson (1996a) even equate voice with source. But in our discussion we will take them as two different concepts and we will return to this issue in the following chapters.

It goes without arguing that the concept of voice plays a crucial role in Bakhtin's dialogism and translinguistics. But in most cases, Bakhtin seems to use this concept on a basis of a priori acceptance of it without a definite clarification of the word. Therefore, it is necessary at this juncture to make a brief account of the different understandings of "voice" of other scholars as well as Bakhtin's, hoping our own conception of the word can get across in the process of the description and clarification.

In contemporary studies of the humanities, voice is really a frequently-used term. Although the notion of voice is unanimously not used in the sense of vocal-auditory signals, in different branches of study, or even in the same field, the notions of the word vary with the changing of contexts and focuses of the researches (Phelan, 2002 [1996]: 19). Diverse as they are, the theoretical accounts of voice from psychology, narratology and rhetoric can bring us some due understandings of the concept, thus enabling us to fashion them into a notion for a more workable model of dialogic analysis of news text.

In psychology, especially those psychological theories viewing human development from Vygotsky's social perspective, voice is used in the sense of identity. Theorists such as Wolf (1990) in this school usually adopt an assumption opposite to Piaget's conception of development; they hold that instead of being egocentric, the selfhood of human beings is *heterogeneous* at the very beginning of socialization. And this heterogeneity of *self* is still observable in adults, which consists of a number of different, simultaneous experiences:

> It is to suggest that, like more observable and public forms of cognition, our most private moments of reckoning are profoundly social: they involve either the interplays of recollected voices of interchanges between several portions of our self—interchanges very similar to and perhaps even stemming from our conversation with others. (Wolf, 1990: 184; adopted from Bredel, 2003: 149)

On this basis, Wolf carries out her investigation into the development of such a complex self-identity. Her observations reveal that in the early stages of development, children use several voices in order to reconstruct problematic events or events with inconsistent self-representations, but when the language acquisition arrives at a certain mature stage, they will move away from the representation of inconsistent experiences in the form of several voices. That is, they have developed relatively stable *authorial selves*, which can integrate the inconsistent experiences into consistent ones. In short, psychological voice is actually another expression of the concept of self-identity (Bredel, 2003).

In narratology, voice is mostly concerning the "question of who it is we 'hear' doing the narrating" (Abbott, 2002: 64-5), and the grammatical person is an important feature of it: it is *first-person*, *second-person*, or *third-person* who is doing the narration. And in narrative theories, especially from English and North American criticism, voice is also very closely associated with the concept of "focalization" or "point of view", referring to the position or quality of consciousness through which we "see" events in the narrative (ibid. : 190). In other words, voice or focalization mainly concerns the question of who is presented as the observer of the events of a narrative—the narrator or a participating character, and the various kinds of discourse associated with different relationships between narrator and character (Fowler, 1996: 169-70; Bruner & Gorfain, 1991: 177-203; Kearns, 1999: Ch. 3). Therefore, in narratology, voice is mainly used to talk about how the story is told: it is told from an independent narrator's point of view, or from a character's point of view, or by alternating between them; and the different voices can be identified from the discourses associated with the parties concerned.

In rhetoric, voice is also used in a relatively narrow sense. Many British and American theorists equate voice with rhetorical purposes or categories. From this perspective, voice is only regarded as the product of the intentional rhetorical activity of an individual consciousness. This intentional activity is linguistically realized in text to accomplish particular rhetorical functions. In short, voices are viewed as textual or rhetorical functions, which are really authorial intentions filtered through various text-forming possibilities. Such a view of voice, therefore, is accused of relatively being devoid of social, cultural, or political significance (Kamberelis & Scott, 2004: 211). This notion of voice is quite accepted by *those SFL* scholars who are now endeavoring to develop a more detailed and comprehensive module of interpersonal function, namely the *Appraisal Theory* (White, 1998; Coffin, 2000).

In contrast to the above widely acknowledged perspectives, Bakhtin has developed a quite different model of voice. From the accounts scattered in his different works (Bakhtin, 1981, 1984, 1986; Bakhtin/ Volosinov, 1986), Holquist and Emerson have drawn a definition-like summary of the gist of Bakhtinian voice: "the speaking personality, the speaking consciousness" (Holquist & Emerson, 1981: 434). Obviously, Bakhtin's notion of voice is also not confined to referring to the concrete qualities of voice, but applies to written as well as spoken communications, and it is concerned with "the broader issues of a speaking subject's perspective, conceptual horizon, intention, and world view" (Wertsch, 1991: 51). The voice or the speaking consciousness is quite different from any notion of an individual author in that it always belongs simultaneously to speech communities and to individual speaker(s). That is to say, voices always exist in a social milieu: no voice can exist in total isolation from other voices. But more importantly, the semantic intention of any voice (or verbal-ideological perspective) is always transformed in some way each time it is used by a new speaker or writer, thus becoming "double-voiced" or, perhaps more accurately, "multiple-voiced" (Wertsch, 1991: 51-2; Kamberelis & Scott, 2004: 212).

In our discussion, we follow the common line running through the above mentioned notions about voice; that is, the voice cannot be reduced to an account of vocal-auditory signals anymore and does not mean the relation between the agent and the action verb (usually transitive)—active or passive voice in traditional school grammar. We accept Bakhtin's broader understanding that voice is actually a semantic category, referring to a certain kind of ideological position or world view. The voice sometimes can be associated with a specific individual, but for the most part of time, it is hard to identify it with a concrete speaking subject in the traditional sense of the word. That is, we do not use the *voice* here in the psychological sense mentioned above: *voice as self-identity*. But our notion of *voice* does draw heavily upon those in narratology and rhetoric: when analyzing the dialogic relationships between *voices*, we do consider the role played by textual dialogicity in the construction of a text, that is, its functions or rhetorical purpose (for example achieving objectivity), though we do not aim at specifying a speaking subject who is telling the story. Thus, our major concerns should be the identification of voices, the dialogic relationships among them, and their textualization. Based on the Hallidayan stratificational model of language-in-use, in our discussion, the textualization of voice is believed to be conducted in this way: voices are realized by utterances in the text, or utterances are engendered by voices in that if a voice can be identified with a stretch of wording in a text (no matter it is a clause, phrase or even a single word in the pure linguistic sense of these categories), then it will actually be associated with a context, thus acquiring the status of a translinguistic utterance or at least the textual representative of a possible utterance. In other words, if a stretch of wording in a text can be interpreted to be associated with a certain voice, it will be contextualized and become a Bakhtinian utterance or at least its textual representative. Thus the stratificational relationship between voice, utterance, and linguistic wording can be illustrated in the figure modeled on Martin (1992: 495):[3]

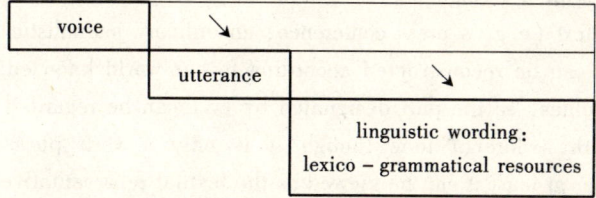

Figure 3.1　Textualization of voice in a Hallidayan mode

As far as the practical analysis of a text is concerned, it seems that in our conception of utterance, it is reduced to a category for the interpretation of text. That is to say, during the textual analysis or interpretation (in the sense of Bakhtinian active understanding), if we identify the existence of a certain voice according to the linguistic markers (i.e. lexico-grammatical expressions) in the text, then a stretch of wording in the text in question will be assigned at least those two properties of utterance which make up its dialogicity—addressivity and expressivity. Therefore, a successful dialogic analysis of text depends on the identification of different voices contained in the text at issue. The successful identification of the existence of a certain voice, then, relies on the identification of its heterogeneity, that is, the difference it bears against other voices in the text. Take another look at example (1), now repeated as (2),

> (2) Unions for refuse collectors are <u>threatening</u> to (**a**) *strike over* what they <u>say</u> is (**b**) *a rising tide of violence that has seen one in five of Britain's* 40,000 *binmen injured in physical attacks at work and more than two thirds verbally abused.* (**c**) They <u>blame</u> *the violence on growing frustration with complex regulations* <u>requiring</u> (**d**) *people to minimize waste and separate recyclable materials. If households fail to sort their waste or put out too much, binmen* are <u>ordered</u> (**e**) *not to take it.*

The underlined parts in the text indicate that the wordings after them or around them (i. e. the italicized parts) are somewhat foreign to the overall reporting voice. The underlined word *threatening* marks out a voice from the unions which is textualized by the italicized part (i. e. *strike over*) designated by the bracketed lower-case letter (a) in bold type; if we take a close look at the text, this stretch of wording can be found to be connected with a foreign source (here the unions) and with a possible foreign context (e. g. a press conference, an ordinary journalistic interview, etc.) that can be reconstructed according to our world knowledge as well as textual clues, so the part designated by (a) can be regarded as an utterance with a foreign tone though it is only a verb phrase "strike over"; [4] or at least it can be viewed as the textual representative of such a possible foreign utterance as *"We are going to go on strike because of the increasing violence against us"*, which can be reconstructed according to the textual and contextual clues. The underlined *say* also marks out the voice from the unions, which is textualized as the stretch of wording designated by (b) though it is only a noun phrase italicized in the text; the underlined *blame* still marks out the voice from the unions, which is textualized as the stretch of wording designated by (c) in the text; [5] the underlined *requiring* marks out a voice from an institution issuing the regulations, which is textualized as the infinitive clause designated by (d); the underlined *ordered* marks out a voice still coming from the unspecified institution, which is textualized as the discrete stretch of wording (i. e. *binmen... not to take it*) designated by (e). Like the stretch of wording designated by (a), the different stretches of wording designated by (b), (c), (d) and (e) can be regarded as foreign utterances coming from their corresponding sources or at least be regarded as the textual representatives of those foreign utterances. That is to say, if a stretch of wording in the text is connected with a foreign voice, then in this way it will be connected with a different source (either specified or unspecified) and enter a reconstructed context different from the context of the written text at issue, thus gaining the status of an utterance (or at least the textual representative of the utterance) be it a connected sentence, clause, a cluster of phrases, or even a stretch of discrete words.

As has just been said, voices are actually semantic and ideological positions, but these positions are actually institutionalized and engendered by the power relations among social agents in the interactions of different walks of life.[6] Power is believed to be distributed unevenly among social agents, which correspondingly creates asymmetries or differences among participants in institutionalized social interactions. For example, experts and professionals talking with clients and lay persons in various sorts of institutional contexts, such as court trials, police interrogations, doctor consultations, classroom interactions, occupy a position of power, authority and expertise. According to Linell & Luckmann (1991: 1-20), it is these asymmetries that engender dialogues of both canonical and non-canonical types among social agents, and Gunther Kress (1989: 12) also argues "that difference [unresolved differences in the individual's discursive history and social positions] is the motor that produces texts". In the world within a text, we assume that the differences or asymmetries of social positions are actually embodied by the differences or asymmetries among different voices. We accept again Kress' understanding of the issue; in this regard he maintains that:

> This difference always has linguistic form, and leads to dialogue, and hence to text. Texts are constructed in and by this difference. Where there is no difference there is silence. In texts the discursive differences are negotiated, governed by differences in power, which are themselves in part encoded in and determined by discourse and by genre. (Kress, 1989: 32)

Since it is hard to identify the concrete speaking subjects in a text (especially in a news text), it can be accepted that it is the differences among voices in the text that motivate the making of a text, and that in a metaphorical sense it is the voices who participate in Bakhtinian dialogues within a certain text or a group of texts.

In summary, drawing selectively upon the notions of voice in psychology, narratology, and rhetoric, we have reinterpreted Bakhtinian notion of voice in the context of Hallidayan *SFL* and postmodern theories of subject or subjectivity. In our dialogic analysis of news text, among Bakhtin's three closely related but insufficiently differentiated terms of *voice*, *subject* and *utterance*, we single out *voice* as the constitutive element of textual dialogicity, for like most postmodern theorists Bakhtin himself has already deconstructed or decentered the Cartesian notion of subject on the one hand, and it is hard to identify the concrete specific speaking subjects (especially in a news text) during the process of making a dialogic analysis of the text on the other hand. In the context of Hallidayan *SFL*, thus the Bakhtinian notion of voice is employed in the following sense: **voice is the ideologically semantic position in the text which is engendered by the institutionalized power relations in social interactions; it is considered to be textualized as a stretch of wording through the mediation of utterance in the sense that when a stretch of wording can be identified with a certain voice, it will be interpreted as an utterance or at least as the textual representative of an utterance; the existence of a voice depends on the existence of other different voices, hence the essentiality of the heterogeneity of the voice, which in text is indicated by some special linguistic resources that are termed "dialogic markers"; and the dialogic relationships among the voices play important rhetorical roles in the construction of the text.**

If we understand the dialogicity of utterance from this angle, then the tension between inter-utterance dialogicity and intra-utterance dialogicity can be resolved. The dialogicity is engendered by the interactions between different voices (rather than the canonical Bakhtinian utterances), and a voice is actually textualized through utterance by lexico-grammatical resources—a word, phrase, clause, sentence, or even sentence group. From the perspective of comprehension, if a word, a phrase, a sentence and so on in the text can be interpreted to signify an alien voice, it will be associated with a foreign context, and thus being interpreted as an alien utterance or at least the textual representative of an alien utterance no matter what linguistic category it belongs to—a word, a phrase, or a sentence. In a measure, utterance can be regarded just as a category for textual interpretation, and it mediates between voice and wording. That is why utterance seems to be the other side of the coin of a materialized wording when we are making a bottom-up textual analysis; and when we are making a top-down observation, utterance seems to be the other side of the coin of voice. [7] Therefore, the two types of dialogic relations identified by Bakhtin in reality are the same thing: both of them are the interaction between different voices inhabiting the text. Only in this sense can Bakhtin's assertion that any utterance is heteroglossic and dialogic in nature be accepted, because each of one's words is related to others; for " [h]e [a speaker or writer] is not, after all, the first speaker, the one who disturbs the eternal silence of the universe" (Bakhtin, 1986: 69). That is to say, there would be no pure utterance totally belonging to a unique speaker; any utterance to some extent is actually "contaminated" by foreign voice(s) and thus can be interpreted dialogically.

In this connection, it should be noted that from now on utterance needs to be distinguished from text: the former is regarded as an intermediate concept between voice and the actual wording; the latter is in fact the actual speech (either in written or oral form) that we are to analyze dialogically.

3.2.2 The dialogic relationship between voices

In a Hallidayan model, the interactions between speaker and listener in a canonical dialogue is theorized as the following: the speaker either gives some information to the listener or demands it from the listener; or the speaker either gives some goods & service to the listener or demands it from the listener; when the thing exchanged is information, the listener can either acknowledge or contradict the offer of information, or the listener can either answer the speaker's question for demanding some information or disclaim it; and when the thing exchanged is goods & service, the listener can either accept the offer of goods & service from the speaker or reject it, or the listener can either undertake the demand of goods & service from the speaker or refuse to do so. Halliday then illustrates these interactions in the following table (Halliday, 2000: 69):

Table 3.1 Hallidayan dialogic model

Role in exchange	Commodity exchanged	Initiation	Expected response	Discretionary alternative
give	goods & service	offer	acceptance	rejection
demand		command	undertaking	refusal
give	information	statement	acknowledgement	contradiction
demand		*question*	*answer*	disclaimer

Obviously, in the Hallidayan model, four types of dialogic relationships have been identified: *offer-acceptance/rejection*, *command-undertaking/refusal*, *statement-acknowledgement/contradiction*, and *question-answer/disclaimer*. According to the things exchanged in the interactions, these four types of dialogic relationships can then be subsumed into two groups: the type of exchanging goods & service and the type of exchanging information. Given that during the process of the exchange of good & service language can mostly play an ancillary role, Halliday holds that the exchange of information is the basic form of linguistic interactions and should receive primary attention because it can give us "a general understanding of the clause in its exchange function" (Halliday, 2000: 71). Considering the fact that the major function of news texts is to supply information, we agree with Halliday on this unequal treatment. Thus only the dialogic relationships concerning the type of information-exchange are relevant in our discussion.

In his translinguistics, however, with the broader sense of dialogue in his mind, Bakhtin has identified three pairs of so-called purely dialogic relationships between two voices: "agreement/disagreement, affirmation/supplementation, question/answer" (Bakhtin, 1984: 188). Although this notion of dialogic relationship in the form of listing is widely accepted, when viewed against Halliday's understanding of dialogic relationships, Bakhtin's three pairs of dialogic relationships appear not to be on the same plane: *agreement/disagreement* and *affirmation/supplementation* are obviously just two alternatives of the *response* to the *initiation* of the exchange of information, while *question/answer* is actually initiation-and-response in the exchange of information. Another point which needs noting is that Bakhtin also seems to concentrate only on the dialogic interactions involving

Halliday's exchange of information. Thus, Bakhtin's dialogic relationships can be compared with Halliday's dialogic format in the way demonstrated by the following table.

Table 3.2　Hallidayan dialogic model and Bakhtinian model compared

Halliday		Bakhtin		
Initiation	Response	Initiation	Response	
statement	acknowledgement		agreement	affirmation
	contradiction		disagreement	supplementation
question	answer	*question*	*answer*	
	disclaimer			

If we take a closer look at the table, it is not difficult to find that both Halliday and Bakhtin have differentiated two kinds of *responses* to the *initiation* in the dialogic interactions: one can be summarized as *supporting*, the other *confronting* (cf. Eggins, 2004: 145). If the *initiation* is issued in the form of a statement, the supporting response in Halliday' model is *acknowledgement*, and the confronting response is *contradiction*; if the *initiation* is issued in the form of a *statement* (modeled on Halliday's format), the supporting response in Bakhtin's model will be *agreement* or *affirmation*, and the confronting response will be *disagreement* or *supplementation*. Correspondingly, when the *initiation* is in the form of *question*, the supporting response is *answer* and the confronting one *disclaimer* in Halliday's model, but Bakhtin fails to distinguish "supporting" from "confronting" in this respect, with his *answer* covering both supporting response and confronting response to a question distinguished by Halliday. According to Bakhtin, however, a real dialogic relationship of question-answer should be understood like this: "*Question* and *answer* are not logical relations (categories); they cannot be placed in one consciousness (unified and closed in itself); any response gives rise to a new question. Question and answer presuppose mutual outsideness. If an answer does not give rise to a new question from itself, it falls out of the dialogue and enters systemic cognition, which is essentially impersonal" (Bakhtin, 1986: 168). That is to say, the Bakhtinian *answer* is just like the Hallidayan *answer* in that they both display the willingness of further interactive cooperations: answer as response triggers more chains of question-answer.

In our discussion, however, in order to avoid some ambiguity and misconception, we just accept Halliday's generalization of the dialogic relationships between two interacting voices: one issues initiation, the other offers its response; and the responses can be classified into the supporting response and the confronting one, both of which can in turn function as initiation to trigger further rounds of dialogic interactions. Therefore, the dialogic relationships can be diagramed as the following:

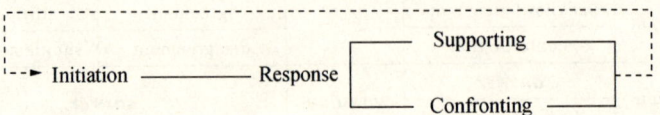

Figure 3.2   Dialogic relationship between textual voices

But in the real-life communication, the relationship between initiation and response is more complicated than the above mentioned dualist understanding (i.e. either supporting or confronting). For the most part of the time, the attitude of the speaker is quite ambivalent; they prefer to stay somewhere between the two poles of "positive" and "negative" (or "agree" and "disagree"). Thus Halliday (2000: 88-92) has theorized the "intermediate degrees" between the two extremes of "yes" and "no" as *modality*, which has abundant lexico-grammatical resources at its disposal to have itself realized in text.

According to Bakhtin, there is no substantial difference between the dialogic relationships of oral interactions and those of written texts, because we can take a broad sense of dialogicity in addition to the narrow-sense one. Addressing the dialogic relationships between the interacting voices in these two senses, he once recorded his idea in the form of note-making:

> The narrow understanding of dialogism [dialogicity] as argument, polemics, or parody. These are the externally most obvious, but crude, forms of dialogism [dialogicity]. Confidence in another's word, reverential reception (the authoritative word), apprenticeship, the search for and mandatory nature of deep meaning, *agreement*, its infinite gradations and shadings (but not its logical limitations and not purely referential reservations), the layering of meaning upon meaning, voice upon voice, strengthening through merging (but not identification), the combination of many voices (a corridor of voices) that

augments understanding, departure beyond the limits of the understood, and so forth. (Bakhtin, 1986: 121; italics in the original)

The above quotation strongly suggests that Bakhtin should hold the opinion that in the text if a voice merges with another one, the relationship between them can be regarded as one agreeing with the other; when two juxtaposed or merged-but-heterogeneous voices do not *contradict* or *confront* each other, they will *agree with* or *support* each other in a broader sense. But more importantly, like Halliday, Bakhtin also emphasizes the existence of "infinite gradations and shadings" in the "combination of many voices." That is to say, contradiction and agreement are just two poles of a continuum or spectrum; they are connected with each other by various intermediate degrees between them rather than absolutely separated and discrete. Thus the above diagram should be revised as the following:

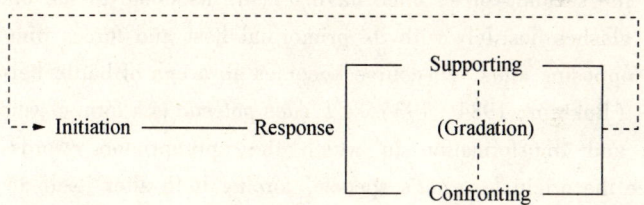

Figure 3.3　Dialogic relationship between textual voices revisited

3.2.3　Dialogic markers in the text

As has just been mentioned above, a successful dialogic analysis of a text depends on the identification of different voices in the text; the *heterogeneity of voice* is textualized through utterance by lexico-grammatical resources; the linguistic resources that can be relied on to identify the different voices are termed *dialogic markers* in the following discussion.

When analyzing Dostoevsky's double-voiced or dialogic discourse, Bakhtin has identified five ways in which foreign voices may be appropriated and transformed into one's own voice: *direct quotation*, *imitation* (or *adoption*), *stylization*, *parody*, and *hidden polemic*. According to Kamberelis & Scott (2004: 213-7), *direct quotation* is a relatively straightforward way of re-envoicement of the discourse of others. The speaker or writer directly appropriates and explicitly marks someone else's discourse by using the reporting clause such as "John said...", or with other more or less explicit cues. *Adoption* is an unselfconscious use of someone else's words, syntax, discourse style, and so on. The language user takes the adopted wording seriously and makes it his or her own, thereby abolishing the distance between the self's and other's discourse. Thus, it represents a near complete merging of two voices. Unlike adoption which blurs or even abolishes the distance between self and other, *stylization* maintains an objective stance toward the other's discourse by maintaining the other as the condition of its appropriation. That is, stylization presupposes other's style, though not explicitly; the speaker or writer appropriates the utterance of other to express the same point of view or create the same effect as the other might have. *Parody*, however, involves the presence of two different and opposing intentions or ideologies within a single utterance. Bakhtin's description of the parodistic utterance is especially succinct and clear: "the second voice, once having made its home in the other's discourse, clashes hostilely with its primordial host and forces him to serve directly opposing aims. Discourse becomes an arena of battle between two voices" (Bakhtin, 1984: 193). *A hidden polemic* is a form of voice appropriation and transformation in which the appropriators' words actively influence the original author's speech, forcing it to alter itself accordingly under their influence and initiative. In constructing a hidden polemic, a speaker or writer recontextualizes the words of another speaker or writer in such a way that the meanings of those words are altered by the new context.

If we take a closer look at these five modes of double-voicedness identified by Bakhtin, however, it is not difficult to find that they are not on the same plane: direct quotation can be accepted as a dialogic syntactic composition characterized by lexico-grammatical and graphological markers, but the rest of them are all about the relationship between two voices on the semantic level. Or from a dualist point of view, dialogic relationships or the heterogeneity of voice can be classified into two groups: lexico-grammatically-marked and non-lexico-grammatically-marked. In Chapter 4, we will focus on the former type, which is assumed to be more relevant to a linguistically-oriented analytical framework for textual dialogicity in our discussion.

3.2.4 Functions of dialogic relationships in the text

When analyzing Dostoevsky's novels, Bakhtin finds that the writer's artistry lies completely on a dialogic way of thinking. In Dostoevsky's novels, dialogues between the voices of the same value shape the characterization, plot, and the narrative structure of the novel, thus creating a new genre of polyphonic novel (Qian Zhongwen, 1998). Apart from this, Bakhtin also points out that dialogicity has another very important function: it enables the novel to acquire objectivity in its supreme form, because life in itself is interactive and dialogic (*An Oeuvre of Bakhtin* (Chinese edition) (5): 50, 366-8). Then a question arising in order should be like this: What role does dialogicity play in the construction of news text (a very important genre in human society)? And this will be our focus in Chapter 5.

3.3 Summary

In this chapter, we have given Bakhtin's dialogic theory a brief description by firstly distinguishing *dialogism* from *dialogue* and *dialogicity*. During our description, we find that there are some seeming contradictions in Bakhtin's account of dialogic relationships. Although we can accept that the discovery of the dialogic relationships within utterance (or intra-utterance dialogicity) is the necessary and inevitable development of his dialogic looking at language-in-use, he is ambivalent about who participates in the textual dialogues or what the constitutive elements of textual dialogicity are. In his works, the following questions are also somewhat insufficiently dealt with: How are dialogic relationships textualized? How are the different voices related to each other? And what role do they play in the construction of a text?

In the context of postmodern theories about subject, we confirm the deconstruction of the subject in the dialogic analysis of text, and prefer voice to the canonical concrete speaking subject to be regarded as the participant of textual dialogues, or as the constitutive element of textual dialogicity. With reference to the notions of voice in psychology, narratology and rhetoric, and modeling on the Hallidayan stratificational understanding of language, we reinterpreted the Bakhtinian voice like this: voice is the ideologically semantic position in the text which is engendered by the institutionalized power relations in social interactions; it is realized in text through utterance, in the sense that when a stretch of wording can be identified with a certain voice, it will be interpreted as an utterance. The motive for the existence of voice is its heterogeneity, or simply, its difference from other voices. The foreignness of one voice from another is indicated by linguistic resources which are termed "dialogic markers"; and the dialogic relationships among the voices play important rhetorical roles in the construction of the text. In short, textual dialogicity refers to the dynamic interactions between different voices, which can be identified by deciphering their linguistic carriers in the text. Thus a successful dialogic analysis of texts such as print hard news depends primarily on the identification of dialogic markers in them.

Notes:
[1] As far as the deconstruction of the traditional autonomous humanist subject is concerned, Lynne Pearce (1994: 9) argues that "what the discourses of [Bakhtinian] dialogism and postmodernism most obviously share is a newly relational view of language (with its roots in Saussurean linguistics), and a theory of subjectivity that rejects the humanist principles of 'wholeness' and 'autonomy'."
[2] Researchers like Frow (1981: 260) also hold that the concept of voice has an advantage over traditional concepts such as point of view, speaking subject, consciousness, and vision in that it is not necessarily "actualized as those of a personified speaker".
[3] Following the common practice in SFL, the downward arrows indicate that the lower plane realizes the upper one.
[4] In our discussion the two adjectives foreign and alien are used in the sense of "different from the speaker, the author or the reporter", and are sometimes used interchangeably with the word other.
[5] The dialogic marker "blame" is believed to not only introduce other's words into the text but also report the content of other's words (or message), so "blame" is also included in utterance (c) which is considered the textualization of the foreign voice from the unions.
[6] According to Bauer (1989: 5), a Bakhtinian view on language use presupposes a consideration of power relations among interacting voices, because "[t]o speak of language, without speaking of power, in a Bakhtinian perspective is to speak meaninglessly, in a void. For Bakhtin, language is thus everywhere imbricated with asymmetries of power."
[7] So in our later discussion we will keep the way of making textual annotations in which we did for example (2) above and use such bracketed bold type lowercase letters to name directly the voices or utterances at issue when doing textual analysis in the framework of translinguistics.

Chapter 4 Dialogic Markers in Print News of English

In the previous chapter, we have mentioned that since voices can be textualized or realized in the text through utterances by lexico-grammatical resources; these resources may not be complete sentences or clauses but just act as the representatives of those utterances. Thus a successful dialogic analysis of a text depends on a fruitful identification of these linguistic representatives, which are marked out by a group of special linguistic devices called *dialogic markers* in our discussion. That is to say, in order to read a text dialogically, in the first place we have to recognize in the text those linguistic parts (no matter what they are—words, phrases, clauses and so on) signifying different utterances and voices with the help of dialogic markers. But before we start our identification and classification of dialogic markers in the setting of print news text, we have to bear in mind some necessary caveats and modifications of our foregoing understanding of dialogicity in the first section of this chapter.

4.1 Voice, difference, and source in news text

In Chapter Three, we singled out *voice* as the participant in textual dialogues in the broader sense (or the constitutive element of textual dialogicity) rather than the other two competing concepts, viz *speaking subject* and *utterance* suggested by Bakhtin when he talks about the dialogic properties of utterance or text in his translinguistics and conducts his dialogic analysis of novel discourse (especially those of Dostoevsky's). The two major reasons for so doing that we have supplied, however, seem not to hold water especially when we are facing the practical analysis of concrete news texts in print form.

True as it is that the autonomous subject has been decentered not only by the postmodern theorists represented by Foucault, Althusser and so forth (Lecercle, 1999; Xin Bin, 2000) but also by Bakhtin, it is also unacceptable that voice can be regarded as a new autonomous center taking the place of the traditional concept of subject. Although voices are conceptualized as ideological or semantic positions inhabiting the text in the present book, they should be occupied by somebody in a concrete case of interaction no matter what stage the interaction is in: production or interpretation. Or a voice should be connected with a source especially in the setting of a news text. Given the interactive nature of our understanding and analyzing news text in the very sense of an active dialogic understanding advocated by Bakhtin in *MPL* (Bakhtin/Volosinov, 1986: 102-3), we have to identify ourselves with a certain ideological or semantic position or in Kress' (1989) words "reading position" when analyzing a concrete news text. But more importantly, during reading, interpreting and explaining the news text, when assuming a certain voice (or adopting a certain reading position), we have to identify our counterpart voices and relate them with certain sources (if not the concrete speaking subjects in the Cartesian tradition). Although researches show that it is almost impossible to pin down the specific man behind each distinct voice in news report, a successful dialogic analysis of news text is indeed preceded by a successful identification of textual voices with their sources; for a description of the manipulation and specific configuration of voices and sources in a news text can be very revealing (Xin Bin, 2000: 167-72; Zeng Qingxiang 2005: 74-92), and moreover it will actually cast enough light on the major theme of postmodern mentality—the relationship between power and discourse, which also constitutes the major concern of CDA. At this juncture, it should be noted that *source* is not used here simply as a substitute for the controversial concept of *subject*. For source can be used to refer to not only the traditional speaking individual but also an institution or an organization (i. e. a group of individuals occupying the same ideological or semantic positions); it can not only be specified but also remain unspecified in the text, or even can be identified with the community as a whole and sometimes it is actually unspecifiable (cf. Thompson, 1996a). *Source* can be regarded as the other side of the coin, one side of which is actually *voice*; it serves as the indication of voice in a specific and concrete case of verbal interaction. Thus, in the setting of news text, voice, the key concept for the dialogic analysis of text, can be understood in this way: voice is the ideologically semantic position in the text which is engendered by the institutionalized power relations in social interactions; it is realized in the text through utterance, in the sense that when a stretch of wording can be identified with a certain voice, it will be interpreted as an utterance; the existence of a voice depends on the existence of other different voices, hence the essentiality of the heterogeneity of voice, which in text is indicated by linguistic resources that are termed dialogic markers; *voices are related to certain sources, specified or unspecified as individual, organization or even the community as a whole in the text*; and the dialogic relationships among the voices play important rhetorical roles in the construction of the text.

Therefore, to recognize the source of a voice is significant with respect to how to tell one voice from another. As has just been mentioned in Chapter 3, the difference between voices is really the motivation of the production and existence of a text. Although this difference is realized linguistically in the text and can be identified with the help of the so-called dialogic markers, a successful identification of the changing of voice-sources can facilitate our recognition of the difference and our accounting for the issue. Thus Bakhtin's idea that the utterance which carries a voice in the text (especially during the process of a dialogic understanding and analysis of the text) can be demarcated by the changing of speaking subjects is modified in the present book like this: *in the setting of news text, the changing of sources will be taken as the demarcation of different voices*. In this connection, it is necessary to repeat how we view the relationship between voice and utterance: *utterance is a unit for dialogic analysis of the text*; when we identify a stretch of wording in the text (a word, a phrase, a clause, a sentence, etc.) with a voice, it will be transformed into an utterance or at least the textual representative of an utterance; that is, it will not be a pure linguistic unit anymore. For example,[1]

(1) (a) Muslims leaders around the world demanded (b) a more personal apology from the Pope last night after the Vatican said (c) he "sincerely regrets" the offence caused by (d) remarks (e) they claimed had insulted Islam. The Vatican tried to damp down (f) fury over (g) the speech, in which the Pope quoted from (h) a medieval text saying the Prophet Mohammed had brought the world "only evil and inhuman" things.

In this short snippet of news report about the Muslims' reaction to the address delivered by Pope Benedict XVI at the University of Regensburg in Germany on Sept. 12, 2006, it is not difficult to identify at least eight voices which are realized in the text by the utterances indicated correspondingly by small case letters: (1) the reporting voice;[2] (2) Pope's apologizing voice; (3) the clarifying voice from Vatican, the top authority of Christianity; (4) Pope's offending remarks; (5) Muslims leader's claiming that the Pope's remarks are insulting; (6) the fury-loaded voices from the Muslim world; (7) Pope's voice of delivering the speech at the University of Regensburg; (8) voice from a medieval text quoted by the Pope saying the Prophet Mohammed had brought the world evil things. Thus, it is fair to say that from the underlined linguistic expressions we can identify the above mentioned voices, hence the corresponding sources and utterances. And at the same time, from a dialogic vantage point, the fine and subtle differences among the voices are expected to be checked against the possible foreign tones carried by their linguistic markers. This is actually what we mean by a double-oriented functional model of dialogic analysis of the text discussed in Chapter 2. With respect to the methodological issue of looking at the text from above, that is, taking a dialogic view at the text, we have already allocated enough space for it in the previous chapters. But as Halliday has pointed out, a complete and genuine analysis of text depends on a detailed linguistic analysis. That is to say, the above rough interpretation and the identification of the voices in the text should be based on enough linguistic accounts or evidence. Thus a relatively systematic account of dialogic markers in news text should be in order.

If we take a closer look at the above example, it is not difficult to find that the dialogic markers in it are almost related to the linguistic phenomenon of one speech reporting another. Its dominant existence in news reporting and its intrinsic function of marking the heterogeneity or foreignness of voice secure its top-priority in our discussion.

4.2 Dialogic markers of speech reporting in news text

During the dialogic analysis of news text, to put speech reporting at the top of our agenda is highly motivated both theoretically and practically.

4.2.1 Speech reporting: a fundamental feature of human language

Speech reporting is not only essential in news text, but in reality an essential mechanism of human language on the whole. It is speech reporting that enables people to convey what was communicated in the past or what is now being communicated or what will be communicated in the future by others. That is to say, people can use language to talk about others' words as well as the material world out there. In linguistics, this fundamental feature of language, namely, its being used to refer to itself (or talk about others' words by commenting on, criticizing, or questioning them) is termed *reflexivity* (Verschueren, 2000: 187-98; Coulmas, 1986: 2). And as Haberland (1986: 219) points out, speech reporting is, indeed, universal to all human languages:

> Most languages we know of seem to have these devices [speech reporting] in one form or other, and even languages which are not too well-equipped, somehow seem to make do with whatever devices they have, mostly relying on context features... reported speech *is* a universal human action.

Like Haberland, Jakobson also maintains that reporting speech, which has the duplex structures of language referring to language, plays a pertinent and indispensable part in the buildup of any human language (Jakobson, 1985: 96). Therefore, without speech reporting, language would be fatally limited in its potential as the major means of human communication (Sakita, 2002: 1-2).

4.2.2 News text: report about others' words

Although news stories are expected to be accounts of major events such as an earthquake, a murder case, a war, etc., we often see in their relevant reports "little of the actual events but much of what various eyewitnesses and officials have to say about the event" (Scollon, 1998: 216). Thus, news reports are generally believed to be full of words belonging to others rather than the reporters themselves. Though there is no doubt that journalists are writers or authors, they are actually not as original as they may appear to be (Waugh, 1995; Xin Bin, 2000: 145-9). According to Bell (1991: 60), a survey of television newscasts, conducted by the Glasgow University Media Group in 1980, found that nearly 20 per cent of the copy read by newscasters and reporters was reported speech. This strongly suggests that news reports rely heavily on other people's accounts of events in their authoring of news items. Fishman (1980: 92) also points out: "This fundamental principle of news fact can be stated like this: *something is so because somebody says it*. Newsmakers take their facts from other people's accounts." Though sounding somewhat radical, this principle does point to the fact that speech reporting plays an essential role in the making of news texts.

The sources of the reported speeches in the news text are generally believed to be composed of reports, declarations, interviews, meetings, press conferences, other media messages, press releases, parliamentary debates, court trials, police documents, and so forth. Some news stories are even entirely cut-and-paste jobs from such sources, or even written by the institution wanting to make something about itself known but published in the name of a reporter, and this is called *preformulating the news* by Jacobs (1999). Van Dijk (1988: 128), therefore, classifies the input sources of news text into the following 12 categories:

1. Dispatches of national and international news agencies.
2. Press releases of institutions, organizations, firms, etc.
3. Press conferences, including invitations for them.
4. Agendas and materials of a large number of legislative bodies, committees, and organizations.
5. Reports from various organizations.
6. Interviews with representatives of organizations.
7. Phone calls with representatives of organizations.
8. Notes of interviews, phone calls, press conferences, etc.
9. Official letters of organizations (often to other organizations), sometimes accompanied by documentation.
10. Articles in a variety of foreign and domestic newspapers.
11. Documentation, including of own newspaper (clippings) [sic].
12. Printed versions of speeches, interventions in meetings, and debates.

Thus, a journalist is as much a compiler as an author, and news texts consist of many previously composed texts from others (Xin Bin, 2000:

147-8). Or in Bell's (1991: 60) words, news text is mainly "talk about talk", and "[i]t consists entirely of what newsmakers have said by way of announcement, protest, plea, or some other speech act."

4.2.3 Bakhtin's understanding of speech reporting

From our discussion about Bakhtin's translinguistics in the first two chapters, we know that in Bakhtin's eyes language-in-use is intrinsically dialogic. According to him, this dialogic nature of language can be fully demonstrated by the examination of speech reporting, which illuminates all aspects of verbal communication (Sakita, 2002: 3). For Bakhtin believes that "[t]he productive study of dialogue presupposes, however, a more profound investigation of the forms used in reported speech, since these forms reflect basic and constant tendencies in the *active reception of other speakers' speech*, and it is this reception, after all, that is fundamental also for dialogue" (Bakhtin/Volosinov, 1986: 117; italics in the original).

According to Bakhtin, speech reporting actually refers to the translinguistic phenomenon of "speech within speech, utterance within utterance, and at the same time also speech about speech, utterance about utterance" (Bakhtin/Volosinov, 1986: 115). The speech which is embedded into another speech is termed *reported speech*, and the embedding speech which takes the reported one as a part is thus termed *reporting speech*, or *authorial context*.[3] Reported speech is regarded by the speaker as an utterance belonging to other speaker (or institution), an utterance that was totally independent, complete in its construction, and lying outside the given context. When the reported speech is transposed from its independent existence into an authorial context (i.e. the reporting speech), it usually retains its own referential content and at least the rudiments of its own linguistic integrity, its own original constructional independence. The reporting speech, or the author's utterance, however, in incorporating the reported other's utterance, brings into play syntactic, stylistic, and compositional norms for its partial assimilation—that is, it is adapted to the syntactic, compositional, and stylistic design of the author's utterance, while preserving its initial autonomy. Among the various forms of the dynamics between reported speech and reporting speech, Bakhtin identifies two contrasting patterns: the linear-style and the pictorial-style speech reporting. "The basic tendency of the linear style is to construct clear-cut, external contours for reported speech" (Bakhtin/Volosinov, 1986: 120). On the contrary, in pictorial speech reporting, "[l]anguage devises means for infiltrating reported speech with authorial retort and commentary in deft and subtle ways. The reporting context strives to break down the self-contained compactness of the reported speech, to resolve it, to obliterate its boundaries" (ibid.). With respect to these two tendencies, texts belonging to different genres show their preferences. Literary texts (especially those of novels, which pay more attention to "verbal art") tend to make a best use of the pictorial speech reporting. But non-literary text (especially those so-called "public texts" such as judicial text, political speech, news reports and so forth) is "less free in its handling of other speakers' utterances" (Bakhtin/Volosinov, 1986: 122), so they turn more frequently to the linear style. They usually require "a distinct cognizance of the boundaries of reported speech. It is marked by an acute awareness of property rights to words and by a fastidiousness in matters of authenticity" (Bakhtin/Volosinov, 1986: 122; cf. Baynham, 1996: 65).[4] The reason for this preference, it seems, is not difficult to understand. In literary texts, for instance, in fiction, reported speeches usually do not come from persons living in the real-life world; that is, all of them are created by the author. But in pubic texts, especially in news reports, the sources of the reported speeches are actually social subjects or institutions out there, and in most cases they are prominent social figures who occupy the higher positions in the social hierarchy (Short, 1988). The so-called "objectivity" of news reports relies heavily on the authenticity of the reported speeches.

Corresponding to the continuum whose two poles are constituted respectively by linear speech reporting and pictorial speech reporting, Bakhtin differentiates direct speech reporting from indirect speech reporting and also regards them as the two poles of the continuum of the linguistic realizations of speech reporting. Linear speech reporting is mostly realized (in the Hallidayan sense of realization) by direct speech reporting and the pictorial speech reporting "is characterized by an exceptional development of mixed forms of speech reporting, including quasi indirect discourse and, in particular, quasi direct discourse, in which the boundaries of the message reported are maximally weakened" (Bakhtin/Volosinov, 1986: 122). Thus, modeling on the Hallidayan mode of language operation and Xin Bin's (2000: 159) understanding of the relationship between direct and indirect speech, the relationship between these two continuums of speech reporting identified by Bakhtin can be illustrated by the following figure:

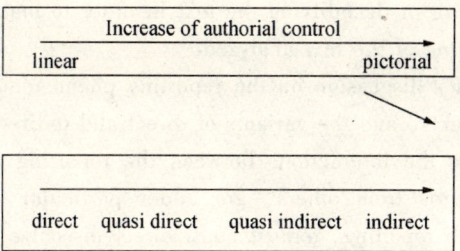

Figure 4.1 Realization of Bakhtinian linear and pictorial speech reporting

From this, it is safe to say that although Bakhtin emphasizes the dynamic interaction between the reporting speech and the reported speech, and takes it as the "active reception of other speakers' speech" happening in "the actual, inner-speech consciousness of the recipient" (Bakhtin/Volosinov, 1986: 117), he also pays much attention to the forms of the syntactic composition of speech reporting. Here is what he actually says on this issue:

> Thus, what is expressed in the forms employed for reporting speech is an active relation of one message to another, and it is expressed, moreover, not on the level of the theme but *in the stabilized constructional patterns of the language itself.*
>
> ...
>
> What we have in the forms of reported speech is precisely *an objective document of this reception.* Once we have learned to *decipher* it, this document provides us with information, not about accidental and mercurial subjective psychological processes in the "soul" of the recipient, but about steadfast social tendencies in an active reception of other speakers' speech, tendencies that *have crystallized into language forms.* (Bakhtin/Volosinov, 1986: 116-7; italicized by the author of this book)

Here, Bakhtin not only directs our attention to the textualization of the relationship between reported speech and reporting speech, but also provides us with some methodological strength for doing dialogic analysis of text, especially for analyzing text in the written form. Different from what

Bek's (1999) anti-codification understanding of Bakhtin's idea of textual analysis, here Bakhtin seems to agree to the necessity of a Hallidayan bottom-up *deciphering* or decodifying the text in order to make an active dialogic understanding of the text analyzed.

But Bakhtin's discussion on the reporting phenomenon is confined to that in literary texts, and the variants of direct and indirect speech, which he believes show the interactions between the reporting authorial context and reported words from others, are under particular attention. These variants of speech reporting, termed quasi direct discourse or quasi indirect discourse, are considered the major linguistic forms polyphonic novels and modern dialogic novels mainly utilize. Thanks to the various variants of direct and indirect speech reporting, human languages (especially Russian) create for literary texts "an extremely favorable situation for the pictorial style of speech reporting", and thus in novel texts " [a]n extraordinary ease of interaction and interpretation between reporting and reported speech is the rule" (Bakhtin/Volosinov, 1986: 127). It is also necessary to note that when talking about speech reporting in his *MPL*, Bakhtin has not yet introduced the concept of *voice* into his discussion. It is in *PDP* where the polyphonic feature of Dostoevsky's novels is under focus that voice is used as an essential concept and analytical tool, but unfortunately it is insufficiently defined and differentiated from those two closely-related concepts of *utterance* and *subject*. Although Bakhtin has mentioned at the stage of *MPL* that the interactional relationships between reported and reporting speech/discourse can reflect the dialogic relationships between their sources, he fails to examine these translinguitic and linguistic phenomena in a dialogic framework. But when a more developed dialogic framework is accomplished at the stages of *PDP* and *PSG*, it seems that Bakhtin does not continue to further his discussion on speech reporting in texts belonging to different genres.

Since our discussion is intended to carry out a Bakhtinian dialogic analysis of print hard news text of English which is characterized by its abundance of speech reporting, we have to fill the gap left by Bakhtin by looking back on speech reporting from the dialogic highland of translinguistics. This in turn will undoubtedly illuminate the dialogicity of hard news text. But as has been mentioned above, a successful dialogic understanding of speech reporting is determined by the successful identification and systematization of dialogic markers which linguistically indicate the difference between the interacting voices.

4.2.4 Dialogic markers in speech reporting

As we have mentioned in Chapter 3, dialogic markers refer to the linguistic resources which indicate the difference between voices or sources. They are closely related and situate themselves to different types of speech reporting.

As for modes of speech reporting, researchers, especially those working in the so-called discourse-pragmatic paradigm, have done enough thorough and insightful researches, for example, Leech & Short (1981: Ch. 10), Coulmas (1986), Short (1988), Clark & Gerrig (1990), Baynham (1996), Thompson (1996a; 2000), and Xin Bin (2000: Ch. 4), to name just a few. Like Bakhtin, they do not view speech reporting as the syntactic transformation in the school grammar class anymore and most of them have identified a similar continuum as Bakhtin's (see the previous section of this chapter) with direct and indirect reporting as its two ends, though different names might be used. For example, direct speech is called quotations in Clark & Gerrig (1990) and somewhere in Thompson (2000), and speech representation is preferred by Leech & Short (1981) and Short (1988). Among them, Xin Bin's (2000) classification of speech-reporting modes is most significant and relevant. Drawing heavily on Bakhtin/Volosinov (1986), Leech & Short (1981), and Fairclough (1988), Xin Bin established a continuum with direct speech (DS) and narrative report of speech acts (NRSA) as its two ends. Between these two poles there are two intermediate modes of speech reporting: free indirect speech (FIS) and indirect speech (IS). But more importantly he assigned this continuum with a scale of "increase of speaker's control" of others' words. Therefore the following figure which encapsulates the relationship among the four modes of speech reporting is in order:

Increase of speaker's control ⟶
DS   FIS   IS   NRSA

Figure 4.2 Xin Bin's continuum of speech reporting

Compared with the modes of speech reporting identified by Bakhtin, Xin Bin's model seems to push the frontier forward and incorporate into his continuum speeches (termed NRAS) which merely report that a speech act, or a number of speech acts, has occurred. "It [NRSA] provides only a minimal statement about what was said and the speaker does not have to commit himself entirely to giving the content of what was said, let alone the form of words in which they were uttered" (Xin Bin, 2000: 158). Another difference between Xin Bin's continuum and that of Bakhtin's is that between direct speech and indirect speech Bakhtin has identified two intermediate modes—quasi indirect speech (QIS) and quasi direct speech (QDS), but in Xin Bin's model there is only FIS. It is quite obvious that Bakhtin makes a finer division than Xin Bin does between direct and indirect speech reporting. Given that we are aiming at a detailed dialogic analysis of news text, it is quite advisable for us to combine these two models of the modes of speech reporting. That is to say, we accept both Xin Bin's expansion of indirect speech (IS) further to NRSA and Bakhtin's finer distinction of quasi direct speech (QDS) from direct speech (DS). Thus our continuum of speech reporting modes can be established as the following:

<pre>
            Increase of inter-voice control
                ─────────────────────────▶
        DS   QDS   IS   NRSA
</pre>

Figure 4.3 A continuum of speech reporting modeled on Bakhtin's and Xin Bin's

In our model, we keep Bakhtin's quasi direct speech (QDS) but incorporate his quasi indirect speech (QIS) or Xin Bin's FIS into Xin Bin's IS, for we find quite reasonable and convincing Xin Bin's observation of the relationship between FIS and IS: "FIS and NASA are in fact the variations of IS which is by nature ambivalent in voice as we cannot be sure whether the words of the original are reproduced or not, or which words are the original and which are not" (Xin Bin, 2000: 160). But we still keep NRSA separate from IS, for NRSA is comparatively reduced too much in form as far as other's speech is concerned. It is also necessary to note that we prefer *inter-voice control* to Xin Bin's *speaker's control* and Bakhtin's *authorial context control* when we are naming the scale of the dynamics between the reported speech/voice and the reporting speech/voice, for we are aiming at a dialogic analysis of speech reporting in news text and voice is regarded as the participant in the textual dialogues (see Chapter 3). And the four modes of speech reporting in our model can be exemplified by the following snippets from the news report hitting the front page of *The*

Sunday Telegraph on September 17, 2006:

(2) Muslims leaders around the world <u>demanded</u> *a more personal apology from the Pope last night.*

(3) "*We want a personal apology from the Pope,*" <u>said</u> Mohammed Habib, of Egypt's Muslim Brotherhood.

(4) "*I believe it is a must for the Pope to retract his erroneous, ugly and unfortunate remarks and apologise both to the Islamic world and Muslims,*" <u>said</u> Mr. Erdogan, Turkey's prime minister.

Here, (2) can be regarded as a NRSA of (3) or (4).

(5) Cardinal Tarcisio Bertone, the Vatican's secretary of state, <u>said</u> *the Pope's remarks had been misinterpreted.*

(6) Cardinal Tarcisio Bertone, the Vatican's secretary of state, <u>said</u>, "*The Pope's remarks have been misinterpreted.*" (the author's transformation from (5))

(5) is regarded as a canonical indirect speech of the direct speech in (6).

(7) He "*sincerely regrets that certain passages of his address could have sounded offensive to the sensitivities of the Muslim faithful, and should have been interpreted in a manner that in no way corresponds to his intentions*".

(8) The statement <u>expressed</u> the Pope's "*esteem*" for Muslims and <u>emphasized</u> that he intended to underline that there was "*no place for violence in religion*".

In (7) and (8), quoted words from others have been put into the quotation marks, which are held to be important markers of direct speech reporting or quotation.[5] But in (7), the wording in quotation marks is combined neatly with the subject of the sentence to form a grammatically well-formed complete sentence; the part quoted from others functions as a compositional part of the sentence. Another thing distinguishing (7) from canonical direct speech reportings such as (3), (4) and (6) is that it shows the absence of a lexico-grammatical reporting signal, namely, one of those underlined words in the above examples. The independence of the quoted two stretches of wordings in (8) is even reduced to a lesser degree—they are just two noun phrases, although they are introduced by the underlined reporting signals (i.e. *expressed* and *emphasized*). If we compare (8) with (5), it is not difficult to find they are almost the same in composition except for the existence of quotation marks in (8). Therefore, we group such hybrid types of speech reportings as (7) and (8) under the somewhat umbrella term of quasi direct speech (QDS), which of course can also be termed quasi indirect speech (QIS), if we look at the things from the other way round. This is probably the main reason why we give up Bakhtin's finer differentiation of QDS from QIS. [6]

Reporting signals in the present book are held to be those linguistic resources which can indicate the foreignness of a voice embodied by a stretch of wording related to them in news text. For example,

(9) David Davies, a Tory MP, said, "*The public are being failed by a system which allows murders and rapist back on to the streets to commit more offenses.*"

(10) Yesterday, after the White House ban was disclosed in the strongly pro-Blair *Sun*, Mr. Howard issued a statement: "*A Conservative government would work very closely with President Bush or President Kerry but my job as leader of the Opposition is to say things as I see them in the interests of our country and to hold our Government to account...*"

(11) The so-called *loyalty test* has been ordered as part of a wide-ranging security review of personnel employed in positions with daily access to top-secret and classified information.

(12) The suspects were said to be under the command of an alleged senior British al-Qaeda agent, Abu Eisa al-Hindi, who is reportedly *one of those still being held*.

(13) According to financial documents filed at Companies House, *the FA has written off £ 17.67 million that it has spent on preparatory work at a site near Burton upon Trent in Staffordshire.*

(14) As an advertisement for a series of such tapes has it, they provide "*A gentle stream of music that floats upon one's consciousness with scarcely a ripple*". (Thompson, 2000: 25)

In the above examples, all the underlined parts are words belonging to different categories: they are obviously verb, noun, adjective, adverb, compound preposition and conjunction respectively. [7] The italicized parts in each example are the utterances embodying others' voices. In (9), the foreign voice marked by the reporting verb *said* can be identified with a specified source, namely, David Davies, a Tory MP; in (10), the foreign voice marked by the reporting noun *statement* can be identified with Mr. Howard; in (11), the foreign voice marked by the reporting adjective *so-called*, however, cannot be identified with a specified source; in (12), the foreign voice marked by the adverb *reportedly* cannot be identified with a specified source either; in (13), the foreign voice marked by the compound preposition *according to* is specified as "the financial documents filed at Companies House", obviously an institution here; and in (14), the foreign voice marked by the conjunction *as* in combination with the verb phrase *has it* is specified as "an advertisement for a series of such tapes".

As for the classification of the reporting signals, Thompson (2000: Ch. 2) has laid a solid groundwork for our discussion of the dialogic markers as reporting signals. On the basis of the famous Corpus of Collins Cobuild and drawing heavily on *SFL*, he has found that reporting verbs are the main reporting signals in any register and genre. And according to the different functions of the reporting verbs, he puts them into two major groups: neutral reporting verbs and evaluative reporting verbs.[8] The neutral reporting verbs used with a significant high frequency in English are: *say*, *tell*, *ask*, *write*, *speak*, *talk*, *state*, and *express*, etc. The reporting verbs with an evaluative sense can be further grouped as:

> (a) reporting verbs or phrases indicating the purpose of the reported speech such as: *acknowledge*, *admit*, *admonish*, *advise*, *affirm*, *allege*, *announce*, *appeal*, *argue*, *assert*, *assure*, *avow*, *beg*, *beseech*, *bet*, *boast*, *brag*, *caution*, *certify*, *challenge*, *claim*, *coax*, *command*, *comment*, *complain*, *concede*, *confess*, *confide*, *confirm*, *contend*, *counsel*, *declare*, *decree*, *demand*, *direct*, *disclose*, *divulge*, *emphasize*, *encourage*, *enjoy*, *entreat*, *exhort*, *explain*, *forbid*, *foretell*, *grumble*, *guarantee*, *implore*, *imply*, *incite*, *inform*, *insist*, *instruct*, *invite*, *joke*, *lament*, *let slip*, *let someone know*, *maintain*, *moan*, *notify*, *object*, *observe*, *offer*, *ordain*, *order*, *plead*, *pledge*, *point out*, *postulate*, *pray*, *preach*, *predicate*, *predict*, *proclaim*, *promise*, *prophesy*, *propose*, *protest*, *reassure*, *recommend*, *record*, *remark*, *remind*,

report, request, reveal, rule, specify, state, stipulate, stress, suggest, swear, teach, testify, threaten, urge, vow, warn, etc.

(b) reporting verbs or phrases indicating the way the reported speech is delivered by the reported source such as: *babble, bawl, bellow, blurt, boom, breathe, burst out, call, chatter, cry, declaim, drawl, exclaim, falter, gabble, gibber, holler, mumble, murmur, mutter, prattle on, quaver, rave, scream, screech, shout, shriek, shrill, snap, stammer, storm, stutter, trumpet, whisper, yell,* etc.

(c) reporting verbs indicating the message of the reported speech such as: *abuse, accuse, attack, belittle, bemoan, besmirch, bewail, blame, castigate, censure, charge, condemn, criticize, curse, decry, defame, denigrate, denounce, deplore, deprecate, dismiss, disparage, insult, lampoon, libel, mock, pillory, rebuke, reproach, reprove, revile, ridicule, satirize, slam, slander, slate, upbraid; acclaim, applaud, bless, commend, compliment, congratulate, endorse, eulogize, extol, flatter, laud, praise,* etc.

(d) reporting verbs indicating both the message and the purpose of the reported speech such as: *admonish, apologize, argue, bellyache, berate, bicker, boast, brag, cheek, chide, complain, confess, equivocate, flannel, greet, gripe, grouch, grouse, grumble, haggle, hail, heckle, jeer, joke, nag, object, pray, preach, protest, quarrel, quibble, reprimand, scold, shush, soft-soap, squabble, swear, taunt, tease, toast, waffle, wheedle, whine, yammer,* etc.

(e) reporting verbs or phrases implying reporter's attitude of approval such as: *acknowledge, admit, concede, confess, disclose, divulge, foretell, forewarn, indicate, let on, let slip, make clear, mention, note, point out, recall, reveal,* etc. ; and reporting verbs or phrases implying reporter's attitude of disapproval or doubt such as: *allege, bluff, claim, distort, exaggerate, fabricate, fib, lie, make out, misinform, misquote,* and *purport,* etc.

(f) reporting verbs indicating the effect aimed at by the reporting speech such as: *cajole, coax, convince, demonstrate, establish, dissuade, nag, persuade, prevail (on/upon), prove, show,* etc.

Apart from the various types of reporting verbs, according to Thompson, some related cognate nouns can also be used as reporting signals, hence dialogic markers in our discussion. Modeling on the classification of verbs, Thompson has also identified three major types of reporting nouns:

(a) reporting nouns indicating the purpose of the reported speech such as: *accusation, acknowledgement, admission, advice, affirmation, allegation, announcement, appeal, assertion, assurance, bet, boast, call, caution, challenge, charge, claim, command, concession, confession, confirmation, contention, criticism, declaration, decree, demand, denial, disclosure, edict, encouragement, excuse, explanation, exhortation, guarantee, hint, implication, insistence, instruction, intimation, invitation, lament, message, news, notification, objection, observation, offer, order, plea, pledge, point, prayer, prediction, proclamation, promise, proposal, proposition, protest, reassurance, recommendation, refusal, remark, reminder, report, request, retort, revelation, specification, statement, stipulation, suggestion, testimony, threat, warning*, etc.

(b) reporting nouns indicating the way the reported speech is delivered by the reported source such as: *bellow, call, chant, chorus, cry, ejaculation, exclamation, howl, murmur, roar, scream, shout, shriek, whisper, yell*, etc.

(c) reporting nouns indicating the message of the reported speech such as: *abuse, accusation, admonition, apology, attack, censure, charge, commendation, commiseration, compliment, condemnation, congratulation, criticism, curse, eulogy, flattery, insult, lampoon, libel, mockery, praise, rebuke, reproach, reproof, ridicule, slander, thanks*, etc.

Compared with verbs and their cognate nouns, only a couple of adjectives are identified by Thompson as reporting signals, for example, *so-called* in (11), and those that can be followed by nominal clauses which are held to be reported speech acts or discussions of feelings or the knowledge of the situation of a certain event. For example, [9]

(15) Many governments, aware that *Al Jazeera is widely considered by Arab audiences to be credible*, have allowed their own sta-

tions to run Jazeera footage of the war to demonstrate their own anti-war credentials.

(16) The prime minister is <u>adamant that</u> *he will not resign.* To do so, he said, would be a betrayal of democracy.

(17) Sometimes parents with little money feel <u>sad that</u> *they can't buy toys for their children.* ((16) & (17) from Thompson, 2000: 29)

In English such several adverbs as *apparently*, *allegedly*, *reportedly*, and *supposedly* can be accepted as reporting signals too, though they tend to be used just to indicate that the utterances they mark embody some foreign voices without specifying the sources from which they come. For example,

(18) A MEMBER of the Marylebone Cricket Club is being investigated by the police after <u>allegedly</u> *threatening with a knife a fellow member who was using a mobile telephone during the recent Test match at Lord's.*

(19) <u>Apparently</u> *he would often sing popular songs when he went to a party.*

(20) <u>Supposedly</u>, *Augustus, an admirer of Virgil, issued an edict that none of his writings be destroyed.* ((19) & (20) from Thompson, 2000: 25)

It should be noted at this juncture that although the above listed reporting signals are identified by Thompson, he did not classify them into different groups from a lexical perspective. His classification of them is actually a hybrid description from simultaneously lexical and syntactical dimensions. That is, in his description, clauses as well as words and phrases can be regarded as reporting signals. For example, (14) now repeated as (21),

(21) <u>As an advertisement for a series of such tapes has it</u>, *they provide "A gentle stream of music that floats upon one's consciousness with scarcely a ripple".*

In (21), Thompson takes as reporting signal the whole clause introduced by *as*—*As an advertisement for a series of such tapes has it*, and termed it *reporting adjunct.* In our discussion, however, we prefer to look at the things from the lexical perspective when talking about the reporting signals. For one thing, it may sound more agreeable to the sense that the word *signal* or *marker* tend to suggest, and for another, when we classify things into different groups, a consistent criterion is usually preferred, though it does not make a significant difference in this case.

4.3 Modality as dialogic markers in news text

Modality holds an important position not only in traditional grammar but also in modern linguistic theories. Though the notion of modality may somewhat vary with different settings in which it appears, it is generally agreed that it is held to provide evaluative modification of the meaning carried by a clause; that is, it can be seen as the question of what people commit themselves to when they make statements, ask questions, make demands or offers (Quirk et al., 1985: 219; Palmer, 1986: 14-33; Halliday, 2000: 88; Fairclough, 2003: Ch. 10). For example,[10]

(22) a. The largest parties in the UK *are advised* by people who remain wedded to a very old notion of how politics works, rooted in the certainties of the 1950s and 1960s.

b. The largest parties in the UK *may be advised* by people who remain wedded to a very old notion of how politics works, rooted in the certainties of the 1950s and 1960s.

c. The largest parties in the UK *seem to be advised* by people who remain wedded to a very old notion of how politics works, rooted in the certainties of the 1950s and 1960s.

d. The largest parties in the UK *are likely to be advised* by people who remain wedded to a very old notion of how politics works, rooted in the certainties of the 1950s and 1960s.

e. The largest parties in the UK *are probably advised* by people who remain wedded to a very old notion of how politics works, rooted in the certainties of the 1950s and 1960s.

It is not difficult for us to know that what the reporter has actually written in (22a) commits himself to the truth of the proposition more than any of its alternatives in (22b), (22c), (22d), and (22e). The differences between them are differences in modality (Fairclough, 2003: 165).

4.3.1 Modality and dialogicity

It should be noted that Halliday (2000: Ch. 4) holds that in verbal interactions there are mainly two kinds of things being exchanged: *proposition* and *proposals*. Thus accordingly, we have two types of modality: *modalization* (or *epistemic modality*) which reflects the speaker's attitude toward the proposition exchanged in the interaction; *modulation* (or *deontic modality*) which reflects the speaker's stance toward the proposal involved in the interaction. Given that news text (especially hard news) is mainly for the sake of information exchange, we will focus on Halliday's modalization or epistemic modality in our discussion. According to Halliday, modalization not only means the speaker's value judgment of the probabilities involved in what he is saying as a proposition, but also reflects the interpersonal distance or affinity between the speaker and the listener or between the writer and the reader, hence being regarded as the linguistic resources to realize interpersonal meanings.

The interpersonal notion of modalization is actually presupposed by a dialogic looking at the issue. Modalization exemplifies the Bakhtinian understanding that text is actually the space where different voices are competing and negotiating with one another: the voice from the speaker, the voice assumed by the reader or the voice from a third party (e. g. another specified or unspecified individual, institution or even the whole community) are dialogically interacting with each other in this textual space. And according to Bakhtin/Volosinov (1986), the competition or negotiation between voices are actually to convey their value judgments for one another, which he terms as "an active understanding" (Bakhtin/Volosinov, 1986: 102). He insists: "No utterance can be put together without value judgment. Every utterance is above all an *evaluative orientation*. Therefore, each element in a living utterance not only has a meaning but also has a value" (Bakhtin/Volosinov, 1986: 105). He also argues that one of the major differences between his dialogic understanding of utterance (i. e. his translinguistics) and the monologic understanding of language (especially the Saussurean abstract linguistics) is that the former pays attention to not only "the expression of a speaker's individual attitude toward the subject matter of his discourse" (ibid.) but also the speaker's evaluation of the related others' words, while the latter's "attention on the abstract system of language is what led most linguists to divorce evaluation from meaning and to consider evaluation an accessory factor of meaning" (ibid.). This value judgment or evaluation is actually a combination of the two intrinsic properties of utterance identified by Bakhtin later in *PSG*, namely, *expressivity* and *addressivity* (see Chapter 1). As we have discussed, the dialogicity of utterance is actually engendered by these two properties of utterance, so it is safe to say the dialogic interactions between voices embodied by utterances are actually the evaluations among the interacting voices: one voice evaluates the other and vice versa. For example, (22a) and (22b) now repeated as (23a) and (23b),

(23) a. The largest parties in the UK *are advised* by people who remain wedded to a very old notion of how politics works, rooted in the certainties of the 1950s and 1960s.

b. The largest parties in the UK *may be advised* by people who remain wedded to a very old notion of how politics works, rooted in the certainties of the 1950s and 1960s.

If we take (23a) as a voice, that is, a semantic position, which is textualized as the utterance (23a),[11] asserting that *the largest parties in the UK are advised by a certain kind of people*, then it may well be that (23b) includes at least two voices: one is actually the assertion expressed in (22a); the other is the voice holding the semantic position to offer its evaluation of the assertion—*the assertion may be true or may not be true*. That is, the truth value of the assertion can be discussed or negotiated, and it is open rather than closed; the two voices are negotiating with each other rather than one controlling the other. Thus the modal verb *may* in (23b) works like a dialogue introducer in an active understanding of the utterance. In the eyes of a textual analyst, it can be said to mark out, or to be exact, to provoke the existence of different voices when a dialogic unraveling is conducted for (23b) (cf. White, 1998: Ch. 3; Li Zhanzi, 2001, 2002: 115-6; Li Shuguang, 2006). The same is true of (22c), (22d), and (22e).

4.3.2 Modality resources as dialogic markers

To make a relatively systematic observation of the linguistic resources which can be used to realize *epistemic modality* or *modalization* in English is really a huge task. Although the classification and range of them remain controversial, it is a fact that the English language does possess abundant resources to express different degrees of interpersonal position toward a proposition. Among the various understandings of the issue, we can roughly identify three modes, that is, *narrow*, *moderate*, and *broad*. The narrow understanding of modality resources just includes the so-called modal verbs such as *can/could*, *may/might*, *must*, and so on; this view is usually held in school grammar textbooks. The broad understanding of modality resources is believed to include such lexico-grammatical resources as *verb tense*, *personal pronoun*, *speech reporting*, *deictic expressions*, *evaluative adjectives* and *adverbs*, some *lexical verbs*, *nouns* as well as *modal verbs* (Fowler & Kress, 1979: 200-7; Palmer, 1986; Simpson, 1993: Ch. 3). Linguists holding a moderate or middle understanding of modality resources seem to just take *modal verbs*, *some lexical verbs*, *a part of nouns*, and *some evaluative adjectives* and *adverbs* as linguistic means of modalization; among others, Quirk et al. (1985), Holmes (1988), Martin (1992), Halliday (2000) and Thompson (1996b) can be subsumed under this group. Within this group, the *SFL* linguists usually follow Halliday's macro-concept of grammatical metaphor to distinguish the congruent forms of modality expressions realized by modal verbs from the metaphorical forms of modality expressions realized by the "uncanonical" non-modal-verb modality resources. In our description of dialogic markers as modality resources we will follow this moderate understanding, but our focus does not lie so much in distinguishing the congruent forms from metaphorical ones as in treating them all as serving the same dialogic interpersonal function.

By using such famous corpuses of English as LOB, Brown, and Lund, Holmes (1988) has carried out a relatively thorough study on the linguistic resources for modalization and made a good list of these resources:

> (a) modal verbs or phrases expressing epistemic modality: (i) expressing certainty: (*be*) *bound to*, *can't/cannot*, *couldn't/could not*, *have to*, *have got to*, *must*, *will*, *would*; (ii) expressing probability: *ought to*, *shouldn't/should not*, *will*, *would*; (iii) expressing possibility: *could*, *may* (*not*), *might* (*not*).

(b) lexical verbs or phrases expressing epistemic modality: *appear, assume, assure, believe, consider, doubt, estimate, expect, feel, guess, hope, imagine, know, look as if/like, presume, reckon, seem, suggest, suppose, tend, think, threaten.*
(c) adverbials expressing epistemic modality:[12] *actually, apparently, at first sight, beyond doubt, certainly, clearly, definitely, doubtless, essentially, in fact, in reality, in theory, in X's opinion, indeed, indubitably, inevitably, maybe, naturally, necessarily, obviously, of course, perhaps, plainly, possibly, presumably, probably, surely, undeniably, undoubtedly, unquestionably, (very) likely, without doubt.*
(d) nouns expressing epistemic modality: *assumption, belief, certainty, chance, danger, doubt, estimate, evidence, explanation, fear, hope, idea, opinion, possibility, speculation, tendency, theory, view.*
(e) adjectives expressing epistemic modality: *apparent, certain, clear, evident, improbable, inevitable, likely, obvious, plain, possible, probable, sure, unlikely.*

The overlapping between the above two types of dialogic markers (i.e. reporting signals and modality resources) is quite evident especially when some lexical verbs and their cognate nouns are under focus. The guiding principle for us to put them into the two categories of reporting and modality is Hallidayan classification of processes: we regard the verbs of verbal processes as the prototypical ones of reporting signals and the verbs of mental processes as the prototypical ones for lexical resources of modality. For example,

(24) a. Sir John believes that *the equipment could play a vital role in averting other tragedies in schools.*
b. Sir John says that *the equipment could play a vital role in averting other tragedies in schools.* (rewritten according to (24a) by the author)

In (24a), belonging to Hallidayan mental process, *believe* works as a dialogic marker of modality, but in (24b), *say*, a typical verb realizing verbal process, is a dialogic marker working as a reporting signal. But according to Halliday (2000: 108-38), verbal process is the process that shares characteristics of both mental process and relational process, or it intervenes between them. That is to say, these processes are connected into something like a cline rather than exist in a discrete way. Another reason for this overlapping is that the usage of a single word may vary with the contexts in which it appears. Furthermore, most of them are polysemous, thus straddling the borderline between different categories.

4.4 Conjunction resources as dialogic markers in news text

Like the notion of modality, the concept of conjunction is also a little controversial. In this book, we accept Thompson's (1996b) understanding of the issue: "Conjunction refers broadly to the combining of any two textual elements into potentially coherent complex semantic unit" (Thompson, 1996b: 156). Obviously, the conjunction here does not refer to the concrete lexical items such as *but*, *and*, *or*, etc., which are also termed conjunctions in grammar textbooks. His conjunction here is actually an uncountable noun and refers to the semantic relationship rather than specific lexical items, but it has to be realized mainly by the following types of lexical items: prepositions, conjunctions, and conjunctive adjuncts.

In *SFL*, conjunction is thought to be used to realize logical-semantic function and the textual function, that is, make a stretch of text coherent. But dialogic relations are conceptualized by Bakhtin as a different type of relations from logical relations between propositions and from "all possible linguistic relations among elements, both in the language system and in the individual utterance" (Bakhtin, 1986: 114). He has emphasized more than once that dialogic relations are different from logical relations and the former can only exist between different translinguistic utterances but the latter exist between linguistic units (Bakhtin, 1984: 183-4, 1986: 124-5). For example,

(25) (a) The sun has risen. (b) But it's still very early. (Bakhtin, 1986: 83)

(26) (a) You can take your time. (b) But I have to get up now. (from the author of the book)

According to Bakhtin, if (25) is spoken by a speaker and can elicit a response like (26) from another speaker, it will be regarded as an utterance, and so is (26). The relationship between (25) as a whole and (26) as a whole is dialogical as well as logical: (26) is in disagreement with (25), or (26) confronts (25). But the relationships between the two sentences within (25) and (26) respectively are only logical rather than dialogic—(25b) and (26b) are the antitheses of (25a) and (26a) respectively, because (25a) and (25b) as a whole are spoken by the same speaker and so are (26a) and (26b). In our developed model of dialogicity, the issue can be reasoned like this: if (25a) and (25b) are interpreted as to realize the single unified voice from a speaker, they form a single Bakhtinian utterance. The same is true of (26a) and (26b).

But as we have already discussed in Chapter 3, Bakhtin seems to be a little self-contradictory about the relationship between dialogicity and utterance. After he emphasizes that dialogic relationship should presuppose inter-utterance relationship, he then argues that "a dialogic approach is possible toward any signifying part of an utterance, even toward an individual word, if that word is perceived not as the impersonal word of language but as a sign of someone else's semantic position, as the representative of another person's utterance; that is, if we hear in it someone else's voice" (Bakhtin, 1984: 184). For example,

(27) A: The sun has risen.

B: (a) The sun has risen. (b) But it's still very early.

That is, if we take (27Ba) as the wording that expresses a foreign voice (i. e. the voice from speaker A) rather than carries the single unified voice of speaker B, then within speaker B's utterance, there will be two voices: one is from speaker A, and the other actually comes from speaker B, hence two utterances (i. e. 27Ba and 27Bb). Thus if we consider the issue from a structuralist point of view, utterance here becomes a hierarchical construction: one utterance can be composed of several componential utterances. If we take a look at the issue from another perspective, it is safe to say that speaker B's speech contains the words from two speakers': (27Ba) is from speaker A, while (27Bb) is from speaker B himself; the latter actually renders the former a negative judgment or evaluation. The existence of the conjunction *but* at the beginning of (27Bb) works like putting quotation marks upon (27Ba), and thus we will have (27B) like this: (a) *"The sun has risen."* (b) *But it's still very early.* That is why we can regard the conjunction *but* as a dialogic marker in this place.

It should be noted again that if we take voice rather than utterance as the constitutive element of textual dialogicity, it will be easier for us to take a universal dialogic look at text regardless of whether it is in the form of canonical dialogue or in the written monologic form (for instance, print hard news text). Our point here is that whether the print text is dialogic or monologic depends on what kind of reading position the analyst takes when he approaches the text. If he takes the vantage point of an active participant who assumes a voice from the other with respect to the voice from the author and engages himself in the interactions presupposed by the text, an active dialogic understanding of the text will be achieved. In this sense, we can say any text can be dialogized. For example,

(28) *The Scottish Secretary, Michael Forsyth,* may (b) *be crude in the way he* bangs on *about* (a) *the dangers of a 'tartan tax' and the 'slippery slope' to independence,* (c) but *in a political vacuum, he who shouts loudest uses up all the oxygen.*
(Hunston, 2001: 180)

If we take a dialogic view at this text, we will find at least three voices: voice (a) from the Scottish Secretary, Michael Forsyth, mainly marked by the speech reporting signal *bang on* and the inverted commas indicating the existence of quasi direct speech—(*there are?*) *the dangers of a "tartan tax" and the "slippery slope" to independence*; voice (b) from an unspecified source, marked by the modal verb *may* together with the conjunction *but*—(*Michael Forsyth's way of saying thing is*) *crude*; voice (c) from the reporter marked by the conjunction *but* together with the modal verb *may*—*even if it is "crude", in a political vacuum, he has no choice but to say things in that way.* The dialogic relationships between the three are like this: by evaluating (a) as "crude", (b) is in disagreement with (a), or at least (b) takes a negative attitude toward (a); but in turn (c) is also in disagreement with (b), although it declines its tone of explicit confrontation with (b) by employing the dialogic marker, the modal verb *may*, to show its willingness to negotiate with (b) about its opposing attitude.

Looking back on what we have just done, we will find that if we take a dialogic look at the text, that is, with the help of dialogic markers such as *bangs on*, *may* and *but*, we can identify at least three voices in the text. We can assume the position of a listener, and in the interaction between the reporter and us, the text can be understood like this: the reporter first reports to us others' utterances, and then gives his own view on the issue. If we assume the position of Michael Forsyth, we will find it pleasant to read the piece, for the writer seems to take his side. If we assume the position of the unspecified speaker, we will find we are involved in a debate with the reporter about the just evaluation of Michael Forsyth's performance. No matter what position we take, however, we have to make our voice textualized, or in simple terms, get it expressed as those italicized parts in the text around the corresponding markers.[13]

Besides the conjunction *but*, which is termed coordinator in school grammar and is thought to create paratactic logical relations in Hallidayan functional grammar, Martin (1992: 194-8) has identified some other hypotactic conjunctions which are thought to be able to realize modalization. They are: *if*, *provided that*, *as long as*; *so that*, *in order to*, and so on. But before we close this subsection, we have to note again that dialogic relationships cannot be reduced just to the logical relationships marked by these linguistic devices of conjunction. Only a different voice can assign the status of utterance to a stretch of wording in the text, and then the conjunction resources which help to identify the existence of different voices are considered dialogic markers like those *BUTs* in (27) and (28) rather than those in (25) and (26).

4.5 Negatives as dialogic markers in news text

Apart from reporting signals, modality resources and some conjunction resources which are held to mark interpersonal overtones of the wording around them in the text and thus are regarded as dialogic markers in our discussion, another important linguistic device that can mark the existence of different voices in text is the negative adverb "not". See the following examples cited from *The Sunday Telegraph*,

(29) (a) She was <u>not</u> (b) blaming the majority of the public, just a minority who were behaving inappropriately at the fountain.

(30) (a) Right now, things don't (b) look promising for those of us who believe this is a war worth waging, but only with broad international support.

If we take a close dialogic look at (29), it is not difficult for us to locate two voices indicated by the underlined negative adverb *not*: (a) the reporter's reporting voice—to deny or nullify an existent opposing proposition held by other's voice; (b) an unspecified other's voice holding the proposition—an accusation which would probably be like: "She was blaming the majority of the public." The same is true in (30): (a) the reporter's reporting voice—to deny or nullify an existent opposing proposition held by other's voice; (b) an unspecified other's voice holding the proposition—the war is justified and needs to gain international support. Thus the existence of the negative particle *not* seems to indicate a debate occurring between the reporter and an anonymous other.

Apart from the prototypical form of negation like (29) and (30) which is made by incorporating the negative particle *not*, there are other forms of negation in the English language. Pagano (1994) has identified two types of negation: the overt referring to the negatives having a formal marker of negation such as *not*, *no*, *nowhere*, etc., and the covert referring to propositions expressing a negative meaning but having a positive form, for example, *I forgot...* The latter type exemplified by "*I forgot...*" is also termed semantic or pragmatic negatives, because it can be understood or paraphrased as *I did not remember...* (Fairclough, 1992a: 122-3) Since our model of dialogic analysis presupposes that any understanding or interpretation depends on formal lexico-grammatical evidence, our discussion of negative dialogic markers is limited to the overt formal ones. In *SFL*, especially in the later developed and enlarged interpersonal module known as *Appraisal Theory*, which draws heavily upon the Bakhtinian notion of heteroglossia, "the negative is construed as carrying a greater interpersonal charge than the positive since it carries with it the possibility of the positive, while the positive references only itself" (White, 1998: 90). For example,

(31) a. The Premier didn't view the documents.
b. The Premier saw the documents.

According to White, (31a) strongly invokes the possibility or at least the claim that "She [the Premier] did view the documents" (ibid.), and "in heteroglossic terms we might say that it implies that someone, somewhere has alleged that the Premier saw the documents" (ibid.). But the positive (31b) does not explicitly invoke any alternative or opposite possibility. White here obviously takes a dialogic view at the issue of negation, although he takes as his premises Hallidayan tri-functional observation of language rather than a Bakhtinian dialogic perspective when aiming at an exploration of the interpersonal engagement in written verbal interaction. The convergence between these two ways of looking at language-in-use is due to the fact that as we have already discussed fully in Chapter 2 they share a lot in understanding the functions language possesses because they are both greatly influenced by Karl Bühler. Though looking at the things from different perspectives and with different focuses: our model of dialogic analysis attempts to recontextualize Bakhtin's translinguistics in Hallidayan *SFL* while the appraisal theory (especially its daughter module *engagement*) aims at a development of *SFL* by drawing on Bakhtinian notion of heteroglossia, the appraisal theory can inevitably provide us with enough insights practically as well as theoretically.

4.6 Summary

After we have made a list of dialogic markers belonging to different linguistic categories, we have to answer an unavoidable question: Do we have exhausted all of them? Or why do we include these rather than others in our discussion?

As to the first question, we should admit that it is impossible for us to make an exhaustive list of dialogic markers here. For one t, the language is developing and as non-native analysts our eyes are put at a disadvantage in a measure due to a lack of necessary intuitive sensitivity with which the native speakers are endowed, though we do have the unique advantage of acuteness in making our observation of the English language with foreign eyes just like a Martian (if there be one) will find something new and unusual in what is taken for granted by people on the earth. For another, our observation depends enormously on a particular dialogic position we will take, so it is unwise to claim that our interpretation and explanation of the text is objective and unquestionable. What is more relevant and significant for us is that we have to base our analysis on enough linguistic evidence by taking a bottom-up looking at the text and expose the things which the text embodies but which would be concealed and disguised if the text is observed in other ways. The second question is closely related to the first one in that there may well be other resources which can also serve as the dialogic markers. But the observations we have made in this book and the resources we have got access to up to now just enable us to go this far. Thus our inventory is open rather than closed.

Another justification for our listing and grouping the dialogic markers is that Bakhtinian translinguistics tends to talk about things above the language level and makes so many linguistic details presupposed. And more importantly, he sometimes draws between translinguistic reading of a text and linguistic analysis of the text a line which seems too forbidding to be crossed. But the dovetail joints between Bakhtin's translinguistic and Hallidayan *SFL* we identified in Chapter Two allow and require us to allocate due space in this book for the discussion of the linguistic resources on which we can rely in the process of making a translinguistic or dialogic analysis of print hard news text.

Furthermore, our listing of dialogic markers in this way is stimulated by Fuller's (1998: 45-9) discussion of discourse negotiation in popular texts of Stephen Jay Gould. She identifies three functional resources of discourse negotiation which are actually inspired by Bakhtinian textual dialogicity: *projection*, *metacomment* and *modality*. And she points out that there exist "three major modes of discourse negotiation which form a functional cline from ideational meaning to interpersonal meaning". We accept her idea that projection (i. e. speech reporting in our discussion) and modality are two crucial linguistic resources to realize textual dialogicity (i. e. negotiation in her words), but we have found that connectives, and negatives can also play important parts in so doing. Another difference between our discussion and hers is that speech reporting, modality, connectives, and negatives are actually the resources to convey the evaluation made by one voice about another. The dialogic relationships between voices are actually making comments or issuing evaluations.

But this listing can only provide us with a basis for making our observation of the dialogicity of print news text from a bottom-up direction. And more importantly, the function possessed by these linguistic resources to mark out different voices is actually context-dependent. That is, not every linguistic form discussed above can unanimously be read as a dialogic marker, as texts can be interpreted in multiple ways by different analysts. But what is certain is that these linguistic resources do have the potential to be interpreted this way.

Notes:

[1] If not specially specified, the examples included in this chapter are from the data collected from *The Sunday Telegraph*.

[2] Given the reporting voice is scattered in the whole text, in our analysis we tend to put a small-case letter at the beginning of the paragraph to indicate its special existence.

[3] When talking about speech reporting, Bakhtin uses the three terms of *speech*, *utterance* and *discourse* interchangeably and even sometimes, the reporting speech is believed to function as a new context for the reported or received speech, and thus also termed *authorial context*. Since our analysis of news text is conducted in the framework of Bakhtinian translinguistics, this way of terming speech reporting is accepted in our discussion in similar situations.

[4] When talking about the different handlings of speech reporting in texts belonging to different genres, Bakhtin differentiate "verbal art" from "rhetoric" as two teleological criteria for classifying genres of text by saying: "The teleology of the authorial context is especially important. In this respect, it is verbal art that most keenly implements all the permutations in sociolingual interorientation. As distinct from verbal art, rhetoric, owing simply to its teleology, is less free in its handling of other speakers' utterances. Rhetoric requires a distinct cognizance of the boundaries of reported speech. It is marked by an acute awareness of property rights to words and by a fastidiousness in matters of authenticity" (Bakhtin/ Volosinov, 1986: 122). It is obvious that "rhetoric" does not mean the art of effective or persuasive speaking or writing here, but refers to the discourse or text which is intended for an effective persuasion on the audience or reader concerning public affairs such as legal issues, social welfares and so on. Thus news text belongs to the genre of "rhetoric" here. This understanding of "rhetoric" can be supported by the Chinese translation of the same text from Bakhtin's original Russian (cf. *An Oeuvre of Bakhtin* (Chinese edition) (2): 475).

[5] In the Hallidayan model of language, quotation marks belong to the graphological expression stratum, which together with other material means are used to materialize/realize the lexico-grammatical configurations (Eggins, 2004: 19, Hu Zhuanglin et al., 2005: 19, 63). In addition to quotation marks, colon can also serve as a dialogic marker. For example, in the headline: *Prince Charles:*

wind farms are horrendous, the colon indicates that the part after it is the wording carrying the voice from Prince Charles rather than the reporter.

[6] Maynard (1997) distinguishes direct speech reportings or quotations like (7) from those like (8) and termed them "syntactically incorporated quotation" and "phrase-labeling quotation" respectively, and holds that they have different functions: the former type is used to echo society's voices and the latter shows embedded heterogeneity. In our discussion, the function of embodying heterogeneity is fundamental and shared by these two types of speech reporting and they are similar as far as the inter-voice control is concerned, thus both of them being grouped into QDS.

[7] We accept the classification of *as* into the category of conjunction in *Oxford Advanced Learner's English-Chinese Dictionary* (6th edition).

[8] Caldas-Coulthard (1994: 305-7) has also distinguished the neutral reporting verbs such as *say*, *tell*, *ask*, etc. , which he argues "introduce a 'saying' without explicitly evaluating it", from those evaluative verbs, which he terms *illocutionary glossing verbs* that convey the presence of the author in the text, and are highly interpretive.

[9] It sounds a little bit far-fetched that adjectives, adverbs and conjunctions can be used to introduce others' words in text, so we provide examples to demonstrate such a usage rather than simply make a list of them as we handle verbs and nouns listed above. Another thing needs noting is that the complementizer *that*, which is used to introduce an indirect speech or representation (or in Hallidayan term, projection), can also be regarded as a dialogic marker, working just like the quotation marks and colon do in direct speeches.

[10] (22a) is the original sentence adopted from *The Sunday Telegraph*, the rest of this group are re-written ones according to (22a) for the purpose of comparison and illustration.

[11] According to Bakhtin (1986: 82), when the individual sentence is analyzed separately from its context, it actually gains the status of an utterance. Thus (23a) and (23b) can be referred to as utterance here.

[12] Researchers like Thompson & Zhou (2000: 122-41) term the resources listed here *disjuncts*, and they argue that these disjuncts can serve both interpersonal function and textual function, but the latter function derives from the former. That is, the intrinsic function of these resources is interpersonal rather than simply being employed to make the text coherent.

[13] If we just assume the listener's position, our voice can be textualized as utterances such as "What is Michael Forsyth's opinion about the latest issue about 'tartan tax'? And what do you think of it?"

Chapter 5 Dialogic Interactions in Print News of English

The identification of dialogic markers provides us with linguistic evidence for recognizing the existence of different voices in a text, or from the perspective of production the dialogic markers are actually the linguistic resources we depend on to realize the dynamic relationships between different voices in the text, the recognition of which is thus the key to a Bakhtinian active understanding of the text. As has been discussed in the previous chapters, a dialogic analysis of a text is expected to focus on the dialogic relationships between heterogeneous voices in the text; the dialogic interactions between voices actually play a crucial part in the construction and acceptance of news reportings, which constitutes an indispensable institutional genre in our social life.

5.1 The dialogic relations in print news

In Chapter 3, we have mentioned that the dialogic relationship between two voices seems to lie at a certain point in the cline from blatantly confronting to ostensively supporting, with an idealized middle point indicating a complete neutrality (i.e. showing neither agreement nor disagreement), which has been exemplified in figure 3.3, and now revised as figure 5.1.

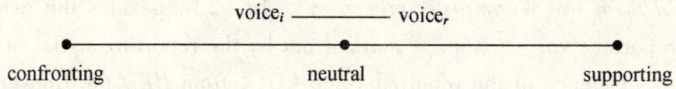

Figure 5.1 Cline of dialogic relationship between voices[1]

In a news text, the actualized voices can be roughly classified into two groups according to their sources: reporter's voice and those from others. Thus the dialogic interactions can correspondingly be subsumed under these two types: the interactions between the reporter's voice and the voices from others (i. e. foreign or alien voices), and the interactions among foreign voices themselves. For example,[2]

(1) (**Rep.** $_r$) Conservative Party chiefs <u>claim</u> (O_i) not to know who sold them two Westminster properties in a multi-million-pound transaction being investigated by the Electoral Commission. (*The Sunday Telegraph*, 01/10/2006: 4)

(2) (**Rep.** $_r$) He <u>said</u> ($O1_{i/i}$) the sale of Platinum was conducted by Citigroup, the investment bank. (**Rep.** $_{r/r}$) <u>However</u>, Citigroup sources <u>told</u> The Sunday Telegraph <u>that</u> ($O2_{i/r}$) they were "unable to find anyone who is aware of this transaction" at the bank. (*The Sunday Telegraph*, 01/10/2006: 4)

In (1) the dialogic marker *claim* indicates that there are at least two voices: one is from the reporter (designated as (Rep. $_r$)), and the other is from the conservative party chiefs (designated as (O_i)). According to our discussion in the previous chapter, the reporting signal *claim* carries an evaluative sense, which is believed to imply the reporter's negative attitude to the correctness or credibility of the reported speech though expressed implicitly, or at least to show that the reporter detaches himself from the responsibility of what is being reported (cf. Thompson, 2000: 57-8; Caldas-Coulthard, 1994: 295). Given the preceding existence of the foreign voice (O_i), we will take it as the voice that initiates the dialogic interaction, and the reporter's voice (Rep. $_r$) correspondingly serves as the voice that responds to it. That is to say, the reporter's voice (Rep. $_r$) in (1) textualized as the utterance which is realized by sentence (1) is in a slight conflict with the voice (O_i) from the Conservative Party chiefs textualized as the utterance that is realized by the part "*not to know who sold them two Westminster properties*". In (2), besides the existence of the reporter's voice (Rep. $_r$) marked out by the reporting signal *said* and *told*, the existence of the reported voice (O1) from *HE* (the Conservative Party chairman, Francis Maude) and the reported voice (O2) from Citigroup is also quite evident. The neutral reporting signals *said* and *told* seem to suggest in a measure the reporter's impartiality between or detachment from (O1) and (O2), but the juxtaposition of (O1) and (O2) shows a sharp conflict between them: Citigroup denies the Conservative

Party chief's claim, thus ($O2_r$) confronting ($O1_i$), so the voice of Citigroup (i.e. ($O2$)) not only initiates the reporter's response, but also gives its own response to the Tory leader's voice ($O1_i$), which at the same time also initiates the reporter's response; that is why they are designated as ($O1_{i/i}$) and ($O2_{i/r}$) respectively. In other words, there are two kinds of interactions here: one takes place between the reporter's voice that issues its response to the party chief's voice and Citigroup's voice, both of which serve as voices issuing dialogic invitations for the reporter; the other takes place between the opposing voices between the party chief's and Citigroup's, with the former seeming to issue its dialogic initiative and the latter supplying its response. And according to our discussion in the previous chapter, the connective *however* can also work as a dialogic marker in the same way as the coordinator *but* does. The existence of *however* actually indicates that the reporting voice takes the side of the denying voice from Citigroup or at least it accentuates the conflict between these two voices. That is to say, due to the existence of the dialogic marker *however*, the reporter's voice seems to be in disagreement with the voice from the Conservative Party chief, and at the same time in agreement with that from Citigroup. Thus the impartiality of the reporting voice between the two confronting sides is blurred or even made leant by the connective *however*.

In written texts, besides the above two types of dialogic interactions, that is, the interactions between the writer's/reporter's voice and foreign voices and the interactions among foreign voices themselves, there exists another kind of interaction—the interaction between the writer's voice and the reader's voice, which has already received enough attention from both linguists and literary critics, for example, Widdowson (1978: 59; 1979: 176; 1984: 48), Kristeva (1986: 45), Kress (1989: Ch. 2), Xin Bin (2000: 115-25), Hoey (2001), and Martin & White (2005: Ch. 3), to name just a few. This kind of interaction is quite different from the former two in that unlike the voices from others and the writer's own voice, both of which can be marked into existence by the dialogic markers and textualized through utterances in the text, the reader's voice is just invoked rather than materialized in the text. The reader's voice is actually the *reading position* identified by Kress (1989: Ch. 2), which the writer sets for his intended readers and which in turn shapes the way the writer conducts his speech. According to Bakhtin (1986: 67-100), this kind of setting a reading voice or position for readers actually refers to the *addressivity* of one's speech, one of the three inherent properties of an utterance. It is the *addressivity* and *expressivity* of an utterance that enable it to interact dialogically with other utterances. It should be noted that in our discussion although we mainly focus on the first two types of dialogic relations in a news text, we have to draw the third one into our picture if we have to make things easier to go, for the third one actually serves as the premise or basis for our analyzing and interpreting a news text from a dialogic perspective.

The relatively complicated relationships between voices nested in (2) suggest that a much more complicated picture of dialogic relationships will come into our view if we look from a dialogic vantage point at a complete piece of news text rather than just an extract from it. That is, we cannot confine our discussion on dialogic relationships to the sentence-long extracts from news texts, because a textual analysis in the framework of Bakhtinian translinguistics and Hallidayan *SFL* presupposes analyzing real texts instead of artificial ones; for focusing on truncated materials is typical of Saussurean linguistics and Chomskyan syntax. But our foregoing discussions can still be justified in the sense that translinguistics and *SFL* do not forbid having linguistic elaborations as their bases or tools. Bakhtinian translinguistics, as we have discussed in the previous chapters, is characterized by its lacking due linguistic considerations; although he himself has not realized this wanting in both his theory and practice, Bakhtin does have mentioned more than once that translinguistics cannot be separated from linguistics but instead it should be based on the findings from linguistics (Bakhtin, 1984: 181; 1986: 99). It goes without arguing that *SFL* is actually formulated and developed through thorough observations of clauses, and clause complexes. Thus a recontextualization of translinguistics which features textual dialogicity as its theoretic essence in the context of *SFL* or vice versa needs to make due preparations by talking about things at the lexico-grammatical level for the subsequent reading and analyzing of complete news texts.

5.2　Genres and social functions of print news

Print news texts mainly appear in newspapers and periodicals such as *The New York Times*, *Financial Times*, *Time*, *Newsweek*, and so on. But newspapers are believed to be the major media channel by which print news texts are circulated. In this book the print news texts analyzed are mainly from *The Sunday Telegraph*, a broadsheet quality newspaper produced in Britain which is available in our university library. Although the term *newspaper* suggests that the content of a newspaper will be primarily devoted to the news of the day or the week, in reality they contain a range of items: news, entertainment and advertising. According to Reah (2002: 1-2), the larger part of a newspaper is usually devoted to items other than news, for example, TV listings and advertising. As far as *The Sunday Telegraph* is concerned, it features the following sections regularly: news, news review & comment, international news, sports, business, travel, home & living, money & jobs as well as a large number of whole page advertisements and those occupying half a page or even only a corner of a page, which are inserted into or blended with other items. It is a common practice nowadays that about half of the content of newspaper is devoted to advertising (Reah, 2002: 3), and there is no exception to *The Sunday Telegraph*.

As for the genres of news, it is generally agreed that there are mainly four basic forms (McNair, 1998: 10; Zhang Delu, 1998: 317; Li Meixia, 2004: 99-104):

1. the *news report*, which aims simply to inform us about happenings of importance and, of course, is in some sense *new* in the world around us;
2. the *feature article*, which presents more in-depth reportage and analysis of a particular subject;
3. the *commentary or column*, in which a journalist presents his or her readers with an (assumed to be) authoritative viewpoint on a particular issue;
4. *editorial*, in which a newspaper or periodical "speaks out" in its "public voice".

Obviously, the texts in the news and international news sections in *The Sunday Telegraph* belong to the genre of news report, which is also termed *hard news*. And this type of news is traditionally and generally expected to provide its readers with *objective new information* rather than to persuade its readers to accept an authoritative viewpoint on some current issues. As has been mentioned in the introduction to this book, our focus is placed on hard news text in order to test the validity of the Bakhtinian dialogic framework recontextualized in the setting of *SFL*, post-modern discourse theories and media studies. If hard news texts can be incorporated by the dialogic framework, then this analytical framework will gain more theoretical and practical strength by taking into its account texts belonging to almost any genre; for the hard news text is believed commonsensically to lie at the positive end of the generic spectrum as far as factuality is concerned (in sharp contrast with the fictional novel texts that have already been fruitfully analyzed dialogically by Bakhtin and his followers). Besides, reading hard news texts dialogically is also expected to shed due new light on the understanding of media issues such as the so-called professional doctrines of objectivity and being-free-of-bias.

5.3　A dialogic analysis of hard news text (1)

The above discussion of the interaction between the reporter's voice and the voices from others seems to suggest that the reporting voice is so pervasive that it actually keeps any foreign voice in the text under its control in a heavily disguised manner for the most part of the time. Take the following news report for example, which is called text (1) in our later discussion.

(a) Prince Charles : (b) wind farms are horrendous
By Andrew Alderson

1. (c) THE PRINCE of Wales believes that (d) wind farms are a "horrendous blot on the landscape" and that (e) their spread must be halted before they irreparably ruin some of Britain's most beautiful countryside.

2. (f) The Sunday Telegraph can reveal that (g) Prince Charles, who has an abiding interest in environmental issues, has told senior aides that (h) he does not want to have any links with events or groups that promote onshore wind farms.

3. (i) The Prince, who believes that (j) Britain needs to rethink its energy policy, is considering making his anti-turbine views public at a time when the issue is on the political agenda and wind farms are spreading throughout the country.

4. (k) Senior aides at Clarence House, where Prince Charles has his private office, say that (l) the heir to the throne has been firmly against wind farms for years, but (m) that (n) he has so far chosen not to enter the public debate on their future.

5. (o) A spokesman declined to (p) comment yesterday but (q) a friend of Prince Charles said: (r) "This is a difficult issue for the Prince because he is in favour of renewable energy and is concerned by the effects of global warming.

But he believes that wind farms are 'a horrendous blot on the landscape'. He thinks that if they have to be built at all they should be constructed well out at sea."

6. (s) The wind farm issue is becoming increasingly contentious.

7. (t) The Government is committed to their spread because it has promised to (u) raise the share of Britain's energy coming from renewable sources to 10 per cent in 2010 and then to 20 per cent in 2020.

8. (v) Renewable sources produce less than four per cent of energy needs at the moment.

9. (w) Stephen Timms, the energy minister, has said: (x) "Wind energy is here and now. It is the most proven green source of electricity generation and can supply a rising proportion of our electricity needs."

10. (y) Michael Howard, the Conservative leader, announced two weeks ago that (z) local people would have a greater say in the sitting of wind farms under a Tory government.

11. (aa) He said that (bb) he would change planning rules to ensure that local opinions could not be overruled or ignored.

12. (cc) The Prince's (dd) views were (ee) welcomed by anti-wind farm campaigners.

13. (ff) Campbell Dounford, the chief executive of the Renewable Energy Foundation, formed last month to press for a review of Britain's energy strategy, said: (gg) "I am delighted to learn of the Prince of Wales's views. His Royal Highness's support on this matter

would be invaluable. He understands there is nothing incompatible with being green and being opposed to wind turbines.

We oppose the huge, dominant use of wind farms onshore because they won't do the job. I am sure the Prince is concerned by the aesthetics of wind farms. The great thing about the Prince is that he doesn't just shoot from the hip. He studies the facts and makes carefully formed judgments."

14. (hh) Some conservation groups (ii) <u>criticized</u> the Prince's stand.

15. (jj) Bryony Worthington, a spokesman for Friends of the Earth, <u>said:</u> (kk) "It's a shame because this will weaken the Prince's green reputation, which has otherwise been very good."

16. (ll) Prince Charles's annual income of almost £ 12 million comes from the Duchy of Cornwall.

17. (mm) (nn) The estate consists of 126, 000 acres, much of it suitable for wind farms in Devon and Cornwall, <u>but</u> (oo) internal Clarence House documents seen by *The Sunday Telegraph* <u>show that</u> (pp) he will not consider having them on his land, or be associated with them whatsoever.

18. (qq) The nearest wind farm to the Prince's country home at Highgrove, Gloucestershire, is seven miles away.

19. (rr) The Prince chooses to spend much of the summer on the Balmoral estate in Scotland which is owned by the Queen. 20. (ss) The nearest wind farm to Balmoral is at Novar, 65 miles away.

21. (tt) Jonathon Porritt, a leading conservationist who advises Prince Charles on environmental issues, is a supporter of wind turbines which he <u>describes</u> as (uu) "beautifully compelling".

22. (vv) (ww) Mr. Porritt, <u>however</u>, <u>believes</u> (xx) the positioning of the farms has been insensitive and <u>that</u> (yy) there needs to be greater consultation with local people.

23. (zz) The first British wind farm was built in Cornwall in 1991.

24. (aaa) There are now 89 in the country and at least 16 more are due to be built over the next two years.

25. (bbb) Work began last week on a 430ft-high turbine—one of the world's tallest—near Lowstoft, Suffolk.

26. (ccc) The £ 3 million project is expected (ddd) to generate electricity for more than 2,000 homes.

(*The Sunday Telegraph*, 08/08/2004: 1)

5.3.1 The distribution of different voices in hard news text (1)

In the above news reporting, 26 sentences are each assigned a number at the very beginning, but those in quotation marks attributed to certain sources, known as direct reported speech (DS) or quasi direct speech (QDS), are treated as a part of the sentence, in which they are introduced into the text by the reporting voice, for instance, sentence 5 and sentence13. Numbering the sentences in this way is just for the convenience of discussion and in agreement with our reading habit shaped by our long-term school grammar education.[3] The different voices including the reporters' reporting voice and those from others are marked out by the underlined dialogic markers and designated correspondingly by the lower-case letters in alphabetical order, which shows the wordings after or around them signify the corresponding utterances and voices. Thus in the following discussion, these bracketed lower-case letters in bold type will also be used to refer to the voices at issue.

The dialogic markers involved in this text can be displayed by the following table:

Table 5.1 The distribution of dialogic markers in hard news text (1)

Dialogic markers		Dialogic markers involved in the text
reporting	verb	believe (1, 3, 22), reveal (2), tell (2), say (4, 5, 9, 11, 13, 15), promise (7), announce (10), criticize (14), show (17), describe (21)
	noun	comment (5), view (12)
	preposition	by (byline, 12)
modality	lexical verb	expect (26)
conjunction		but (4, 5, 17), however (22)
complementizer		that (1, 2, 3, 4, 10, 11, 17, 22)
punctuation		colon (headline, 5, 9, 13, 15), quotation marks (1, 5, 9, 13, 15, 21)

With the help of the above dialogic markers, it is not difficult to identify the wordings in text (1) that signify different voices, which can be attributed to certain specified sources or remain unspecified as shown by table 5.2.

Table 5.2 Voices inhabiting hard news text (1)

Source of the voice	Voices in text (1)
Reporting: reporter and his institution's	a, c, f, g, i, k, m, o, q, s, t, v, w, y, aa, cc, ff, hh, jj, ll, mm, oo, pp, qq, rr, ss, tt, vv, zz, aaa, bbb, ccc (32/56)
Prince Charles His aides His spokesman His friend	b, d, e, h, j, dd (6/56); l, n (2/56); p (1/56); r (1/56)
Government Stephen Timms (the energy minister)	u (1/56); x (1/56)
Michael Howard (the Conservative leader)	z, bb (2/56)
Anti-wind farm campaigner e.g. Campbell Dounford (the chief executive of the Renewable Energy Foundation)	ee (1/56); gg (1/56)
Conservation group e.g. Bryony Worthington (spokesman for Friends of the Earth)	ii (1/56); kk (1/56)
Jonathon Porritt (a leading conservationist who advises Prince Charles)	uu, xx, yy (3/56)
Unspecified	nn, ww, ddd (3/56)

From the table, we can see: the reporting voices are dominant, the total number of which makes 32 and makes up 57 per cent out of the total of 56 voices in the text; voices from Prince Charles and his side that oppose the governmental policy to build wind farms makes up about 17 per cent; the number of voices from the government and its minister that defend its policy of building wind farms makes up about 4 per cent; the voices from the Opposition leader (Michael Howard) that criticize the governmental policy and practice also make up about 4 per cent; the voices from unnamed anti-wind farm campaigners and its representative Campbell Dounford, an NGO leader (the chief executive of the Renewable Energy

Foundation) who supports Prince Charles, make up nearly 4 per cent; the voices from other NGOs opposing Prince Charles make up nearly 4 per cent, too; voices from Jonathon Porritt, the leading conservationist who advises Prince Charles on environmental issues but now criticizes the governmental policy, make up nearly 5 per cent. Besides the above mentioned voices, there are three foreign voices from unspecified sources: voice (nn) invoked by the conjunction *but* in sentence 17, suggesting the feasibility of building the wind farms on the estate of Prince Charles; voice (ww) invoked by the connective *however* in sentence 22, suggesting that Jonathon Porritt should have supported the building of wind farms rather than criticizing the governmental policy; voice (ddd) marked out by the dialogic marker *expected* in the last sentence of the text suggests its position of favoring building the wind farms; these three voices make up about 5 per cent out of the total of 56 voices in text (1).

5.3.2 The interactions among the foreign voices in hard news text (1)

It is obvious that the voices from others (i.e. the foreign voices) in text (1) can be divided into two groups according to the positions they hold toward the governmental policy of building wind farms in Britain. The dialogic relationships among them can be illustrated by figure 5.2.

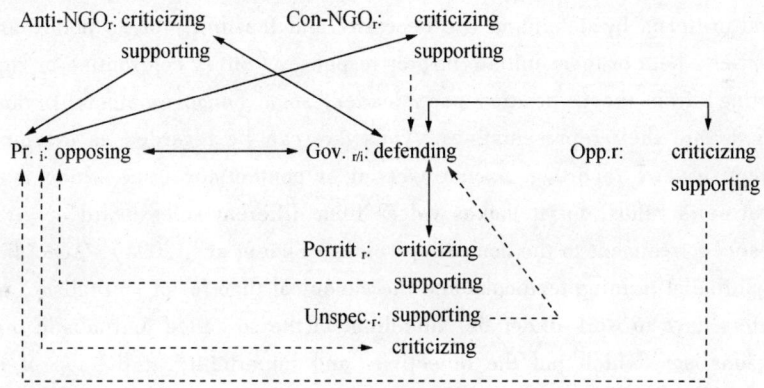

Figure 5.2   The dialogic interactions among foreign voices in hard news text (1)

In the figure, Pr. stands for the concerted macro-voice from Prince Charles and his staff, which is understood to initiate the dialogic interaction; Gov. stands for the macro-voice from the government, which is understood to give its response to the criticizing voice from the prince but at the same time to invite both negative and positive responses from other voices; Opp. stands for the voice from Michael Howard, the leader of the Opposition, which is understood to make a critical response to the defending voice from the government; Anti-NGO stands for the voice from the nongovernmental anti-wind-farm organizations and their representative that endorses the position of the prince and at the same time opposes the governmental policy ostensively; Con-NGO stands for the voice from the nongovernmental conservation organizations and their representative that is understood to make a critical response to the prince's voice. Unspec. stands for the three unspecified voices marked out by *but*, *however*, and *expected*, namely, (nn) in sentence 17, (ww) in sentence 22, and (ddd) in sentence 26. The single-directional arrows in the figure indicate a relationship of ostensive support; the double-directional arrows suggest a relationship of ostensive confrontation; the dotted single-directional and double-directional arrows indicate relationships of confronting and supporting in disguise.

Figure 5.2 shows us that this news report is constructed like a dialogic interaction taking place among different parties: the interaction is initiated by the voice of Prince Charles, which intends to criticize the governmental policy on building wind farms in Britain; the latter responds to the royal criticism by defending the necessity and feasibility of its policy and practice; both of them initiate further responses (either confronting or supporting) from the Opposition party leader, some nongovernmental organizations and their representatives. Thus this can be regarded as a typical objective news report on a controversial or contentious issue which is of great news value, for it makes voices from different sides heard or gives balanced treatment to the competing voices (Fico et al., 2004). According to journalist training textbooks and the canonical theories of journalism, reporters have to work under the guidelines of the so-called journalistic professionalism, which put the objectivity and impartiality at the top of its ethical agenda (Huang Dan, 2005: 68-117; Xie Jing, 2005: 92-122). This requirement can be well reflected in what Schaffer et al. (1998: 132) have said in their textbook for training journalistic professionals: "Reporters report facts. They must be careful to maintain objectivity—that is, *to report only facts, not their own opinions. The reporter's job is to look at news from a distance and from all sides.* In a news story, whether it is hard news or soft news, the reporter must present only the facts about an issue or event and let readers draw their own conclusions. *The reporter's personal views and values should not be part of a news story.*" (italicized by the author of this book)

Although journalists are trained to observe the principle of presenting their readers with an impartial news report and let readers themselves make their own judgments, more and more modern media researchers have found that the pure objectivity and impartiality preached by the canonical journalistic professionalism is simply a beautiful myth or fiction, which simply does not exist in the press at all. News is actually what is created by the politicians, journalists and the various institutions they belong to (Tuchman, 1978; Johnson-Cartee, 2005). But these researchers approach the problem from the perspective of the power possessed by the media to make a subjective selection of what is to be published, which results in setting the social agenda and even leading to social changes, for instance, influencing the floating voters' decisions through the reports in favor of the candidate they support and thus getting him elected in the expectation that the candidate's policy will make a difference to the status quo. In the latest two or three decades, a host of linguists from the school of Hallidayan *SFL* or those doing textual analysis by employing Hallidayan *SFL* have made great endeavors to deconstruct the myth of objectivity of news reports, for example, Trew (1979), Fairclough (1992a; 1995; 2001), Fowler (1991), White (1998), Xin Bin (2000; 2005), and Martin & White (2005), to name just a few. But most of them mainly focus on the ideology-loaded lexis in the news text (especially the appraisal theory developed by Martin, White and their colleagues). Those linguists working under the framework of Critical Discourse Analysis (CDA) developed by Roger Fowler and Norman Fairclough, however, do not confine their analyses to the lexis in the text but take the syntactic structures into their considerations; and under the influence of Bakhtinian dialogism and the postmodern discourse theories, analysts, among others, such as Fairclough and Xin Bin have expanded the frontiers of news text analysis to its intertextual resources, which has provided us with abundant revealing insights into the bias and ideological struggles between the lines in news text. But the media bias or ideological and power imbalance loaded in print hard news text has so far not yet been observed from the perspective of the dialogic interaction between the reporting voice and the reported voices.

It cannot be denied that even in a Bakhtinian reading of a literary text (novel text in particular), an author still exists behind the lines, though the status of the traditional omnipotent author is challenged and questioned and the characters are believed to be given enough independence from the author in the so-called polyphonic novels created by Dostoevsky (Qian Zhongwen, 1987; Zhang Jie, 1989; Mey, 2000; Zeng Jun, 2004: 38-64). It may be a widespread misconception that Bakhtin has completely deconstructed the authorship of novels; for when talking about the discourse in fictional prose Bakhtin once argued that "a prose writer can distance himself from the language of his own work, while at the same time distancing himself, in varying degrees, from the different layers and aspects of the work. He can make use of language without wholly giving himself up to it, he may treat it as semi-alien or completely alien to himself, while *compelling language ultimately to serve all his own intentions*" (Bakhtin, 1981: 299; italicized by the author of this book). Although the problem of authorship of a news text is much more complicated (see the previous two chapters), a reporter, or several reporters is entitled to or has to put his or their names on the byline, though the text is usually a co-authored product, which involves more persons in the organization. But somebody has to sign his name and takes responsibility (Ferguson & Patten, 1993: 74-82; Zang Guoren, 1999: 72-153). According to Bell (1991: 55), "[w]ithin a news organization people's roles are meshed into the one authority structure" and " [m]ost newsmakers speak on behalf of a group or organization"; that is to say, behind the lines of a news text the reporting voice, which is usually attributed to the bylined reporter, is actually a concerted *macro-voice* consisting of different voices from the hierarchies within the news-production organization.

But in text (1), what kind of relationships exists between the macro-reporting or reporter's voice and those foreign voices demonstrated in figure 5.2? Or how does the reporting voice interact with those voices from others? Looking at the annotated text (1) and table 5.2, it is not difficult to find that the reporting voice not only is dominant in the number of its occurrence, but more importantly exerts a tight control over the reported voices mainly in the way of putting them into the frame it deliberately sets for these foreign voices.

5.3.3 Framing: the reporter's voice taking foreign voices under its control

As we have discussed in section one of this chapter, dialogic markers like *claim* in the text can in a measure indicate whether the reporting voice is in a supporting or confronting dialogic relationship with the reported foreign voice. Out of the 23 cases of local dialogic interactions in the text, the dialogic marker *believe* which belongs to the resources of modality has been used three times. Although it is hard to say in sentences 1, 3, and 22 the reporter's voice shows any inscribed attitude toward its corresponding foreign voices (i.e. confronting or supporting them), the existence of *believe* at least indicates that though it intends to keep a distance from the reported voices the reporting voice in a measure takes it as a fact that the party involved holds a belief in something. This invoked attitude, if realized by an utterance which is then materialized by the concrete wording into being, may go like "*He believes and endorses the idea, but it doesn't mean I have the same opinion*", and this attitude toward or evaluation of other's voice is very likely to be triggered by the intended reading position or readers' voice which can probably be textualized as "*What is Prince Charles'/Mr. Porrit's opinion on building wind farms? And what do you think of it?*"

The neutral reporting verb *say* has been used six times to introduce the foreign voices into the text. Like the modality marker *believe*, *say* in sentences 4, 5, 9, 11, 13, and 15, *tell* in sentence 2 and *show* in sentence 17 are also used to attribute the responsibility for what is reported to others; the using of them enables the reporter to assume a neutral position at the scale of dialogic interaction displayed by figure 5.1. But the cases involving the evaluative reporting verb *criticize* in sentence 14 and *announce* in sentence 10 are a little bit different: in sentence 14, by using the evaluative reporting verb *criticize* the reporting voice shows its inscribed attitude toward the foreign voice from some conservation groups: *what they have said is nothing else but criticisms*; in sentence 10, by using the evaluative reporting verb *announce*, the reporting voice suggests to the readers what is reported is of significant importance and that its source may possess a certain amount of social influence. But these two are at most judgments of other's verbal behavior, which can hardly indicate whether the reporting voice agrees or disagrees with the reported voices. The other two reporting nouns, that is, *view* in sentence 12 and *comment* in sentence 5, function in the similar way the verb *criticize* and *announce* do—to classify the verbal behaviors of others but not to take sides in the related local contexts without showing explicit support or confrontation. But the reporting verb *reveal* in sentence 2 is very likely to invoke a negative association with the reported voice (i. e. (h)) that there is something that needs to be covered up, and *promise* in sentence 7 shows that the reporting voice takes what is reported as a promise made by the government, suggesting in a measure a responsible image of the government.

The above descriptions of the local dialogic interactions between the reporter's voices and those from others seem to tell us that the reporting voice in most cases takes a neutral position toward the reported foreign voices, and thus text (1) seems to be a typical objective news reporting. Even though we have made some suggestions that there may be some bias in it; that is, the reporting voice seems to take sides sometimes, they are based on inadequate evidence, thus sounding subjective or even far-fetched.

The limitations of analyzing the local interactions between reporting voice and foreign voices for revealing what lies behind the news text as a whole have actually already been pointed out in Bakhtin's *PSG* when he talks about the role played by the context in dialogic understanding of an utterance and about the differences between linguistic sentence and translinguistic utterance (Bakhtin, 1986: 67-100). But as we have already mentioned, local dialogic descriptions can pave the way for our global reading and analyzing a news text as a whole.

According to van Dijk (1977), a text is constructed in a similar way as a grammatical clause or sentence does; any coherent text (especially a written one) is characterized by a macro-structure in which a macro theme or topic controls a series of topics or local macro-themes. Different genres show different macro-structures or schemata (or superstructures), and a good case in point is news text (van Dijk, 1988: Ch. 2). In his widely referenced book *News as Discourse*, van Dijk developed a social-cognitive-based model of the generic structure of news text. His model is based on the notion of "importance" that is regarded as the key organizing principle of the textuality of news reporting in journalist training textbooks. The notion of "importance" as the key organizing principle is well reflected in the term "inverted pyramid" which organizes information from the most important to the least important. Thus MacDougall states:

> The striking difference between traditional news writing in the United States and other forms of written composition, such as the essay, poetry, drama, novel and short story, continues to be this: whereas the authors of these other forms of composition usually begin with minor or incidental details and work to a climax near or at the end of their compositions, the news writer reverses this plan of organization. That is, the climax or end of the story comes first. Given a schedule of facts to arrange in the form of a newspaper article, the writer selects the most important fact or climax of the story and puts it at the beginning. The second most important fact comes second, the third most important fact third and so on. (MacDougall, 1982: 98; adopted from White, 1998: 65-6)

According to the training textbooks, apart from the headline, the most important part in a news text is usually the opening paragraph or sentence which is termed *lead*; the lead of the news reporting is said to single out the news point or angle of the story and to summarize its essential news elements, which are usually embodied by the so-called five Ws and an H—*who, what, when, where, why* and *how* (Schaffer et al., 1998: 123; Itule et al., 2003: 74). Thus the organizing principle of the body of the news report is the order of importance rather than the chronological sequence of common narratives.

It is obvious that van Dijk's analysis is conducted within a cognitive theory of text comprehension and based on the total acceptance of the organizing principle held by news-writing training textbooks. Although he does have mentioned the existence of subjectivity in the derivation of macrostructure of a text in the process of comprehension, he really persuades newspaper readers to read the news text in the way the news practitioners expect them to do—the most important thing is put at the beginning, which can be separated from the following; that is, "partial reading in that case will not result in partial understanding but only in missing a few, lower-level details" (van Dijk, 1988: 44). Another problem with van Dijk's analysis is that his acceptance of the importance-first or "inverted pyramid" organizing principle of news text is in a little contradiction with his identification of the structure of news. According to him, a news text usually includes: 1. Summary: Headline and Lead; 2. Episode: Main Events in Context and their Backgrounds; 3. Consequences; 4. Verbal Reactions; 5. Comment; and "since topics may be realized cyclically in installments, this is also the case for superstructure categories. That is, a Main event category may be expressed in several positions throughout the text" (van Dijk, 1988: 56-7), that is to say, news categories are realized in the news text in a discontinuous or sporadic way rather than in the way an important unit is followed by units of less importance that can be omitted either in editing or in a skimming reading, which is believed to make little significant difference as far as the main essence of the news text is concerned. Therefore, in most cases, the news item cannot be read in the way of making deletion (the so-called macro-rule advocated by van Dijk) but has to be read in the way of making addition—to take every part of the text as a significant component and to take the text itself as a whole. That is to say, in our discussion, the rule of specification, the opposite way to the macro-rule of deletion, is believed to be in operation not only in the process of production but also in the process of comprehension of news text; for a critical dialogic reading of news text, aiming at revealing something taken for granted by the general reading public, has to look from a different perspective at what the training textbooks set as common sense. A critical dialogic reading of a news text, therefore, will not see the notion of "importance" as some innate property which naturally and theoretically has been attached to certain elements to a greater degree and to others to a lesser degree; this essential notion of "importance", if we keep it when talking about things, should be accepted as a dialogically and ideologically determined construct. If van Dijk's model of news text is believed to focus on its information or "factuality", the dialogic reading of it, which is conducted within the Bakhtinian translinguistics in combination of Hallidayan *SFL*, will care as much about "opinions" (interpersonal values or the addressivity and expressivity of news reporting) as about "facts" (experiential or referential values of news reporting).

Thus news reportings like text (1) do have structures, which are not constructed in an "inverted pyramid" manner and whose leads are not arrived at by deleting less important details. The lead of text (1) is the

Chapter 5 Dialogic Interactions in Print News of English 137

reporter's presentation of Prince Charles's two voices (i.e. (d) and (e)), which are specified and developed by the subsequent voices from himself and his staff (i.e. (h), (j), (l), (n), (p) and (r)).[4] When reporting these voices from the prince and his side, the reporting voice tries its best to conduct it in a neutral way though making its summaries about the manner in which the concerned party speaks, and which, as has been discussed above, is believed to be able to suggest some evaluative sense. After this presentation of the voices from the prince's side, the reporting voice (voice(s) in text (1)), which sets the stage for the performances of the competing voices in the following section of the text, comes to the fore (in sentence 6) rather than merges with the reported voices and remains in the background as it does in the first part of the text (that is, the part consists of sentences 1, 2, 3, 4 and 5). Afterwards, voices from the government and its minister (i.e. (u), (v) and (x)), which can be accepted as the responses to the critical voices from the prince and his staff and sound quite like defending, are reported into the text.[5] As a response to the governmental defending voice, the voices from the Opposition Party leader (i.e. (z) and (bb)), Michael Howard, who criticizes the governmental policy of ignoring the opinions of local residents when building wind farms, are introduced into the text. Then the reporting voice (cc) in sentence 12, like voice (s), intervenes into the picture to introduce more competing voices (i.e. (ee) and (gg), the latter specifying the former) by making an evaluative summary—the voices of the prince is positively responded by anti-wind farm campaigners; in the similar manner, the reporting voice (hh) in sentence 14, intervenes to introduce voices from conservation groups (i.e. (ii) and (kk), the latter specifying the former), which criticize the prince's voice or position. After the presentation of competing voices from different sides, nearly the remaining one-third of the text (from sentence 16 to 26) is occupied by the reporting voices except for these: 1) the conjunction *but* in sentence 17 invokes voice (nn) from an unspecified source, which debates with the reporting voice (oo); 2) in sentence 21, the critical voice from Jonathon Porritt (i.e. (xx)), the leading conservationist, who advising Prince Charles on environmental issues, is known as a supporter of wind farms (which is evidenced by his own voice (uu)) and thus expected to endorse the governmental policy; but unfortunately this time he criticizes the governmental policy of building wind farms in the same way as the Opposition Party leader does; 3) an unspecified voice (ww) invoked by the conjunction dialogic marker *however*, which may expect Jonathon Porritt to support the governmental policy and persuade the prince to change his anti-wind farm attitude; and 4) in sentence 26, the last sentence of the text, voice (ddd) from the unspecified general public which hopes high for the productivity of the wind turbine project is drawn into the picture. The reporting voice in this section which follows the foregoing neutral-sounding presentation of voices from those competing sides seems to have provided us with more information concerning the two major parties in conflicts—Prince Charles and the government. In the description of the relationship between Prince Charles and the wind farms, highlighted are his economic, aesthetical, and recreational interests and correspondingly his objection to building the wind farms on his land or even on the land neighboring his estate (see sentences 16, 17, 18 and 20), but when describing the governmental policy of building wind farms (from sentence 23 to the last), the reporting voice just lists a series of numbers which mirror the progress of the project and its expected productivity. This juxtaposition of the "additional" details of the competing two sides, with one party looking at the issue from the perspective of its own interests but the other aiming at producing more green energy, is obviously not made at random. This way of specification is quite revealing in that it shows which side the reporting voice will take—people are taught to keep their distance from or even to condemn selfishness from their childhood. And they are now worrying about the catastrophic effects on their environment wreaked by burning fossil fuels to get their energy supply. The acid rain, the melting of the ice caps in both poles of the globe and El Nino all force them to shift to the green energies such as wind energy and solar energy. It almost has become a forbidden attitude (especially in those developed countries such as Britain, a key member of a group of developed countries that initiated *The Kyoto Protocol* to deal with global warming) of opposing the development and utilization of green energies, let alone objecting it for the sake of one's self interests.

But under the general constraint of being free of inscribed sides-taking or evaluation (especially negative evaluation), the reporter has to wrap up his attitude in this type of presenting the voices in text (1). If we take the arrangement of different voices in the text as a kind of structure, then the sides-taking of the reporting voice is achieved structurally and thus dialogically in the sense that the reporting voices, being orchestrated in the later part of the text into a macro-voice, serve as a comment on or an evaluative summary of the foregoing conflicting voices: it gives a negative response to the macro-voice from the side of Prince Charles and correspondingly a disguised positive response to the macro-voice from the government. If we take a closer look at the whole text, it is not difficult to find that the reporting voice (which is believed to disperse into the whole text) actually provides a framework in which the foreign voices are fitted into their pre-designated slots. The reporting voice also works as a thread running through the beads of foreign voices and making them connected into a whole: it remains in the background by merging with the foreign voices and if needed it also comes to the fore to make necessary comment a nd transition. It is in constant interaction with foreign voices and does show its bias in a covert manner by structuring the voices in the way to invoke the desired effect of persuasion—to support the government and to criticize Prince Charles, a fake advocate of renewable green energy who has to show his real face when his interests are at stake. Thus the framing or structuring effect of the reporting voice on the foreign voices can be demonstrated by figure 5.3.

In figure 5.3 Rep. stands for the macro-reporting voice responding to foreign voices, and the rest of the indicators are the same with those in figure 5.2. The letters in bold type are used to indicate voices involved in the text, with the one before the hyphen referring to the local reporting voice that is used to introduce into the text the corresponding foreign voice or voices (that is, those after the hyphen). The arrows are used in the same way as those in figure 5.2, with the solid ones indicating inscribed dialogical interactions and the dotted ones suggesting invoked interactions. Given that the reporter works with *The Sunday Telegraph*, voice (f) and (g) are both treated as reporting voice, thus being indicated by a slash. And as has been mentioned above, voice (v) can be both regarded as a reporting voice and as the reported governmental voice simultaneously in a global reading of the text, hence the designation of "v-v" in the figure.

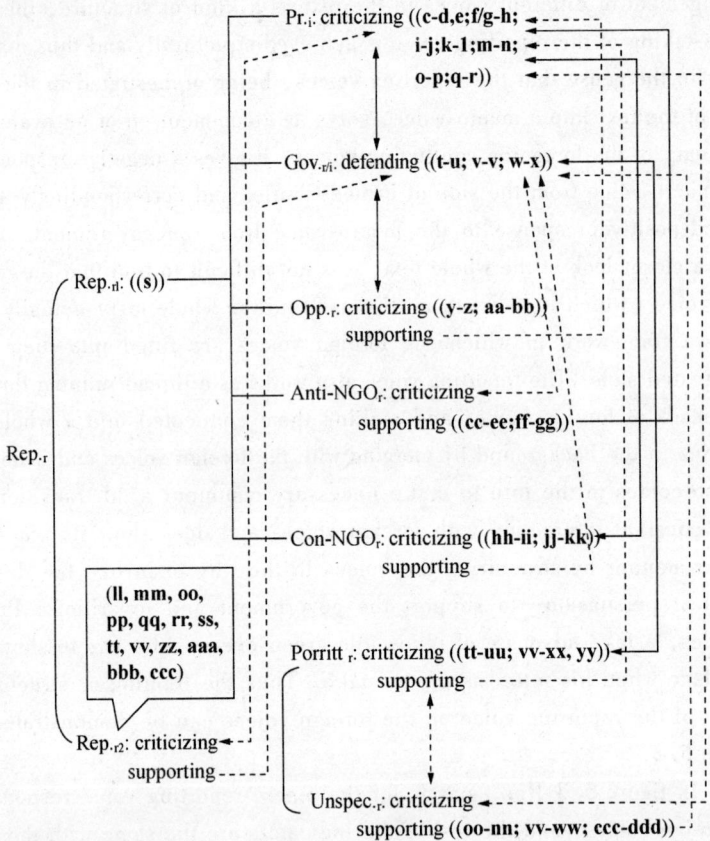

Figure 5.3 Framing effect of the reporting voice in hard news text (1)

Figure 5.3 can tell us that from a dialogic point of view text (1) consists of two sections. The first section is constructed around the reporting voice (s) textualized as sentence 6, which works like an announcer who introduces to his audience the warring parties in "the drama on stage"; the second section is constructed around the reporting voice dispersing itself into the voices listed in the figure, which work together to make a macro-comment on the performances of different foreign voices presented in the first section though this comment is delivered in a covert and smart way. That is to say, the macro reporting voice plays two roles in text (1): it first works as a neutral announcer or presenter but then joins in the play and takes sides. From the perspective of journalist training textbooks and van Dijk's model which put at the top of their agenda the representation of the happenings in the outside world, the second part of text (1) is of lesser importance and can be omitted not only in production but also in comprehension because it is about further details about the controversial issue which can be understood correctly according to the first part of the text or even can be understood quite well from the lead. But the dialogic reading of the text, which attaches due importance to the interpersonal interactions, shows greater interest in the second part of the text, which is believed to be able to "betray" the bias carried by the reporting voice. But this "betrayal" is planted by the reporting voice itself through building the voices into the construction we have displayed in figure 5.3. This construction in which the various voices are embedded actually forms a context for the understanding of the interactions between voices in the text. And the effect produced by the reporting voice on the foreign voices through these interactions is usually termed *framing*, which is believed to be able to shape the communicative status of the foreign voices.

5.4 A dialogic analysis of hard news text (2)

The dialogic analysis of text (1) shows us that between the objective-neutral-sounding lines of hard news text the reporter can get across his attitude toward the reported foreign voices through strategic structuring of different voices (including his own). But another more important and popular way of showing attitude in disguise is to manipulate foreign voices in the way of ventriloquation. Take text (2) for example,

(a) (b) Public have fouled Diana memorial fountain, says minister

By Melissa Kite

1. (c) (d) IRRESPONSIBLE behavior by members of the public is to blame for the closure of the Diana, Princess of Wales Memorial Fountain, the Cabinet minister in charge of the project said yesterday.

2. (e) Tessa Jowell, the Secretary of State for Culture, Media and Sport, told The Sunday Telegraph that (f) the memorial had been spoilt by people who had allowed their dogs to run in it and

dropped rubbish, including nappies, into the water.

3. (g) She added that (h) it was "a pretty sad situation" that people appeared to need to be told how to behave at the fountain, and insisted that (i) when the memorial reopened it should be treated as a place of remembrance.

4. (j) The fountain in Hyde Park was closed 10 days ago after two adults and a child were hurt when they slipped while paddling. 5. (k) The £ 3.6 million fountain was drained and has since been the subject of an investigation by health and safety officers.

6. (l) "We accept that there are problems that the Royal Parks have got to sort out," (m) Ms Jowell said. 7. (n) "Once these are sorted, people have got to be responsible in the way they let their children play in the fountain.

The critical issue is that this is a memorial. It requires both a management regime by the Parks and good sense by members of the public. I don't think any responsible person would want to see people allowing their dogs in it. How can we maintain the purity of the water if some people allow their dogs to paddle?"

8. (o) (p) The fountain, designed by Kathryn Gustafson to express the late princess's spirit and love of children, opened a month ago, but (q) has suffered problems ranging from blockages to complaints about the water quality and slipperiness of the granite floor. 9. (r) It is understood that (s) when the fountain does reopen, rules will be posted banning animals and littering. 10. (t) Children will be told to (u) paddle in areas of the fountain where the surface is flat.

11. (v) Ms Jowell insisted that (w) (x) she was not (y) blaming the majority of the public, just a minority who were behaving inappropriately at the fountain. 12. (z) "Of the thousands of people who have enjoyed this small number appear to have behaved irresponsibly," (aa) she said. 13. (bb) "This is a place for reflection, contemplation and remembrance, as well as a place for people to enjoy bringing their children."

14. (cc) Rosa Monckton, the princess's close friend and chairman of the committee that selected the fountain, welcomed the (dd) comments. 15. (ee) She said: (ff) "Tessa is quite right. You

would have thought that people would have shown a little bit more respect given that it is a memorial. (**gg**) But it should remain open— (**hh**) we should not be browbeaten by the health and safety police who interfere too much already in our everyday lives. "

(*The Sunday Telegraph*, 01/08/2004: 1)

5.4.1 The distribution of different voices in hard news text (2)

Text (2) is annotated in the same way as text (1) has been done. The dialogic markers involved in text (2) can thus be demonstrated by table 5.3.

Table 5.3 The distribution of dialogic markers in hard news text (2)

Dialogic markers		Dialogic markers involved in the text
reporting	verb	say (headline, 1, 6, 12, 15); tell (2, 10); add (3); insist (3, 11); blame (11)
	noun	comment (14)
	preposition	by (byline)
modality	lexical verb	understand (9)
conjunction		but (8, 15)
negative		not (11, 15)
complementizer		that (2, 3, 9, 11)
punctuation		colon (15); quotation marks (3, 6, 7, 12, 13, 15)

From table 5.3, we can see that a wide range of dialogic markers are used in text (2).[6] But as expected, the neutral reporting signals such as *say*, *tell* and *add* are used more frequently in text (2) (8 cases out of the total 15 sentences) than text (1) (7 cases out of the total 26 sentences), and the evaluative reporting signals which are used to summarize the illocutionary force of the reported speech such as *insist* and *blame* are comparatively less frequent (3 out of total 15); only one nominal reporting signal *comment* is involved and the prepositional reporting signal *by* is also used just once. There is also just one case of the lexical modality verb *understand*, two cases of the conjunction *but* and two cases of the negative particle *not*. With the help of the above dialogic markers, it is not difficult to identify the wordings in the text that signify different voices, which can be attributed to certain specified or unspecified sources, as shown by table 5.4.

Table 5.4 Voices inhabiting hard news text (2)

Source of the voice	Voices in text (2)
Reporting: reporter and the institution's	a, c, e, g, j, k, m, o, q, r, t, v, aa, cc, ee (15/34)
Tessa Jowell	b, d, f, h, i, l, n, w, x, z, bb, dd (12/34)
Rosa Monckton	ff (1/34)
unspecified community	s, u (2/34)
unspecified others	p, y, gg, hh (4/34)

As in text (1), the reporting voice in text (2) is still dominant, and the voices from Tessa Jowell, the Secretary of State for Culture, Media and Sport, also occupy a relatively high proportion (12 out of the total 34, about 35 per cent). The one case of a specified voice from Rosa Monckton, Princes Diana's friend and the chairman of the committee that selected the fountain occupies about 3 per cent of the total, two cases of voices identified as coming from unspecified community occupying 6 per cent, and four cases of voices from unspecified others invoked by the conjunction *but* and the negative particle *not* 12 per cent. Thus it is safe to say text (2) differs from text (1) in that it is a report mainly about a social VIP's (cabinet minister Tessa Jowell) words and opinions on an issue—the irresponsible behaviour of some members of the public leading to the closure of the Memorial Fountain for Diana, rather than about competing opinions from different parties on a controversial issue. At first glance, it seems that the reporter still adopts a very neutral and objective voice without showing any traces of expressing his bias. He gives a large portion of textual space to the minister, and Rosa Monckton, another very important person, who responds positively to the minister's voices. But is it really the case that the reporter neither makes his evaluations nor shows his attitude toward the foreign voices and the issue under discussion? To be more specific, can we know from the text whether the reporter agrees with the minister or not about the claim that the behaviour of some members of the public is irresponsible? In simple words, does the author also take sides in text (2)? If the answer is yes, how can he do this under the professional constraint of being free of bias stipulated by the training textbooks?

5.4.2　Evaluation as sides-taking

In the profession of journalism, the doctrine of objectivity requires the reporters to avoid being involved into the political issue and taking sides. In order to stick to this principle, some major media groups even sign contracts with their employees, which forbid them from expressing their views on political issues and from participating in political activities (Hackett et al., 2005 [1997]: 34-5). In making a news report, one effective way to avoid being regarded as showing bias or taking sides, according to the training textbooks, is to avoid using the value-laden words which are believed to convey the reporter's judgment on the reported human behaviors, things or events. On their "blacklist" are those adjectives and adverbs which are used to describe things and events but at the same time betray the reporter's attitude, for example, *definitely*, *largely*, *quickly*, *eagerly*, *unfortunately*, *especially*, *really*, *wonderful*, *just*, *tragic*, *greatly*, *finally* and *only* (Schaffer et al., 1998: 132-5). According to *Appraisal Theory*, the words like those listed by Schaffer and his colleagues are the words which are used to realize the so-called *inscribed attitude* or *evaluation*, and the unmediated *inscribed attitude* (including *affect*, *judgment*, and *appreciation*) is seldom found in hard news texts; in hard news reports, inscribed evaluations are usually attributed to some external sources.[7] And each kind of evaluation moves along the scale from the negative to the positive, which is called *graduation* (Martin & White, 2005: 164-83). If the judgment is made about the behaviour of a certain person, it is quite understandable that the negative or positive attitude taken by the appraiser clearly indicates which side he will take—our instinct tells us to keep our distance from the person whose behaviour we think is disgusting. For example, in text (2), the adjective *irresponsible* is obviously a word which conveys an inscribed negative judgment of a person's behaviour, which is subsumed under the category of *social sanction* about the propriety of the ethical values of one's behaviour. But this negative judgment of the behaviour of some members of the public is not accredited to the reporter but attributed to the cabinet minister, Tessa Jowell through the mechanism of speech reporting.

Besides the inscribed evaluations, Martin and White have also identified a range of other mechanisms to realize *invoked attitude* or *evaluation*, which include the interactions among the sub-systems of attitude, that is, *affect*, *judgment* and *appreciation*. For example, the sentence "*he played responsibly*" is an inscribed positive judgment (a positive judgment of the *propriety* of one's behavior) but at the same time it invokes an *appreciation* of one's performance as a thing like "*it was a responsible innings*". In addition to these interactions between the three sub-systems of attitude, invoked evaluation also refers to the phenomenon that the ideational meanings of the text can trigger evaluations. For example, an objective tone of describing a disgusting behavior may well mirror some degree of negative evaluation from the reporter or writer and thus trigger a like response in the reader (Martin & white, 2005: 61-8).[8] For example, in text (2), the wording in the headline "public have fouled Diana memorial fountain" is very likely to provoke a negative judgment of the behaviour of the concerned party; such kind of wording that can invoke a certain kind of evaluation is termed *token* in appraisal theory, and it is thought to be able to suggest the same inscribed judgment effected by the adjective *irresponsible* in this context. That is to say, the wordings like this can also indicate the speaker's sides-taking attitude.

5.4.3 Sides-taking through ventriloquation

A dialogic reading of a text, however, focuses on the interactions between different voices in it. Or roughly speaking, it is about a speaker's attitude towards others' speeches rather than toward a material object, or toward people's activities out there. That is, what we care is mainly what attitude one voice takes toward another. In canonical dialogues, confronting and supporting responses to other's speech can be made roughly in two ways: one way is obviously to agree and disagree, or to support and confront other's words clearly and directly; the other is to say one thing and mean another. The latter indirect type of making response to other's speech has already been well studied in pragmatics. For example (Levinson, 2001: 97, 111),

(3) A: Can you tell me the time?
B: Well, the milkman has come.
(4) A: I do think Mrs Jenkins is an old windbag, don't you?
B: Huh, lovely weather for March, isn't it?

These are two well-cited examples in the discussion of the notion of *conversational implicature* originating with Paul Grice in the literature of pragmatics. These two mini-conversations are the same in that speaker B answers in an indirect way to the question asked by speaker A and the implied meanings of speaker B's utterances,[9] that is, their *implicatures*, are motivated by the same Gricean maxim called *relevance*. But the relationship between the two utterances in (3) differs from that between the two utterances in (4). The implicature of speaker B's utterance in (3), which can be successfully inferred by speaker A in the context, can be that "I cannot tell you the exact time but I have noticed the milkman has come, so 'the time is at least after whenever the milkman normally calls' (Levinson, 2001: 107)." That is to say, speaker B in reality successfully answers speaker A's question. Thus from a dialogic point of view, speaker B's voice supports rather than confronts the voice of speaker A, for the former actually makes a positive response to the latter. The implicature of speaker B's utterance in (4) can be that "I cannot badmouth others with you, because this is against my principles." It is safe to say that the seemingly irrelevant answer given by speaker B in (4) actually provides a negative response to speaker A's voice; or the voice of speaker B can be said to be more in confrontation with speaker A's voice than in agreement with it in (4). That is to say, no matter how one voice responds to another, directly or indirectly (in a inscribed way or in a invoked manner), the dialogic relationship between two interacting voices still move along the scale from blatantly confronting to ostensively supporting demonstrated by figure 5.1.

The difference between the implicature of speaker B's utterance in (3) and that in (4) and the corresponding difference in the dialogic relationships between the two utterances are due to the fact that the indirect ways speaker Bs adopt to respond to speaker As' questions may well be motivated by different reasons. In (3) it is quite possible that it is inconvenient for speaker B to consult a watch or a clock to give speaker A a complete and precise answer, while in (4) it is very likely that speaker B wraps up his negative response to speaker A's question in talking about an irrelevant thing, which can reduce threats to speaker A's "positive faces" (to disagree with speaker A or at least to reserve his opinion on the topic). The degree to which one's utterance causes threats to others' "faces" is determined by the social distance between the speakers and the relative power possessed by them. Generally speaking, the larger the social distance between the speakers and the wider the gap in power possessed by them in a certain community or institution, the more indirect way the interlocutor in the lower social position will adopt in order to sound more polite (He Zhaoxiong et al., 2000: 225-30; Watts, 2003: 85-95). But when the interactions enter a wider social sphere and the private conversations become public discourse, the constraints (coming from the social distance and power relations) on the way the interlocutors conduct their verbal interactions on public issues will be more complicated and influential. In the case of journalistic discourse in newspapers, the way the texts are constructed can mirror these constraints very well. Although the journalistic professionalism and training textbooks insist that news-writing should be based on an objective description of what is reported, it has been shown that "because the institutions of news reporting and presentation are socially, economically and politically situated, all news is always reported from some particular angle" (Fowler, 1991: 10). Thus the objectivity of news reporting is believed to be a beautiful myth. But in the journalistic practice, the maxim of being objective and free of bias is still regarded as the top ethical decree not only by the profession but by other social groups including the general reading public and the government as well, because it can protect newspapers from possible troubles caused by the reports they have published and the government can also benefit from it in the sense that the public, who also believe news reports should be objective, will be easier to be persuaded into accepting the reports about the governmental policy if they are conducted in favour of the government. Thus the objectivity of news report sometimes becomes a tool with which the power manipulates the media. That is to say the notion of objectivity has become something that is performed and exerted by the concerned social institutions. Therefore it is safe to say that the objectivity has been reduced to a compromise between power and truth (Huang Dan, 2005: 111). This compromise is actually the root cause that determines the way the newspaper and its reporters construct a news text. The reporters construct news reportings from particular angles, which presuppose their attitudes toward what is reported, but the social power relations and then the institutional formula of saying things, that is, its *genre*, force them to follow the expected institutional indirect way of constructing news texts.

To wrap up the reporter's angle or attitudes toward what is reported in hard news text can be conducted in three major ways. The first is to select what is to be reported and what should be screened from the public eyes, which certainly reflects the institutional bias of the newspaper toward our social life; this selection and screening is called agenda-setting in media studies. And this agenda-setting bias has already been well-studied not only by journalism critics but also by discourse analysts, for example, among others, Tuchman (1978), Fowler (1991), Johnson-Cartee (2005), and Huang Dan (2005). After selecting what is to be reported, the reporters will construct their texts under the pressure of the institutional genre of this profession—they are supposed to make their reports at least sound objective and free of bias. There are perhaps several ways or resources for reporters to wrap up their personal or institutional angles, judgments, appraisals, or attitudes in the objective-sounding wording of their texts, but we just focus on two of them. The first one is to put different voices into a deliberately-set frame to invoke an expected judgment in their readers, and this has already been discussed when we make a dialogic reading of text (1). The second more linguistically-oriented way of looking at news bias on which we are focusing now is to find out how reporters express their own opinions through the mouths of others. Speaking one's own words through the mouths of others actually refers to the linguistic phenomena ranging from *quotation*, *speech reporting* or *speech projection* to even *thought representation* (Leech & short, 1981: 318-51; Coulmas, 1986; Short, 1988; Halliday, 2000: 250-73). [10] In Bakhtinian translinguistics, when viewed from a different perspective, this phenomenon is termed *ventriloquation* (Bakhtin, 1981: 299; Wortham & Locher, 1996; Maynard, 1997; Lauerbach, 2006). [11] The major difference between *speech reporting* and *ventriloquation* is this: speech reporting/projection/representation is viewed in the way that the reporter can make a faithful, bias-free and altruistic representation of other's speech (Waugh, 1995), while ventriloquation is viewed in the way that the reporter, just like a ventriloquist on stage, makes the one whose words are reported his "dummy" —the person who says what the reporter (the ventriloquist) wants to say.

Looking at the reported speeches in text (2) from the perspective of ventriloquation rather than projection or representation is actually engendered and advocated by the idea of social constructionists that reality and truth is socially constructed mostly by discourse. Thus the *factuality* and *fictionality* are actually different scales of a continuum. In any kind of text or discourse, the authorial construction maintains its presence to various degrees (Jørgensen & Phillips, 2002). If we take this view to look at speech reporting, we will find that even quoting directly is a creative activity primarily controlled by the quoter rather than a representation of someone else's (i. e. the quotee's) verbatim speech. Thus, in daily dialogue, Tannen (1989) has found that direct quotation (direct speech) is a misnomer since it is not actually "reported". Instead what is generally meant by "direct speech" is spontaneous speech creatively constructed by the speaker at the time of talking. When it comes to the quoting activities in news text, media researchers such as McGlone (2005a, 2005b) argue that it is impossible for quoted words in news text (no matter what type it is, direct speech or quasi-direct speech, let alone indirect speech and narrative speech act) to be verbatim because what is quoted is severed from its original context. On the basis of empirical evidence, he found that this way of quoting or excerpting of words from their original context certainly "distorts the source's intentions". Thus he borrows the term *contextomy* to refer to this phenomenon of the false reproduction of the original words in journalistic discourse.[12] That is to say, even the direct speech in news text, which is believed to be under the least authorial control from the reporting voice, is actually something severed from its original context and recontextualized in the new context created by the reporting voice. Once the words are recontextualized in a new context, according to Bakhtin (1986: 67-100), they will become the components of a new utterance and will be interpreted differently in the context of this new utterance as a whole. In this sense, the sources whose words are quoted and fitted into the newly constructed text will be reduced to "dummies", whose "mouths" are employed and manipulated by the reporter who really wants to speak what he attributes to the sources. These dummy-roles played by the sources (whose words are quoted, for example, the cabinet minister, Tessa Jowell in text (2)) will be exemplified by text (2) if we rewrite the text by only deleting the reporter's words which are used to introduce or indicate the sources of the reported words as shown by the following:

(1) IRRESPONSIBLE behavior by members of the public is to blame for the closure of the Diana, Princess of Wales Memorial Fountain.

Synopsis: *Irresponsible behavior caused the closure of Princess of Wales Memorial Fountain.*

(2) The memorial had been spoilt by people who had allowed their dogs to run in it and dropped rubbish, including nappies, into the water.
(3) It was a pretty sad situation that people appeared to need to be told how to behave at the fountain, and when the memorial reopened it should be treated as a place of remembrance.

Specification 1:
What's the behaviour?
And why is it irresponsible?

(4) The fountain in Hyde Park was closed 10 days ago after two adults and a child were hurt when they slipped while paddling. The £ 3.6 million fountain was drained and has since been the subject of an investigation by health and safety officers.

Specification 2:
When, why and how was the fountain closed by whom?

(5) We accept that there are problems that The Royal Parks have got to sort out. Once these are sorted, people have got to be responsible in the way they let their children play in the fountain.
(6) The critical issue is that this is a memorial. It requires both a management regime by the Parks and good sense by members of the public. I don't think any responsible person would want to see people allowing their dogs in it. How can we maintain the purity of the water if some people allow their dogs to paddle?

Extension of specification 1:
1) *concession*: *Problems with the fountain*;
2) *argument*: *The purpose of the decent behaviour the fountain (memorial) demands*;
3) *suggestion*: *How to behave responsibly at the fountain.*

(7) The fountain, designed by Kathryn Gustafson to express the late princess's spirit and love of children, opened a month ago, but has suffered problems ranging from blockages to complaints about the water quality and slipperiness of the granite floor. When the fountain does reopen, rules will be posted banning animals and littering. Children should paddle in areas of the fountain where the surface is flat.

Extension of specification 2: *more detailed information about the fountain*: *its purpose, closure, and future requirements.*

(8) I am not blaming the majority of the public, just a minority who were behaving inappropriately at the fountain. Of the thousands of people who have enjoyed this small number appear to have behaved irresponsibly. This is a place for reflection, contemplation and remembrance, as well as a place for people to enjoy bringing their children.

(9) You would have thought that people would have shown a little bit more respect given that it is a memorial. But it should remain open—we should not be browbeaten by the health and safety police who interfere too much already in our everyday lives.

Comment: *Clarification and restatement of the position.*

The above rewritten version of text (2) can be read as a coherent passage, with the first paragraph presenting a synopsis, or in van Dijk's term, the macro theme of the text—*irresponsible behavior of the public caused the closure of Princess Diana's memorial fountain*. Paragraph (2) serves as a detailed specification of how those irresponsible people behaved, and paragraph (3) makes a negative evaluation of this kind of behaviour. Paragraph (4) provides more detailed information to elaborate the synopsis by specifying the causal relationship between people's behaviour and the closure of the fountain, the time of this closure, how it was closed, and who did it. Paragraphs (5) and (6) serve as an extension of the specification of the synopsis provided by paragraphs (2) and (3) by emphasizing the inappropriateness of the behaviour after giving a concession which is then followed by a suggestion for the appropriate way to enjoy the fountain. Paragraph (7) is the extension of the second round of specification (i. e. specification (2) presented by paragraph (4) for the synopsis, which gives us further details of the fountain: its purpose, the problems it faces, and its future requirements). Paragraphs (8) and (9) serve as the concluding comment of the passage through clarification and restatement of the author's position on the issue—*only that small number of people who behave irresponsibly are to blame and the memorial purpose of the fountain should be respected*. Therefore, modeling on van Dijk's textual structure, the relationship between the paragraphs of the rewritten version can be illustrated by the following figure 5.4.

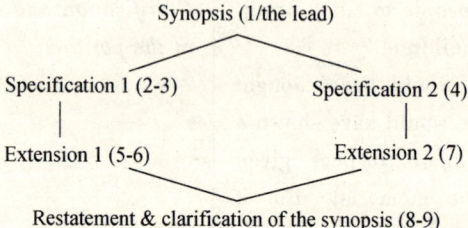

Figure 5.4 The textual structure of the rewritten version of hard news text (2)

It seems that the deletion of the parts consisting of the reporting signals (one major type of dialogic markers) and the sources of the foreign voices do not deprive the remains of text (2) of its textuality; that is, the remains can still make a coherent text. This strongly suggests that the words from the cabinet minister and the friend of Princess Diana are not quoted at random. They are the words the reporter needs to construct a coherent text. That is to say, the words from the quoted sources at most serve as the building materials, so to speak, the bricks and beams. But when the bricks of wording are assembled and a new building of text is completed, the verbal bricks are not their original ones at all, for they have received new functions assigned by the textual building as a whole. They are used to embody the idea of the constructor. And the stage metaphor of ventriloquation, as we have made above, will be that the reporter works just as the ventriloquist and the reported sources as his dummies. That is, the words quoted are just the words the reporter wants to say, but in news text the social power relations and institutional genre stipulate that these words should be spoken by the mouths of others, especially those of the social VIPs, who are believed to be able to bring more credibility to the things at issue.

The plausibility for reading text (2) from the perspective of ventriloquation can also be found in the layout of different reporting modes in it even from a representationist point of view. In Chapter 4 we have classified speech reportings into four major types; and they form a continuum as far as the inter-voice control is concerned, which has been demonstrated by figure 4.3, now repeated as figure 5.5.

$$\xrightarrow{\text{Increase of inter-voice control}}$$
DS　　QDS　　IS　　NRSA

Figure 5.5   A continuum of inter-voice control in speech reporting

Figure 5.5 tells us that when two voices, that is, the reporting voice and the reported voice (or foreign voice), are realized in the text by using direct speech (DS), the reporting voice exerts the least control of the reported voice. The textual form of the latter is usually separated from that of the former by the so-called quotation marks, which, from the representationist's point of view, is believed to indicate that what is reported is the verbatim speech of others. On the contrary, in the indirect speech (IS), the reporting voice has the reported voice under its tighter control, and in the narrated speech act (NRSA), the control is so complete that the reporting voice merges with the reported voice completely. In text (2), DSs can be found in sentences 6, 7, 12, 13 and 15; the former four cases are from the cabinet minister, Tessa Jowell, who criticizes the irresponsible behaviour of some members of the public, occupying about 28 per cent of the space of text (2) (132 words out of the total 466); the last case in sentence 15 is from Rosa Monckton, the princess's close friend and chairman of the committee that selected the fountain, making up 11 per cent of the textual space (49 words out of the total 466). ISs can be found in the headline, sentences 1 (the lead), 2, 3, 9 and 11: except the IS in sentence 9 in which the reported speech (to be exact the reported idea) is from an unspecified source that can be the community, the general public including the reporter, or the minister, and so forth, the rest are all from the minister, occupying nearly 24 per cent of the textual space (111 words out of the total 466). NRSA can be found in sentences 10 and

14, making up nearly 4 per cent of the textual space (14 words out of the total). Quasi direct speech (QDS) refers to the wordings like the first half of sentence 3 in text (2), which blends the form of IS with that of DS and is also attributed to the minister, making up about 4 per cent of the textual space (20 words out of the total 466). Thus more than half of the space of text (2) (56 per cent) is given to the voices from the cabinet minister: they are realized by DS that makes up 28 percent of the textual space, by IS that makes up 24 percent of the textual space, and by the blending form of QDS that makes up 4 per cent of the textual space.

The headline and the lead of the text, which are believed to be the most important parts of a hard news text, are presented in the same way: the part which is used to realize the reporting voice (that is, the part which is used to attribute the reported indirect speech to the cabinet minister) is put at the end of the sentence. Therefore, it is quite possible that at first glance we will mistake the reported words for the reporter's own words, thus mistaking the foreign voice for the authorial voice. Though the attribution is made at the end of the sentence, which is expected to be able to correct the reader's first "false reading", psychological researches show that "unlike computers human information processors do not 'overwrite' acquired knowledge that is later revealed to be false or questionable, but rather treat the altered truth value as an addendum to this stored knowledge" (McGlone, 2005a). This lasting effect caused by the first impression is termed "cognitive obstination", "interpretive obstinacy" or "interpretive perseverance" in psychology, which is also applied to textual analysis, especially when free direct speech in literary text is under consideration (cf. Mey, 2000: 29-34, 120, 203). That is to say, the "false reading" will usually be stored in our mind and the information provided by the later attribution cannot eliminate this preconception completely. Although in the second paragraph (also the second sentence of the text) the source (still the minister) is indicated before her words, the words of the minister are still presented in the form of IS, which shows the authorial control over the foreign voice to a substantial extent. Paragraph 3 (also sentence 3) is still used to report the voice of the minister, but this time the blending form of QDS is used, which is followed still by IS. Paragraph 4 is dominated by the reporting voice (j) and (k), which are believed to provide a specification for the lead. This paragraph is then followed by two paragraphs of direct quotations from the minister, which, as we have just discussed, actually provide extended information to specify the synopsis of the lead. Paragraph 7, which is dominated by the reporting voice (of course also invoking the presence of a certain unspecified foreign voice), serves a similar function as paragraph 4 does. Paragraph 8 is again given to the voice of the minister, which is first realized in the form of IS and then in the form of DS. Thus the arrangement of the modes of speech representation that are employed to realize the minister's voice in text (2) can be illustrated in the following figure 5. 6.

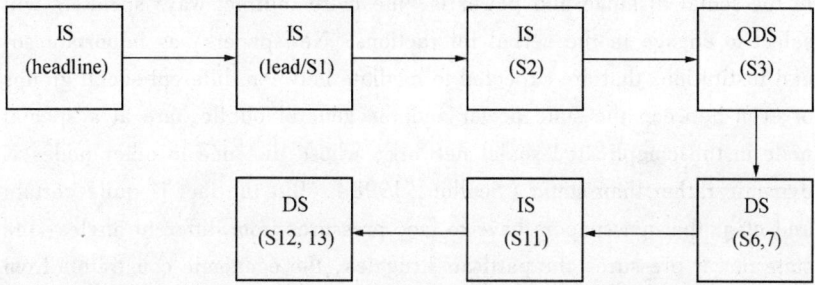

Figure 5. 6 The layout of reporting modes in hard news text (2)

If we take a close look at figure 5. 6 against figure 5. 5, we will find that in text (2) the reporting voice firstly exerts a tighter control over the reported minister's voice, and then the authorial control is reduced gradually roughly through QDS to DS. Given that the authorial control is achieved mainly by merging the reporting voice with the reported foreign voice (thus the former appropriating the latter, that is, (a) appropriating (b), and (c) appropriating (d)), it is safe to say that figure 5. 6 strongly suggests that what the minister has said is also the words the reporter wants to say, because it will be against our common sense that one will merge his voice with the voices of those people whose positions he opposes. As we have mentioned in Chapter 3, according to Bakhtin, when two juxtaposed or merged-but-heterogeneous voices do not *contradict* or *confront* each other, they will *agree with* or *support* each other in a broad sense, so this merging at least suggests that the reporting voice shares the same position with the reported voice. Considering the important position of the headline and lead in the reading habit of general public, this arrangement of reporting modes in text (2) can lend some strength to the understanding that what the minister says is also the thing that the reporter wants to say. He supports the position held by the minister.

Reading hard news texts from the perspective of ventriloquation actually reduces speech reporting to a linguistic device that invites someone else's voice for the sake of advancing one's own. Thus the reported words are nothing but the reporter's views in disguise. The *raison d'être* for ventriloquation in hard news text lies in the factors which determine the way speakers adopt to initiate a verbal interaction or respond to other's words. As we have mentioned at the beginning of this section, the wider the gap in the social distance and power is, the more indirect ways speakers will select to engage in the verbal interactions. Newspapers, as important social institutions that are expected to mediate between different social groups or even between the state power and the general public, are at a special node in the complicated social network, whose distance to other nodes is dynamic rather than static (Scollon, 1998). But the fact is quite certain and clear that newspapers have to face pressures from different angles: the state power pressure, the partisan struggles, the economic constraints from the advertisers in this highly commodified world, and the expectations of their subscribers for faithful information about the society they live in and so forth. Thus news reports are understandably compromises resulting from the competitions among these different forces. This negotiated compromise requires the news producers to show their support and confrontation in disguise: that is, to criticize through other's mouth and to praise through other's mouth, too. If the news text is read in this way, the appraisal resources discussed by *Appraisal Theory* can actually be regarded as the indicators of the authorial attitude toward the issue reported. In text (2), thus, the inscribed and invoked negative judgment of some-members-of-the-public's behaviour as "irresponsible" can be said to be held by the reporter and his organization too.

In the similar vein, if we read the text in a dialogic manner, we have to pay attention to the foreign voices reported and invoked by the dialogic markers embedded in the reported speeches (even those within the quotation marks), so the foreign voices such as (y) in sentence 11, (gg) and (hh) in sentence 15 have also been identified when we annotate text (2) dialogically, because they are under the same authorial control. That is to say, voice (x) triggered by the negative particle *not*, which may hold that the reported words of the minister are blaming too many people, is the position the reporting voice wants to oppose too. Voice (gg) engendered by the conjunction *but* within the quotation marks in sentence 15, which may hold that the fountain can be closed to the public, is also what the reporter wants to debate with and object to. Similarly, voice (hh) indicated by the negative particle *not* after (hh), which may hold that we had better obey the requirements of health and safety police not to go to the fountain, is also what the reporter wants to say "no" to.

Therefore, the sides-taking effect is quite evident: the reporting voice supports the reported minister's voices which criticize the irresponsible behaviour of some members of the public. Or to be exact, the reported minister's voices support the reporter's voice that attempts to criticize those whose irresponsible behaviour caused the closure of the memorial fountain for Princess Diana, who is highly respected and remembered by the general public in Britain after her death. At the end of text (2), the support to the minister's voice is actually expressed distinctly, but still it is conducted in the way of ventriloquation: the reporter speaks of his support to the minister's position through the mouth of Rosa Monckton, the princess's close friend, to criticize the irresponsible behaviour. Thus the dialogic interactions in text (2) can be illustrated by figure 5.7.

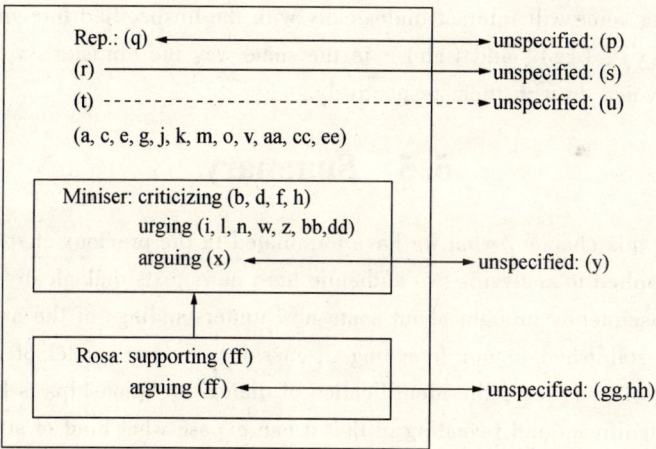

Figure 5.7 The dialogic interactions in hard news text (2)

Figure 5.7 demonstrates the dialogic interactions between voices indicated by the lower-case letters in brackets in text (2). The ventriloquation-motivated reading tells us that together with the reporting voices that possess context-setting function, the reported voices from the minister and Rosa, which are put into two separate boxes in the figure, actually make up significant components of the macro-reporting voice (i.e. the Rep. in the figure), which is designated by the biggest box in which the two separate component boxes standing for the voices from the minister and Rosa are embedded. The local interaction between the reporting voice (q) and unspecified foreign voice (p) marked and engendered by the conjunction *but* in sentence 8 is understood to be confronting. The reporting voice (r) is believed to support the unspecified foreign voice (s) marked and engendered by the modality verb *understand*; and the reporting voice (t) is also thought to give support to the foreign voice (u) marked and engendered by the reporting verb *tell*, but the supporting attitude of the reporting voice is invoked in the context rather than inscribed lexically, thus being indicated by the dotted arrow in the figure. The other local interactions between minister's voice (x) and the unspecified foreign voice (y), and between Rosa's voice (ff) and the unspecified foreign voices (gg) & (hh), as we have discussed above, also show that they are in conflict with each other. If we accept the ventriloquation reading of the text, then the macro reporting voice will interact dialogically with the unspecified foreign voices (i.e. (y), (gg), and (hh)) in the same way the minister's voice and Rosa's voice do with them respectively.

5.5 Summary

In this chapter, what we have formulated in the previous chapters has been applied to analyzing two authentic hard news texts dialogically, which has consequently brought about some new understandings of the analytical model established in our foregoing discussions. In our model of dialogic reading of news text, the identification of dialogic relationships is believed to be significant and revealing in that it can expose what kind of attitude is held by one voice toward another. Keeping an eye on the attitude-making expressions in news text is thought to be the major task of textual analysis of journalist discourse with a critical spirit, because news text is said to be neutral and free of biased evaluations in the training textbooks and this myth-like professional doctrine as a commonsensical preconception has already been planted into the minds of the general reading public. Therefore, a dialogic reading of news text with a critical eye is accordingly to expose the attitude-showing (especially those performed in disguise) in the process of dialogic interactions between different voices inhabiting the textual space.

The relationship between two voices, as we have said, moves along the scale from "confronting" to "supporting" (or from "negative" to "positive"), and in theory the middle point of the scale is the state of being neutral (i.e. neither confronting nor supporting). According to the journalist training textbooks, this middle point is what the reporting voice (the voice of the newspaper including the reporter of course) should pursue and keep when interacting with the reported foreign voices. That is to say, the reporting voice is expected to try as much as possible not to show its attitude toward the reported foreign voices—it should be neutral instead of taking sides (for example, to express agreement or disagreement, to criticize or to praise, and so forth). But according to Bakhtinian translinguistics, human utterance is far from value-free; the attitude borne by one utterance toward another is actually the addressivity and expressivity of the utterance. In our model, the notion of voice is theorized as the semantic position in the text which is believed to be realized by Bakhtinian utterance; and the utterance is actually the textual side of the voice, through which the voice enters a text and inhabits there. The addressivity and expressivity of utterance are in reality motivated by the voice, which is saturated with ideological conflicts and power imbalances. Given the dynamic nature of social life, it is almost impossible for a voice to keep neutral toward another voice when they meet in the social and then textual space that is full of competitions and struggles. In this sense, as far as the inter-voice interactions are concerned, showing attitude by taking sides is absolute; in other words, remaining completely neutral is relative and even fictional. Researches in pragmatics also show that in daily verbal interactions attitude-showing is usually made covert by the influence coming from the social distance and relative power between the participants; they often say one thing but mean another, or more academically, the illocutionary force does not match the locutionary act. But when it comes to the written hard news text, which claims to be neutral and free of sides-taking, how does the reporting voice express its attitude toward the reported foreign voices under the guise of keeping free of evaluation-making?

In this chapter, through analyzing two complete authentic texts from *The Sunday Telegraph*, we have found two major ways adopted by the reporting voice to show its attitude in disguise. Text (1) makes a good example for showing attitude and taking sides by fitting foreign voices into the frame set by the reporting voice, which can successfully invoke the expected value-judgment in the readers of the text. Another way of showing attitude is in fact closely related to the first one, which is exemplified by text (2). Through a dialogic analysis of text (2), we have shown that in news text what the reported voices say is actually what the reporting voice wants to say. The latter performs just as a ventriloquist does and the former just work as dummies. It is because of the possibility of ventriloquation that the reporting voice has access to framing the foreign voices in its favour to say what it wants to say while staying behind the attributed sources, which are believed to grant the journalistic text the needed legitimacy and credibility. Besides, ventriloquation in the form of speech representation in hard news text can also make the narrative more lively: "introducing participants as speakers conveys both the human and the dramatic dimension of news events." (van Dijk, 1988: 87)

The analyses of text (1) and text (2) also display a certain kind of methodological significance concerning the dialogic reading of a text. Through the analyses of these two concrete authentic hard news texts, it has been found that the local dialogic interactions discussed in chapters 3 and 4 are actually under the control of the global dialogic relationships among the voices in the text. Therefore, the former should be interpreted in accordance with the latter, and only in this way can the dialogic analysis of news text be relevant.

Notes:

[1] The voice which initiates the dialogic interaction is designated as $voice_i$, and the voice which responds to the initiation is designated as $voice_r$ in the figure and also in the following discussion.

[2] In these two extracts, Rep. stands for *the reporter's voice*, and O stands for *other's voice*; the index *r* means *responding*, and *i* means *initiating*.

[3] The pure linguistic categories such as *sentence* or *clause*, as has just been discussed in the foregoing chapters, are still needed as analytical tools even when we are making a translinguistic analysis of a text. For one thing linguistics, according to Bakhtin, complements translinguistics as far as the concrete analysis of language resources is concerned, and for another only when textual analysis is based on linguistic analysis can it be regarded as real analysis, according to Halliday (2000: F42-F43).

[4] In order to talk about things in the common media vocabulary, we still use the word *lead* to refer to the opening paragraph or sentence of a news report.

[5] Voice (v) is regarded just as the reporting voice when the dialogic interactions in the text are read locally, but when taking a global view, (v) sound more like the voice from the government, for it is inserted between the voice from the government and its minister (i. e. (u) and (x)). This ambiguity of the source of the voice is sometimes made deliberately to convey opinions in a covert way, which characterizes news text.

[6] Different from the annotation of text (1), here we take reported speeches from others into our consideration. That is, we also pay some attention to the dialogic interactions embedded in others' speech, so the dialogic markers in the reported speeches are also included in this table, for example, the negative particle *not* in sentence 11. The reason why we do so will be discussed later.

[7] According to White, hard news text is characterized by this lacking of inscribed evaluations; compared with hard news text, feature news text (or news analysis) is characterized by " authorially-sourced social esteem ", and editorial or commentary news text is characterized by having " no co-textual constrains on judgment (free occurrence of unmediated social sanction and social esteem)"; and these three typical types of using appraisal resources appearing correspondingly in the three typical types of news discourse, namely, hard news, features and editorials, are termed *reporter voice*, *correspondent voice* and *commentator voice*, with the latter two subsumed under the umbrella term *writer voice*, which runs parallel to *reporter voice* (Martin & White, 2005: 173-4). As we have discussed in Chapter 3, the term of *voice* used here is different from our conception of voice; in appraisal theory, voice is used to describe the rhetorical style of news discourse as far as using the appraisal resources is concerned (White, 1998).

[8] As far as the relationship between ideational meaning (referential meaning) and evaluative meaning is concerned, Bakhtin looks at the things from the other way round. According to him, " referential meaning is molded by evaluation; it is evaluation, after all, which determines that a particular referential meaning may enter the purview of speakers—both the immediate purview and the broader social purview of the particular social group" (Bakhtin/Volosinov, 1986: 105).

This way of looking at the relationship between ideational and interpersonal sphere of language (in Hallidayan terms) is quite in agreement with Bakhtinian translinguistics which has interpersonal dialogicity as its core.

[9] As we have discussed in Chapter 1, the term utterance in modern pragmatics refers to almost the same thing as the Bakhtinian utterance does, except that the Bakhtinian utterance takes the written text as utterance, for instance, a complete novel, a piece of news report, etc., which is believed to be composed of various utterances when different voices can be detected from its lines. In our discussion utterance is used in the way that if a stretch of wording can be identified to be associated with a voice in the text, then it becomes utterance, and otherwise, it remains a lexico-grammatical category—a word, phrase, clause or sentence. Here, utterance is used still in the sense of the canonical pragmatics, but since in these two cases utterances are realized by single sentences and are associated with a single voice from speaker A or B, the pragmatic utterances and the translinguistic utterances converge here.

[10] In the literature about these linguistic phenomena, quotation mostly only refers to those involving the so-called quotation marks, which are also called direct speeches especially in school grammars. Speech reporting has a wider range, which is sometimes used interchangeably with speech representation, and this way of naming the thing is preferred by stylists such as Geoffrey N. Leech and Michael H. Short (Leech & Short, 1981). Thought reporting or representation refers to the phenomenon that what is reported or represented is not one's speech but one's ideas, in Halliday's words, a mental rather than a verbal process. For example, *Dr. Singleman always believed that his patient would recover*. Halliday (2000) prefers the term *projection* in his functional grammar to *reporting* and *representation* when he talks about the same linguistic phenomena. In Chapter 4 of this book, thought/idea projection/reporting is regarded as a type of modality. But in the later discussion, speech/thought reporting, speech/thought representation, and speech/thought projection will be used interchangeably for they are all related to inter-voice interactions.

[11] Researchers use different derivatives from the English root *ventriloquist* to refer to this phenomenon: when translating Bakhtin's *Discourse in the Novel*, which is collected in *The Dialogic Imagination*, Holquist uses its verb form *ventriloquate* (Holquist & Emerson, 1981: 299), and Wortham & Locher (1996) follows him by using the verb form *ventriloquate* and noun form *ventriloquation*; Maynard (1997) prefers the noun form *ventriloquism*, and Lauerbach (2006) the verb form *ventriloquize* and its gerund *ventriloquizing*. In our discussion, we will follow Holquist and Wortham & Locher's way of naming the things.

[12] The term *contextomy* is coined by historian Milton Mayer, who compared the practice of "quoting out of context" to surgical excision, "to describe its use by

Julius Streicher, editor of the infamous Nazi broadsheet newspaper, *Der Sturmer in Weimar-era Germany.*" "*One of the early tactics Streicher used to arouse anti-Semitic sentiments among the weekly's working-class Christian readership was to publish truncated quotations from Talmudic texts that, in their shortened form, appear to advocate greed, slavery and ritualistic murder.*" (McGlone, 2005b)

Conclusion

Addressing the seeming contradiction between Bakhtin's hypothetical assertion that any text is dialogic in nature and his distinction of certain novel texts from other genres of texts by the criterion that the former type of text is dialogic while the latter one monologic, this book intends to recontextualize Bakhtin's translinguistics in the setting of modern linguistics (Hallidayan *SFL* in particular), aiming at a more workable framework for analyzing hard news text dialogically. Hard news text is commonsensically subsumed under the category of monologic and authoritative text, which in contrast to novel text lies at the other end of the cline of text that is thought to command *factuality* to the maximum (see figure 0.1). If this type of text can be handled by the recontextualized framework of translinguistic dialogicity, then the problem left by Bakhtin will be solved.

During the process of assembling Bakhtin's translinguistic ideas dispersed in his works written over different periods of time, we have found that Bakhtin adopts an out-and-out sociological perspective on human language, which results in his emphasis on the actual speech (i.e. *utterance*) rather than the abstract system and structure (i.e. *langue*) that is enshrined by Saussure as the only legitimate object of linguistic studies. In contrast to Saussurean linguistics, Bakhtin advances his translinguistics that selects the concrete actual speech as its object, the most relevant property of which is its dialogicity. Among such key notions in translinguistics as *utterance*, *voice*, *genre*, and *dialogic relationship*, three of them, namely, *voice*, *utterance* and *dialogic relationship* are found to be most relevant to the current textual analyses which feature substantial requisite linguistic analyses, but these translinguistic notions need to be recontextualized and developed in Hallidayan *SFL* because Bakhtin fails to specify them in a systematic and unified way; for his formulations on these key translinguistic notions are dispersed in his philosophical and poetic theorizations on literary text and even sometimes they are thought to be in conflict with each other when used in different contexts. That is to say, if a wider range of texts than the literary texts (which are the focus of Bakhtin and his followers) are to be incorporated into translinguistics for dialogic analyses, these three essential translinguistic concepts need to be adapted and developed by taking nutrients from the contemporary linguistic findings, especially those from Hallidayan *SFL*.

Apart from piecing together Bakhtin's sporadic translinguistic ideas and identifying some of their ruptures that hinder them from making a systematic and workable analytic framework expected to cover a wider range of texts than the literary ones, another major achievement of this book is the establishment of the compatibility between Bakhtin's translinguistics and Hallidayan *SFL*. Through careful observations and comparisons, we succeed in finding that Bakhtin's translinguistics and Hallidayan *SFL* have a lot in common as far as the following aspects are concerned: both of them share a non-Aristotelian philosophical tradition of looking at human language; they both attach due importance to context in which language is used; both influenced by Karl Bühler, they have made quite similar observations on the functions of language; and both of them have recognized the importance of the concept of genre when selecting the actual speech as the object of study from a sociological perspective. The establishment of the interface between Bakhtin's translinguistics and Hallidayan *SFL* is considerably significant, because *SFL* is found to be able to bridge the gap between Bakhtin's translinguistics and the discoveries of contemporary linguistic findings, particularly the fruitful observations of the lexico-grammatical resources of human language, of which Bakhtin's translinguistics is notoriously in need. In this sense we have carried out what Bakhtin has proposed but failed to put into practice—to incorporate linguistically-oriented textual analyses into translinguistics in the way that lexico-grammatical analyses serve as the linguistic basis for translinguistic interpretations, and in turn translinguistics provides the lexico-grammatical analyses with an interpretive framework, just as Bakhtin (1984: 181) has pointed out "they [linguistics and translinguistics] must complement one another, but they must not be confused." In so doing, a double-oriented model of dialogic analysis of text is established.

In Bakhtin's translinguistics, the dialogicity of a text actually refers to the dynamic relationships between different voices inhabiting the text. Although this notion of voice plays such an essential part in his theorization on textual dialogicity, unfortunately, he fails to define what *voice* really is, let alone how *voice* is realized by the lexico-grammatical resources in the process of textual production and how a voice can be identified out of lexico-grammatical expressions in the text when it is read in a dialogic way. In Chapter 3, these problems are tackled by drawing heavily on Hallidayan *SFL*. At first the key notion of voice is regarded as the constitutive element of textual dialogicity and is then defined as *semantic position in the text which is engendered by the institutionalized power relations in social interactions*. In simple terms, voice is regarded as the participant of textual dialogues, which metaphorically refer to the interactions between different semantic positions in the text. Modeling on Halliday's understandings of the dialogic relationships in daily verbal interactions, Bakhtinian translinguistic-dialogic relationships are found to form a cline from blatantly *confronting* to ostensively *supporting*. Methodologically speaking, the most significant achievement of this chapter is that Bakhtin's utterance is theorized as an intermediate category mediating between voice and lexico-grammatical resources (or the actual wordings in a text). That is to say, text and utterance are differentiated from each other for the time being in the way that text is regarded as the object for analysis while utterance is used as a tool for making dialogic interpretation of the text. Or if we still keep the Bakhtinian treatment of *text as utterance*, then utterance becomes a concept with hierarchical composition: a text/utterance can be regarded as a texture woven from componential utterances. But this structural understanding of utterance can be accepted only on the condition that it is methodologically relevant rather than ontologically significant, because only when an alien voice is associated with a stretch of wording in a text in the process of interpretation can it be accepted as an utterance; for foreign voice, namely, a different semantic position, actually needs to be reconstructed by the reader and at the same time it is associated with a different context from the one the text at issue inhabits. That is to say, a written text ontologically is just an utterance produced by a concrete writer, but when it is read dialogically, foreign voices will be identified out of it and thus some stretches of wording will be read into utterances produced by different sources other than the bylined author. The mediating role played by utterance which is illustrated by figure 3.1 in Chapter 3 should be understood in the way that when making a bottom-up reading of a text, we associate a certain stretch of wording with a foreign voice with the help of some special linguistic resources working as markers, and then we reconstruct an utterance in a top-down manner by putting this stretch of wording into a different context and developing it into a relatively complete utterance especially when the wording is syntactically fragmented. Therefore, before applying this framework to analyzing hard news text, we have to make a relatively systematic observation of the special linguistic resources that can mark out the traces of foreign voices in a text. On the basis of the findings attained by such *SFL* linguists as Thompson (2000) and Holmes (1988), we have made a long list of what we call *dialogic markers* in the English language and at the same time made some trial analyses of the local dialogic interactions embodied in the snippets extracted from complete hard news texts as examples. On the basis of the preparatory work done in the preceding chapters, in Chapter 5 two complete hard news texts are analyzed in the dialogic framework developed in Chapter 3. The dialogic relationships between the reporter's voice and those reported foreign voices are under our focus there; the interactions between them show us that the reported foreign voices in hard news text are actually under a tight control exerted by the reporting voice. The reporter's control over foreign voices is found to be achieved mainly through the following two ways: (1) to fit the foreign voices into a smartly designed frame to invoke an expected or even forced value judgment in the readers; (2) to ventriloquate what the reporter wants to say through reported foreign voices. Thus the dialogic reading of hard news text has actually deconstructed the journalistic professional commitment to be objective and free of bias. In this sense, the so-called hard news text actually reports what the reporter wants to say under the guise of reporting others' words. Therefore, a dialogic reading of a hard news text actually reveals that the so-called factual text is also created into being by the reporter and his organization to air their opinions and judgments rather than just simply mirroring the reality out there. If we take the tight authorial control of the text as a characteristic possessed by monologic text, then in this sense hard news text can be considered monologic rather than dialogic. Or it is dialogic on the surface, but monologic in essence. That is probably why Bakhtin does not include hard news text in his prototypical genre of embodying textual dialogicity. Thus Bakhtin's contradiction mentioned above seems to have been resolved.

The so-called findings or achievements summarized above, however, will be of limited significance unless their implications are considered. Firstly, as a fundamental genre of text, hard news reports in newspapers are claimed and expected to supply the general reading public with the most objective, bias-free, and balanced information about the relevant happenings in the society. Therefore, according to the training textbooks, whatever perspective we take to view hard news text—logic-semantic, sociological, ethical or even legal, hard news text should display an extreme degree of factuality. So in their daily practice, the reporters are forced to try as hard as possible to attribute evaluation-laden expressions which are the major means of airing bias to credible sources (usually social VIPs). Given that the abundance of different voices is characteristic of a dialogic or heteroglossic text, hard news text should be the type of text that is most dialogic in nature because it is full of so many reported words from others and more importantly these reported words are actually spoken by the concrete sources out there. But as has just been mentioned above, a Bakhtinian dialogic reading of hard news text reveals that such professional commitment and promise of journalism is actually a beautiful myth. In the journalistic world, however, journalism practitioners are still educated to stick to the principle of keeping objective and free from bias. Newspapers are still claimed to be the discursive sphere for the whole public although it is possessed by private owners in western countries. For example, the so-called quality newspapers such as *The New York Times* are believed by a lot of practitioners to have strict rules to implement those professional doctrines (Li Zijian, 1999). But on the contrary, researches and scandals also show that even in America where journalistic freedom is protected by the first constitutional amendment,[1] newspapers are still actually manipulated by the state power or at least keep a close symbiotic and even conspiratorial relationship with the government and sometimes shows partisan leanings (Zhang Juyan, 2004; Coe et al., 2004; Hackett et al., 2005 [1997]; Ryan, 2006). Another important factor that exerts substantial impact on news production is the economic demands made on newspapers in such a highly commodifized world, in which new media such as television and the Internet pose great peer pressure. Newspapers have to pay attention to their circulations and the advertisers' likes and dislikes. Tabloid newspapers' "infotaining" style and reader-centeredness also join the forces to make the broadsheets present something creative and individual (Conboy, 2006). All of these have made enormous impact on the writing of news text in newspapers. A good case in point is the increasing use of "artifacts of spoken discourse to engage a reader"; this trend has been disclosed by Colleen Cotter through a longitudinal observation of the using of sentence-initial connectives in news reports on the newspapers of English (Cotter, 1996). Thus it is safe to say that the tension between the inside professional commitment and the outside pressures is quite evident, which forces news producers to adopt a relatively more proactive rhetoric to deal with the dilemma—they have both to be free of bias and to produce original and individual texts; they have to entertain as well as inform their readers. Thus under the cover of dialogic interactions between the reporting voice and reported voices and the dialogic interactions among reported voices themselves reporters have to plant their evaluations, judgments, and sides-takings.

Our dialogic reading, therefore, is intended to reveal this contradictory nature of hard news text—dialogic on the surface but monologic in essence. This kind of reading is actually in agreement with Bakhtin's dialogic reading of novel text. It is generally accepted that Bakhtin's dialogic reading of novel text has set a model for us to acquire a critical eye for things we usually take for granted. The commonsensical knowledge we are educated to accept as norms is actually the ideological controls exerted on us by various social powers. We are trained into "credulous" and obedient social subjects (or good citizens) by newspapers, televisions, the speeches of those baby-kissers, advertisements, and so forth, because the power-engendered ideological controls have been legitimatized and habitualized into the form of common sense, which is believed to be the most effective force to keep the stability and status quo of a society (Thompson, 1984: Ch. 2; Fairclough, 1992c: 7-17; Xin Bin, 2000: Ch. 1, 2005: Ch. 4). Though we cannot say that all the ideologically habitualized common sense is negative, the commonsensical norms sometimes indeed are manipulated by the powerful to take advantage of those who possess less social resources. As we have mentioned above, as essential mediators between the state power and the general public, newspapers, which have been given too much habitualized commonsensical trust, are sometimes really tempted or even forced to conspire with the powerful groups—the governments, the commercial tycoons, and the advertisers, to keep the outsiders in the dark and supply them with the news they have to consume. Although it is said that American people have a lot of complaints about the press (Geis, 1987: 13-6), Shannon E. Martin (2003) still found that even in an era when people's reading habits have been unprecedentedly changed because of new technology, news reading public still flocked to the newspaper stands after the September 11, 2001 so that "every major daily newspaper in the United States reported publishing extra copies and special editions to meet the demands of readers who wanted what only newspapers seemed able to supply in the immediate and protracted aftermath of the tragedy" (Martin, 2003: viii). All this shows us that living in such a highly mediated society we have to keep a critical eye when facing what has been presented to us by the media (especially by the most trusted so-called quality newspapers); otherwise, we will be kept outside of the social interactions and thus unable to effect a change in the society. This critical eye is actually what Fairclough's (1995: Ch. 10) term *critical literacy* refers to. Here, the word *literacy* means a lot as far as the significance of the present book is concerned.

In short, what we have done in our discussion can be understood from the following two perspectives. Firstly, Bakhtin's translinguistic ideas have been pieced together and recontextualized in the setting of Hallidayan *SFL* to be developed into a more workable linguistically-oriented framework for analyzing and interpreting hard news text. Secondly, Bakhtin's seemingly contradictory assertions have been resolved in the sense that dialogic reading of a text is actually a way of keeping a critical eye upon those commonsensical norms. If a novel text is commonsensically believed to be created out of the mind of the author, namely, being fictional and monologic in nature, a dialogic reading will show us it is actually a "realism in the higher degree" (Bakhtin, 1984: 61); on the contrary, if a hard news text is commonsensically believed to be an exact representation of the actual happenings out there in the world, namely, being factual and dialogic in nature, the actual dialogic analysis will show us it is in reality "fictional" in the higher degree, namely, being "fictional" in disguise. Thus "reading news as fiction" will actually enable us to keep distance to a certain extent from what we are presented with by the newspapers and other media channels. But it should be noted that reading news as fiction does not necessarily mean news is actually fiction. As a *critical-literacy-cultivating reading strategy*, dialogic reading focuses on the fictional side of the news, and fictionality and factuality differ from each other only in degree. In other words, fictionality and factuality actually coexist symbiotically in a textual space with one usually outweighing the other. What a critical dialogic reading does is try to throw light on the suppressed one of them.

The research done in this book is actually at an initial stage. A number of questions are in need of more careful considerations. Firstly, there may be some danger of appropriation suspected of misunderstanding in our interpretation of Bakhtin's translinguistic theory. Secondly, the dialogic model established by modeling on Hallidayan understanding of daily verbal interactions needs to be tested by analyzing different genres of texts, and more importantly the gradation of the dialogic relationships between the two poles of blatantly confronting and ostensively supporting in the model remains untried even in our analyses of the two authentic hard news texts. Thirdly, there may well be far more linguistic resources that can be used to mark out alien voices and more ways for reporters to air their judgments in disguise than framing and ventriloquation discussed in this book. Furthermore, it is very likely that Hallidayan *SFL*'s potential for recontextualizing Bakhtin's translinguistics into a more workable framework for textual analysis has been underplayed and thus needs to be realized in a more systematic way. And if this research was based on an adequate data base of hard news text from a wider range of sources, the interpretations made in our analysis would be more convincing. Finally, the dialogic analytical model and its application to the analysis of hard news text should take cultural factors into consideration, so some comparative studies on this issue between Chinese and English are also worth our future efforts.

Notes:

[1] For example, in 2003, Jayson Blair, a reporter with *The New York Times*, fabricated a news report and got it published, which stirred heated discussions on the objectivity of news reporting and the professionalism of journalism. (Hindman, 2005)

References

［俄］巴赫金，1998，《巴赫金全集》（钱中文主编），石家庄：河北教育出版社。
白春仁，2000，边缘上的话语——巴赫金话语理论辨析，《外语教学与研究》第 3 期。
［英］贝尔特，1998，《二十世纪的社会理论》，上海：上海译文出版社 2002 年。
［美］费伦，1996，《作为修辞的叙事》，北京：北京大学出版社 2002 年。
丰林，2001，超语言学：走向诗学研究的最深处，《北京科技大学学报（社会科学版）》第 1 期。
顾曰国，1999，使用者话语的语言学地位综述，《当代语言学》第 3 期。
［美］哈克特等，1997，《维系民主？——西方政治与新闻客观性》，清华大学出版社 2005 年。
何兆熊等，2000，《新编语用学概要》，上海：上海外语教育出版社。
何自然，2000，《语用学新解·导读》，北京：外语教学与研究出版社。
胡壮麟，1994a，《语篇的衔接与连贯》，上海：上海外语教育出版社。
胡壮麟，1994b，巴赫金与社会符号学，《北京大学学报（哲学社会科学版）》第 2 期。
胡壮麟，2000，《理论文体学》，北京：外语教学与研究出版社。
胡壮麟，2001，走近巴赫金的符号王国，《外语研究》第 2 期。
胡壮麟等，2005，《系统功能语言学概论》，北京：北京大学出版社。
黄旦，2005，《作者图像：新闻专业主义的建构与消解》，上海：复旦大学出版社。
黄国文，1988，《语篇分析概要》，长沙：湖南教育出版社。
黄国文，2001，《语篇分析的理论与实践——广告语篇研究》，上海：上海外语教育出版社。
黄国文、葛达西（Ghadessy），2006，《功能语篇分析》，上海：上外语教育出版社。
［英］霍尔，1997，《表征——文化表象与意指实践》，北京：商务印书馆2003年。
李彬，2001，巴赫金的话语理论及其对批判学派的贡献，《国际新闻界》第6期。
李曙光，2006，新闻语篇对话性初探——情态语言资源视角，《外语与外语教学》第6期。
李悦娥、范宏雅，2002，《话语分析》，上海：上海外语教育出版社。
李战子，2001，学术话语中认知型情态的多重人际意义，《外语教学与研究》第5期。
李战子，2002，《话语的人际意义》，上海：上海外语教育出版社。
李战子、高一虹，2002，功能语法与批评性话语分析的结合点——第28届国际系统功能语法大会述评，《外语研究》第3期。
李子坚，1999，《纽约时报的风格》，长春：长春出版社。
凌建侯，1999，试析巴赫金的对话主义及其核心概念"话语"，《中国俄语教学》第1期。
凌建侯，2000，话语的对话性，《外语教学与研究》第3期。
凌建侯，2001，巴赫金话语理论中的语言学思想，《中国俄语教学》第3期。
凌建侯，2002，从哲学-语言学看巴赫金与马克思主义的关系，《北京大学学报（哲学社会科学版）》第2期。
刘涵之，2004，巴赫金超语言学思想刍议，《新疆大学学报（社会科学版）》第3期。
刘亚猛，2005，《追求象征的力量》，北京：三联书店。
宁一中，2000，论巴赫金的言谈理论，《外语教学与研究》第3期。
钱中文，1987，复调小说：主人公与作者——巴赫金的叙述理论，《外国文学评论》第1期。
钱中文，1998，《巴赫金全集·理论是可以常青的》，石家庄：河北教育出版社。
王加兴，1998，巴赫金言谈理论阐析，《南京大学学报（哲学·人文·社会科学版）》第4期。
王文忠，2002，言语体裁理论的形成与发展，《解放军外国语学院学报》第3期。
谢静，2005，《建构权威·协商规范——美国新闻媒介批评解读》，上海：复旦大学出版社。
辛斌，2002，巴赫金论语用：言语、对话、语境，《外语研究》第

4期。
辛斌,2005,《批评语言学:理论与应用》,上海:上海外语教育出版社。
徐盛桓,2001,《语用学导论·导读》,北京:外语教学与研究出版社。
杨喜昌,1999,巴赫金语言哲学思想分析,《解放军外国语学院学报》第2期。
臧国仁,1999,《新闻媒体与消息来源——媒介框架与真实建构之论述》,台北:三民书局。
曾军,2004,《接受的复调》,桂林:广西师范大学出版社。
曾庆香,2005,《新闻叙事学》,北京:中国广播电视出版社。
张德禄,1998,《功能文体学》,济南:山东教育出版社。
张会森,1999,作为语言学家的巴赫金,《外语学刊》第1期。
张杰,1989,复调小说作者意识与对话关系——也谈巴赫金的复调理论,《外国文学评论》第4期。
张杰,2004,巴赫金对话理论中的非对话性,《外国语》第2期。
张巨岩,2004,《权利的声音:美国的媒体和战争》,北京:三联书店。
赵一凡,1993,话语理论的诞生,《读书》第8期。
朱永生,2005,《语境动态研究》,北京:北京大学出版社。
朱永生、严世清,2001,《系统功能语言学多维思考》,上海:上海外语教育出版社。
朱永生、郑立信、苗兴伟,2001,《英汉语篇衔接手段对比研究》,上海:上海外语教育出版社。
朱永生、严世清、苗兴伟,2004,《功能语言学导论》,上海:上海外语教育出版社。
Abbott, H. P. 2002. *The Cambridge Introduction to Narrative*. Cambridge: Cambridge University Press.
Agger, B. 1998. *Critical Social Theories: An Introduction*. Oxford: Westview Press.
Allen, G. 2000. *Intertextuality*. London and New York: Routledge.
Alpatov, V. 2004. The Bakhtin Circle and Problems in Linguistics. In C. Brandist et al. (eds.), *The Bakhtin Circle: In the Master's Absence*. Manchester and New York: Manchester University Press, pp. 70-96.
Bakhtin, M. M. 1981. *The Dialogic Imagination: Four Essays by M. M. Bakhtin*. C. Emerson & M. Holquist (eds. and trans.). Austin:

Texas University Press.
Bakhtin, M. M. 1984. *Problems of Dostoevsky's Poetics*. C. Emerson (ed. and trans.). Minneapolis: University of Minnesota Press.
Bakhtin, M. M. /V. N. Volosinov. 1986. *Marxism and the Philosophy of Language*. L. Matejka & I. R. Titunik (trans.). Cambridge: Harvard University Press.
Bakhtin, M. M. 1986. *Speech Genres and Other Late Essays*. C. Emerson & M. Holquist (eds.), V. W. McGee (trans.). Austin: Texas University Press.
Bauer, D. 1989. *Feminist Dialogics: A Theory of Failed Community*. Albany, NY: State University of New York Press.
Baynham, M. 1996. Direct Speech: What's it Doing in Non-narrative Discourse? *Journal of Pragmatics* 25: 61-81.
Bek, S. T. S. 1999. Bakhtin and Halliday: A Case of Misrepresentation. *Dialogism* 2: 60-86.
Bell, A. 1991. *The Language of News Media*. Oxford UK and Cambridge MA: Blackwell.
Booth, W. C. 1961. *The Rhetoric of Fiction*. Chicago: University of Chicago Press.
Booth, W. C. 1984. Introduction. In C. Emerson (ed. and trans.), *M. M. Bakhtin's Problems of Dostoevsky's Poetics*. Minneapolis: University of Minnesota Press, pp. xiii-xxvii.
Brandist, C. 2004. Voloshinov's Dilemma: On the Philosophical Roots of the Dialogic Theory of the Utterance. In C. Brandist et al. (eds.), *The Bakhtin Circle: In the Master's Absence*. Manchester and New York: Manchester University Press, pp. 97-124.
Brandist, C. et al. (eds.). 2004. *The Bakhtin Circle: In the Master's Absence*. Manchester and New York: Manchester University Press.
Bredel, U. 2003. Polyphonic Constructions in Everyday Speech. In T. Ensink & C. Sauer (eds.), *Framing and Perspectivising in Discourse*. Amsterdam/Philadelphia: John Benjamins Publishing Company, pp. 147-70.
Brown, G. & G. Yule. 1983. *Discourse Analysis*. Cambridge: Cambridge University Press.
Bruner, E. M. & P. Gorfain. 1991. Dialogic Narration and the Paradoxes of Masada. In I. Brady (ed.), *Anthropological Poetics*. Savage:

Rowman & Littlefield Publishers Inc, pp. 177-203.
Caldas-Coulthard, C. R. 1994. On Reporting Reporting: The Representation of Speech in Factual and Factional Narratives. In M. Coulthard (ed.), *Advances in Written Text Analysis*. London: Routledge, pp. 295-308.
Chouliaraki, L. & N. Fairclough. 1999. *Discourse in Late Modernity: Rethinking Critical Discourse Analysis*. Edinburgh: Edinburgh University Press.
Clark, K. & M. Holquist. 1984. *Mikhail Bakhtin*. Cambridge: Harvard University Press.
Clark, H. H. & R. J. Gerrig. 1990. Quotations as Demonstrations. *Language* 66 (4): 764-805.
Coe, K. et al. 2004. No Shades of Gray: The Binary Discourse of George W. Bush and an Echoing Press. *Journal of Communication* 54 (2): 234-52.
Coffin, C. 2000. *History as Discourse: Construals of Time, Cause and Appraisal*. Unpublished PhD thesis. From http://www.library.unsw.edu.au/~thesis/.
Conboy, M. 2006. *Tabloid Britain: Constructing a Community through Language*. New York: Routledge.
Cook, G. 1999. *Discourse and Literature*. Shanghai: Foreign Language Education Press.
Cotter, C. 1996. Engaging the Reader: The Changing Use of Connectives in Newspaper Discourse. In J. Arnold et al. (eds.) *Sociolinguistic Variation: Data, Theory, and Analysis: Selected Papers from NWAV 23 at Stanford*. Stanford: CSLI Publications, pp. 263-78.
Coulmas, F. 1986. Reported Speech: Some General Issues. In F. Coulmas (ed.), *Direct and Indirect Speech*. Berlin: Mouton de Gruyter, pp. 1-28.
Danow, D. K. 1991. *The Thought of Mikhail Bakhtin: From Word to Culture*. New York: St. Marin's Press.
Eco, U. 1992. Between Author and Text. In S. Collini (ed.), *Interpretation and Overinterpretation*. New York: Cambridge University Press, pp. 67-88.
Eggins, S. 2004. *An Introduction to Systemic Functional Linguistics* (2nd edition). New York and London: Continuum.

Emerson, C. 1997. *The First Hundred Years of Mikhail Bakhtin*. Princeton: Princeton University Press.
Fairclough, N. 1988. Discourse Representation in Media Discourse. *Sociolinguistics* 17: 125-39.
Fairclough, N. 1992a. *Discourse and Social Change*. Cambridge: Polity Press.
Fairclough, N. 1992b. Discourse and Text. *Discourse and Society* 3 (2): 193-217.
Fairclough, N. 1992c. Introduction. In N. Fairclough (ed.), *Critical Language Awareness*. London and New York: Longman, pp. 1-29.
Fairclough, N. 1995. *Media Discourse*. New York: Edward Arnold.
Fairclough, N. 2001. *Language and Power*. Harlow: Pearson Education Limited.
Fairclough, N. 2003. *Analysing Discourse: Textual Analysis for Social Research*. London: Routledge.
Ferguson, D. L. & J. Patten. 1993. *Journalism Today*. Lincolnwood: National Textbook Company.
Fico, F. et al. 2004. Influence of Story Structure on Perceived Story Bias and News Organization Credibility. *Mass Communication & Society* 7 (3): 301-18.
Fishman, M. 1980. *Manufacturing the News*. Austin: University of Texas Press.
Foucault, M. 1972. *The Archeology of Knowledge*. A. M. Sheridan Smith (trans.). New York: Pantheon Books.
Fowler, R. 1986. *Linguistic Criticism*. New York: Oxford University Press.
Fowler, R. 1991. *Language in the News: Discourse and Ideology in the Press*. London and New York: Routledge.
Fowler, R. 1996. *Linguistic Criticism* (2nd edition). New York: Oxford University Press.
Fowler, R. & G. Kress. 1979. Critical Linguistics. In R. Fowler et al. (eds.), *Language and Control*. London, Boston and Henley: Routledge & Kegan Paul, pp. 185-213.
Fromkin, V. & R. Rodman. 1993. *An Introduction to Language*. London: Harcourt Brace College Publishers.
Frow, J. 1981. Voice and Register in Little Dorrit. *Comparative Literature*

33: 258-70.
Fuller, G. 1998. Cultivating Science: Negotiating Discourse in the Popular Texts of Stephen Jay Gould. In J. R. Martin & R. Veel (eds.), *Reading Science: Critical and Functional Perspectives on Discourse of Science*. New York and London: Routledge, pp. 35-62.
Gardiner, M. 1992. *The Dialogics of Critique: M. M. Bakhtin and the Theory of Ideology*. London: Routledge.
Gardiner, M. E. 2003. Editor's Introduction. In M. E. Gardiner (ed.), *Mikhail Bakhtin (Vol. I)*. London: Sage Publications, pp. ix-xxx.
Gee, J. P. 1999. *An Introduction to Discourse Analysis: Theory and Method*. London: Routledge.
Geis, M. L. 1987. *The Language of Politics*. New York: Springer-Verlag.
Georgakopoulou, A. 2005. Bakhtin in Sociolinguistics and Discourse Studies: Readings and Open Issues. From http://www.lancs.ac.uk/fss/organisations/lingethn/.
Goffman, E. 1974. *Frame Analysis*. New York: Harper and Row.
Greenberg, J. H. 1973. Linguistics as a Pilot Science. In E. P. Hamp (ed.), *Themes in Linguistics: The 1970s*. The Hague: Mouton, p. 59.
Gregory, M. J. 1967. Aspects of Varieties Differentiation. *Journal of Linguistics* 3: 177-98.
Gregory, M. 2001. "Phasal Analysis" Yesterday, Today and Tomorrow? In *The 28th International Systemic Functional Congress—Interfaces: Systemic Functional Grammar and Critical Discourse Analysis*. Abstract Book. ISFC28, Ottawa: Carleton University.
Grice, P. 2002. *Studies in the Way of Words*. Beijing: Foreign Language Teaching and Research Press.
Haberland, H. 1986. Reported Speech in Danish. In F. Coulmas (ed.), *Direct and Indirect Speech*. Berlin: Mouton de Gruyter, pp. 219-53.
Halliday, M. A. K. 1964. The Linguistic Study of Literary Texts. In J. Webster (ed.), *Linguistic Studies of Text and Discourse*. London: Continuum, pp. 5-22.
Halliday, M. A. K. 2000. *An Introduction to Functional Grammar* (2nd edition). Beijing: Foreign Language Teaching and Research Press.

Halliday, M. A. K. 2001. *Language as Social Semiotic: The Social Interpretation of Language and Meaning*. Beijing: Foreign Language Teaching and Research Press.

Halliday, M. A. K. 2002a. *On Grammar*. London: Continuum.

Halliday, M. A. K. 2002b. *Linguistic Studies of Text and Discourse*. London: Continuum.

Halliday, M. A. K. 2003. *On Language and Linguistics*. London: Continuum.

Halliday, M. A. K. & R. Hasan. 1985. *Language, Context, and Text: Aspects of Language in a Social-semiotic Perspective*. Oxford: Oxford University Press.

Halliday, M. A. K. & R. Hasan. 2001. *Cohesion in English*. Beijing: Foreign Language Teaching and Research Press.

Halliday, M. A. K. et al. 2004. *An Introduction to Functional Grammar* (3rd edition). London: Edward Arnold.

Hanks, W. F. 1989. Text and Textuality. *Annu Rev Anthropol* 18: 95-127.

Harris, Z. 1952. Discourse Analysis. *Language* 28: 1-30.

Hasan, R. 1985. Meaning, Context and Text: Fifty Years after Malinowski. In J. D. Benson & W. S. Greaves (eds.), *Systemic Perspectives on Discourse (Vol. I)*. Norwood: Ablex Publishing Corporation, pp. 16-49.

Hindman, E. B. 2005. Jayson Blair, The New York Times, and Paradigm Repair. *Journal of Communication* 55 (2): 225-41.

Hirschkop, K. 2001. Bakhtin's Linguistic Turn. *Dialogism* 5, 6: 21-34.

Hodge, R. & G. Kress. 1993. *Language as Ideology* (2nd edition). London: Routledge & Kegan Paul.

Hoey, M. 2001. *Textual Interaction: An Introduction to Written Discourse Analysis*. London and New York: Routledge.

Holmes, J. 1988. Doubt and Certainty in ESL Textbooks. *Applied Linguistics* 9 (1): 21-44.

Holquist, M. 2002. *Dialogism: Bakhtin and His World* (2nd edition). London and New York: Routledge.

Holquist, M. 2003. Answering as Authoring: Mikhail Bakhtin's Trans-Linguistics. In M. E. Gardiner (ed.), *Mikhail Bakhtin (Vol. II)*. London: Sage Publications, pp. 183-95.

Holquist, M. & C. Emerson. 1981. Glossary for *The Dialogic Imagination*: *Four Essays by M. M. Bakhtin*. Caryl Emerson & Michael Holquist (eds. and trans.). Austin: Texas University Press, pp. 423-34.

Hunston, S. 2001. Evaluation and the Planes of Discourse: Status and Value in Persuasive Texts. In S. Hunston & G. Thompson (eds.), *Evaluation in Text*: *Authorial Stance and the Construction of Discourse*. Oxford: Oxford University Press, pp. 176-207.

Hutchings, S. C. 2004. The Russian Critique of Saussure. In C. Sanders (ed.) *The Cambridge Companion to Saussure*. Cambridge: Cambridge University Press, pp. 139-56.

Hymes, D. 1974. *Foundations in Sociolinguistics*: *An Ethnographic Approach*. Philadelphia: University of Pennsylvania Press.

Itule, B. et al. 2003. *News Writing and Reporting*. Beijing: Press of Renmin University of China.

Jacobs, G. 1999. *Preformulating the News*: *An Analysis of the Metapragmatics of Press Releases*. Amsterdam/Philadelphia: John Benjamins Publishing Company.

Jakobson, R. 1985. The Fundamental and Specific Characteristics of Human Language. In R. Jakobson's *Selected Writings* 7: *Contributions to Comparative Mythology*. Berlin: Mouton de Gruyter, pp. 93-7.

Johnson-Cartee, K. S. 2005. *News Narratives and News Framing*: *Constructing Political Reality*. New York: Rowman & Littlefield Publishers, Inc.

Jørgensen, M. & L. Phillips. 2002. *Discourse Analysis as Theory and Method*. London: Sage Publications.

Kamberelis, G. & K. D. Scott. 2004. Other People's Voices: The Coarticulation of Texts and Subjectivities. In N. Shuart-Faris & D. Bloome (eds.), *Uses of Intertextuality in Classroom and Educational Research*. Greenwich: Information Age Publishing, pp. 201-50.

Kearns, M. 1999. *Rhetorical Narratology*. Lincoln and London: University of Nebraska Press.

Kress, G. 1989. *Linguistic Processes in Sociocultural Practice*. Oxford: Oxford University Press.

Kristeva, J. 1986. Word, Dialogue and Novel. In T. Moi (ed.), *The Kristeva Reader*. Oxford: Basil Blackwell, pp. 34-61.

Kundera, M. 1986. *The Art of the Novel*. Boston and London: Faber and Faber.
Lachman, R. 2004. Rhetoric, the Dialogical Principle and the Fantastic in Bakhtin's Thought. In F. Bostad et al. (eds.), *Bakhtinian Perspectives on Language and Culture*. New York: Palgrave Macmillan, pp. 46-64.
Lähteenmäki, M. 1998. On Meaning and Understanding: A Dialogical Approach. *Dialogism* 1: 74-91.
Lau, R. W. K. 2004. Critical Realism and News Production. *Media, Culture & Society* 26 (5): 693-711.
Lauerbach, G. 2006. Discourse Representation in Political Interviews: The Construction of Identities and Relations through Voicing and Ventriloquizing. *Journal of Pragmatics* 38: 196-215.
Lecercle, J. J. 1999. *Interpretation as Pragmatics*. New York: St. Martin's Press.
Leech, G. N. 1983. *Principles of Pragmatics*. London and New York: Longman.
Leech. G. N. & M. H. Short. 1981. *Style in Fiction: A Linguistic Introduction to English Fictional Prose*. London: Longman.
Leeuwen, T. V. 2005. Three Models of Interdisciplinary. In R. Wodak & P. Chilton (eds.), *A New Agenda in (Critical) Discourse Analysis*. Amsterdam: John Benjamins Publishing Company, pp. 3-18.
Levinson, S. C. 2001. *Pragmatics*. Beijing: Foreign Language Teaching and Research Press.
Li Meixia. 2004. *Genre and Its Integrative Analysis Model in English Print-Media News Settings*. Beijing: Social Science Press of China.
Linell, P. & T. Luckmann. 1991. Asymmetries in Dialogue: Some Conceptual Preliminaries. In I. Marková & K. Foppa (eds.), *Asymmetries in Dialogue*. Savage: Barnes & Noble Books, pp. 1-20.
Linell, P. 1998. *Approaching Dialogue*. Amsterdam and Philadelphia: John Benjamins Publishing Company.
Lock, C. 2001. Double Voicing, Sharing Words: Bakhtin's Dialogism and the History of the Theory of Free Indirect Discourse. In J. Bruhn & J. Lundquist (eds.), *The Novelness of Bakhtin: Perspectives and Possibilities*. Copenhagen: University of Copenhagen Museum Tusculanum Press, pp. 71-87.

Lodge, D. 1990. *After Bakhtin: Essays on Fiction and Criticism*. London and New York: Routledge.

Lyons, J. 1981. *Language and Linguistics: An Introduction*. London: Cambridge University Press.

Marková, I. 1990. Introduction. In I. Marková & K. Foppa (eds.), *The Dynamics of Dialogue*. New York and London: Harvester Wheatsheaf, pp. 1-22.

Marková, I. 2003. Dialogicality as an Ontology of Humanity. In C. B. Grant (ed.) *Rethinking Communicative Interaction*. Amsterdam/ Philadelphia: John Benjamins Publishing Company, pp. 29-51.

Marková, I. & K. Foppa 1991. Conclusion. In I. Marková & K. Foppa (eds.), *Asymmetries in Dialogue*. Savage: Barnes & Noble Books, pp. 259-73.

Martin, J. R. 1985. Process and Text: Two Aspects of Human Semiotics. In J. D. Benson & W. S. Greaves (eds.), *Systemic Perspectives on Discourse* (Vol. 1). Norwood: Ablex Publishing Corporation, pp. 248-74.

Martin, J. R. 1992. *English Text: System and Structure*. Amsterdam: John Benjamins Publishing Company.

Martin, J. R. 2000. Close Reading: Functional Linguistics as a Tool for Critical Discourse Analysis. In L. Unsworth (ed.), *Researching Language in Schools and Communities, Functional Linguistic Perspectives*. London: Cassell, pp. 275-304.

Martin, J. R. & D. Rose. 2003. *Working with Discourse*. London: Continuum.

Martin, J. R. & P. R. R. White. 2005. *The Language of Evaluation: Appraisal in English*. New York: Palgrave Macmillan.

Martin, S. E. 2003. Introduction. In S. E. Martin & D. A. Copeland (eds.), *The Function of Newspapers in Society*. London: Praeger, pp. vii-xi.

Matejka, et al. 1986. Translator's Preface. In *Marxism and the Philosophy of Language*. L. Matejka & I. R. Titunik (trans.). Cambridge MA: Harvard University Press, pp. vii-xii.

Matejka, et al. 1986. Translator's Introduction. In *Marxism and the Philosophy of Language*. Ladislav Matejka & I. R. Titunik (trans.). Cambridge MA: Harvard University Press, pp. 1-6.

Maynard, S. K. 1997. Textual Ventriloquism: Quotation and the Assumed Community Voice in Japanese Newspaper Columns. *Poetics* 24: 379-92.

McGlone, M. S. 2005a. Quoted out of Context: Contextomy and Its Consequences. *Journal of Communication* 55 (2): 330-46.

McGlone, M. S. 2005b. Contextomy: The Art of Quoting out of Context. *Media, Culture & Society* 27 (24): 511-22.

McNair, B. 1998. *The Sociology of Journalism*. London: Arnold.

Mey, J. L. 2000. *When Voices Clash: A Study in Literary Pragmatics*. Berlin and New York: Mouton de Gruyter.

Mey, J. L. 2001. *Pragmatics: An Introduction*. Beijing: Foreign Language Teaching and Research Press.

Morris, P. 1994. Introduction. In P. Morris (ed.), *The Bakhtin Reader*. London: Edward Arnold, pp. 1-24.

Morson, G. & C. Emerson (eds.). 1989. *Rethinking Bakhtin: Extension and Challenge*. Evanston: Northwestern University Press.

Muntigl, P. & A. Horvath. 2005. Language, Psychotherapy and Client Change. In R. Wodak & P. Chilton (eds.), *A New Agenda in (Critical) Discourse Analysis*. Amsterdam: John Benjamins Publishing Company, pp. 213-39.

Nielsen, G. M. 2002. *The Norms of Answerability*. New York: State University of New York Press.

Ongstad, S. 2004. Bakhtin's Triadic Epistemology and Ideologies of Dialogism. In F. Bostad et al. (eds.), *Bakhtinian Perspectives on Language and Culture*. New York: Palgrave Macmillan, pp. 65-88.

Paducheva, E. V. 1998. Bakhtin and His Influence on His Contemporary Linguistics. *Elementa* 4: 45-63.

Pagano, A. 1994. Negatives in Written Text. In M. Coulthard (ed.), *Advances in Written Text Analysis*. London: Routledge, pp. 250-65.

Palmer, F. R. 1986. *Mood and Modality*. London: Cambridge University Press.

Pearce, L. 1994. *Reading Dialogics*. London and New York: Edward Arnold.

Pettit, P. 1977. *The Concept of Structuralism: A Critical Analysis*. Berkeley and Los Angeles: University of California Press.

Podestá, A. 2001. A Tribute to the Father of Discourse. From http://www.shareeducation.com.ar.

Pötter, H. 2004. Objectivity as (Self-) censorship: Against the Dogmatization of Professional Ethics in Journalism. *The Public* 11 (2): 83-94.

Quirk, R. et al. 1985. *A Comprehensive Grammar of the English Language*. New York: Longman.

Reah, D. 2002. *The Language of Newspapers*. London and New York: Routledge.

Robins, R. H. 1989. *General Linguistics*. London: Longman.

Robins, R. H. 2001. *A Short History of Linguistics*. Beijing: Foreign Language Teaching and Research Press.

Rutland, B. 2003. Bakhtinian Categories and the Discourse of Postmodernism. In M. E. Gardiner (ed.), *Mikhail Bakhtin (Vol. III)*. London: Sage Publications, pp. 104-13.

Ryan, M. 2006. Mainstream News Media, an Objective Approach, and the March to War in Iraq. *Journal of Mass Media Ethics* 21 (1): 4-29.

Sakita, T. I. 2002. *Reporting Discourse, Tense, and Cognition*. London and New York: Elsevier.

Saussure, F. de. 2001. *Course in General Linguistics*. Beijing: Foreign Language Teaching and Research Press.

Saeed, J. I. 2000. *Semantics*. Beijing: Foreign Language Teaching and Research Press.

Schaffer, J. et al. 1998. *Journalism Matters*. Lincolnwood: National Textbook Company.

Schiffrin, D. 1994. *Approaches to Discourse*. Cambridge: Blackwell.

Schultz, E. A. 1990. *Dialogue at the Margins: Whorf, Bakhtin, and Linguistic Relativity*. Madison: The University of Wisconsin Press.

Scollon, R. 1998. *Mediated Discourse as Social Interaction: A Study of News Discourse*. London and New York: Longman.

Short, M. 1988. Speech Presentation, the Novel and the Press. In W. V. Peer (ed.), *The Taming of the Text*. London and New York: Routledge, pp. 61-81.

Simpson, P. 1993. *Language, Ideology and Point of View*. London: Routledge.

Swales, J. M. 2001. *Genre Analysis: English in Academic and Research Settings*. Shanghai: Shanghai Foreign Language Education Press.

Tannen, D. 1989. *Talking Voices: Repetition, Dialogue, and Imagery in Conversational Discourse*. New York: Cambridge University Press.
Thibault, P. J. 1991. *Social Semiotics as Praxis: Text, Social Meaning Making, and Nabokov's Ada*. Minneapolis: University of Minnesota Press.
Thompson, G. 1996a. Voices in the Text: Discourse Perspectives on Language Reports. *Applied Linguistics* 17 (4): 501-30.
Thompson, G. 1996b. *Introducing Functional Grammar*. London: Arnold.
Thompson, G. 2000. *Reporting*. Beijing: Foreign Languages Press.
Thompson, G. & J. Zhou. 2000. Evaluation and Organization in Text: The Structuring Role of Evaluative Disjuncts. In S. Hunston & G. Thompson (eds.), *Evaluation in Text: Authorial Stance and the Construction of Discourse*. Oxford: Oxford University Press, pp. 121-41.
Thompson, J. B. 1984. *Studies in the Theory of Ideology*. Cambridge: Polity Press.
Trew, T. 1979. "What the Papers Say": Linguistic Variation and Ideologies Difference. In R. Fowler et al. (eds.), *Language and Control*. London: Routledge & Kegan Paul, pp. 117-56.
Tuchman, G. 1978. *Making News: A Study in the Constitution of Reality*. London: The Free Press.
Unger, S. 2004. Saussure, Barthes and Structuralism. In C. Sanders (ed.) *The Cambridge Companion to Saussure*. Cambridge: Cambridge University Press, pp. 157-73.
Ure, J. & J. Ellis. 1977. Register in Descriptive Linguistics and Linguistic Sociology. In O. Uribe-Villegas (ed.), *Issues in Sociolinguistics*. The Hague: Mouton, pp. 197-243.
van Dijk, T. A. 1977. *Text and Context: Explorations in the Semantics and Pragmatics of Discourse*. London and New York: Longman.
van Dijk, T. A. 1988. *News as Discourse*. Hillsdale, N. J.: Lawrence Erlbaum Associates Publishers.
van Dijk, T. A. 2001. Multidisciplinary CDA: A Plea for Diversity. In R. Wodak & M. Meyer (eds.), *Methods of Critical Discourse Analysis*. London: Sage Publications, pp. 95-121.
Verschueren, J. 2000. *Understanding Pragmatics*. Beijing: Foreign

Language Teaching and Research Press.
Watts, R. J. 2003. *Politeness*. Cambridge: Cambridge University Press.
Waugh, L. R. 1995. Reported Speech in Journalistic Discourses: The Relation of Function and Text. *Text* 15 (1), pp. 129-73.
Wertsch, J. V. 1991. *Voices of the Mind: A Sociocultural Approach to Mediated Action*. Cambridge: Harvard University Press.
White, A. 2003. Bakhtin, Sociolinguistics and Deconstruction. In M. E. Gardiner (ed.), *Mikhail Bakhtin (Vol. III)*. London: Sage Publications, pp. 114-32.
White, P. R. R. 1998. *Telling Media Tales: The News Story as Rhetoric*. Unpublished PhD thesis. From http://www.grammatics.com/appraisal/index.html.
Widdowson, H. G. 1978. *Teaching Language as Communication*. Oxford: Oxford University Press.
Widdowson, H. G. 1979. *Explorations in Applied Linguistics (1)*. Oxford: Oxford University Press.
Widdowson, H. G. 1984. *Explorations in Applied Linguistics (2)*. Oxford: Oxford University Press.
Widdowson, H. G. 2004. *Text, Context, Pretext: Critical Issues in Discourse Analysis*. Oxford: Blackwell Publishing.
Wolf, D. 1990. Being of Several Minds: Voices and Versions of the Self in Early Childhood. In D. Cichetti & M. Beeghly (eds.), *The Self in Transition: Infancy to Childhood*. Chicago: University of Chicago Press, pp. 183-211.
Wortham, S. & M. Locher. 1996. Voicing on the News: An Analytic Technique for Studying Media Bias. *Text* 16 (4): 557-85.
Xin Bin. 2000. *Intertextuality from a Critical Perspective*. Suzhou: Suzhou University Press.
Young, L. & C. Harrison. 2004. Introduction to the Collection. In L. Young & C. Harrison (eds.), *Systemic Functional Linguistics and Critical Discourse Analysis*. London: Continuum, pp. 1-11.
Zima, P. V. 2002. *Deconstruction and Critical Theory*. London and New York: Continuum.